THE
BEARS
OF
BROOKS
FALLS

THE
BEARS
OF
BROOKS
FALLS

Wildlife and Survival
on Alaska's Brooks River

MICHAEL FITZ

Countryman Press

An Imprint of W. W. Norton & Company
Independent Publishers Since 1923

For information about special discounts for bulk purchases, please contact
W. W. Norton Special Sales at specialsales@wwnorton.com or 800-233-4830

Manufacturing by Versa Press
Production manager: Devon Zahn

Countryman Press
www.countrymanpress.com

An imprint of W. W. Norton & Company, Inc.
500 Fifth Avenue, New York, NY 10110
www.wwnorton.com

Library of Congress Cataloging-in-Publication Data

Names: Fitz, Michael, author.
Title: The bears of Brooks Falls : wildlife and survival on Alaska's Brooks River / Michael Fitz.
Description: New York : The Countryman Press, [2021] | Includes index. |
Includes bibliographical references and index.
Identifiers: LCCN 2020055539 | ISBN 9781682685105 (paperback) |
ISBN 9781682685112 (epub)
Subjects: LCSH: Brown bear—Alaska—Brook River. | Natural history—Alaska—Brook River.
Classification: LCC QL737.C27 F576 2021 | DDC 599.78409798/4—dc23
LC record available at https://lccn.loc.gov/2020055539

10 9 8 7 6 5 4 3

CONTENTS

A PERSONAL DISCOVERY

On the lip of Brooks Falls stands a bear eagerly seeking salmon. Grazer is no rookie here and it shows. She walks to the lip without hesitation and stands firmly against the force of rushing water. She knows exactly where to place her feet and exactly when to lunge, but her skills will be put to the test this year. She's fishing to fuel more than just her own survival.

Her three young cubs sit warily on the near bank and watch their mother intently. At their vulnerable age, barely two months out of the womb-like den, her success is their success. Mother's milk has been their sole source of calories since they were born in midwinter. Grazer nursed them through spring, using her last precious stores of body fat to fuel their growth and provide them with the strength to embark on the family's migration to the river. Until the salmon arrived, her meals were mostly grass—roughage that can't sustain the family's nutritional needs indefinitely.

Several other bears occupy the water below the falls. Two large and very dominant males, known as 747 and 856, bully their way to the most pre-ferred fishing spots. The others jostle for access to any place they can fit in. Enough salmon are here to keep the bears' attention, but not enough to allow them to become sated. They wait patiently for their prey to make a mistake.

Instinct compels the salmon to brave the waterfall and return to their spawning grounds. Since hatching three to five years ago, the fish have spent years running a gauntlet of predators, but Brooks Falls presents a new challenge. They've encountered nothing quite like it on their journey as near-adults. Now they must overcome the 6-foot-high obstacle or die trying.

Suddenly, a salmon shoots from the water beneath Grazer. She leans toward the fish as it strives to reach the upper lip, but its leap lacks the energy and trajectory necessary to surmount the waterfall and the salmon crashes back into the foam. A moment later, another salmon makes an attempt. Its aim is accurate enough and its momentum is great enough to jump beyond the top of the falls, perhaps its last major obstacle before spawning, if only mom wasn't in the way. With precision, Grazer catches the fish in her jaws and bites down hard. The salmon struggles but not for long. Grazer moves away from the waterfall's edge and devours the whole 5-pound fish in less than a minute. Soon, it will be digested and processed into the fatty milk needed to nurse her growing cubs.

On the Alaska Peninsula, where exceptional landscapes are commonplace, a small river and its namesake waterfall attract attention far beyond its scale. Physically, Brooks River rarely inspires superlatives. Barely a mile and a half long and 50 yards wide, it hasn't carved any deep and torturous canyons. It isn't prone to flood nor does it begin from a tumultuous cascade high in the mountains. Its water is not appropriated for human thirst, agriculture, shipping, or hydropower. Even the river's single waterfall could be regarded as ordinary in a land filled with active volcanoes, pristine lakes, and a wild, storm-lashed coastline.

Yet, Brooks River is unlike any other place.

Almost 300 miles southwest of Anchorage, Brooks River reigns as the biological and cultural heart of Katmai National Park and Preserve. Katmai is the fourth largest national park in the United States and is larger than any in the contiguous 48 states, yet in the minds of many a small waterfall has become its singular feature. Brooks Falls is no Niagara Falls, Yellowstone Falls, or Yosemite Falls, but what this small waterfall lacks in physical grandeur it exceeds in life. Brooks Falls, and the spectacle that takes place here, is synonymous with wild Alaska.

During my time as National Park Service ranger at Brooks Camp, and later as the resident naturalist with explore.org, I've never tired of the scene at the waterfall—the fish overcoming tremendous odds to survive and procreate; the bears grabbing salmon out of the air, competing for space, and raising their cubs. Many of the same bears fish at the river day after day, year after year, and I watched them for hours learning who outranked who, how they fished, how they lived. I began to recognize their individuality, seeing, perhaps for the first time, that wild animals weren't mindless automatons acting solely on instinct. They were individuals with personas, personalities. Out of ignorance and a lack of awareness I never realized such a possibility, like I had been sleepwalking and Brooks River woke me.

The public, perhaps rightfully so, expects rangers to be scholars for the parks. Through my effort to meet this lofty expectation, I realized the story of the river's bears and salmon is complicated, both biologically and historically. For bears, the tale contains miraculous feats of adaptation, as hibernation allows them to survive months without eating or drinking. It shows a mother's willingness to sacrifice for her cubs and an adolescent's ability to remember her lessons. Freshly emancipated from their mother's protective sphere, the world of a subadult bear is one of strife and learning, where they must overcome many challenges to survive to adulthood. The bears experience hunger in ways humans do not, as they are prompted by the need to eat a year's worth of food in six months or less. They are intelligent, adaptable, individualistic, charismatic, and can tell us much about life if we simply watch them and are willing to learn from them.

While the river's bears receive the bulk of our attention, few organisms on Earth are as important to an ecosystem as salmon are to Brooks River. As anadromous fish, they leave the river to feed and grow in the ocean before returning to spawn. Using inherent instincts lacking in humans, they navigate across thousands of miles of ocean. Upon returning to the river, adult salmon compete fiercely, maybe even more so than bears, for the opportunity to spawn and pass on their genes. Their return ends in death but guarantees life for the next generation. It's a journey that feeds every strand in Brooks River's food web, supports a billion dollar sustainable fishery in nearby Bristol Bay, and creates nearly all the experiences people seek at Brooks River.

Both bears and salmon are inseparably enmeshed in the area's culture, and the spectacle at Brooks Falls is not entirely natural. People influence the behavior and abundance of the animals that make the scene so special. The infrastructure needed to support thousands of visitors and their recreational activities invite conflict with bears. Managing bears and people in such a small area is especially challenging, provoking a decades-long and often emotional debate about the river's future.

Like one of Katmai's first champions, Robert Griggs, Katmai holds an eternal grasp over my psyche. Years after first discovering Brooks River for myself, it's hard for me to imagine my life without it. I've watched bears and salmon for thousands of hours and witnessed many memorable events, but my first moments at Brooks River stick with me even now.

I first ventured to Katmai in early May 2007, barely 10 days after first arriving in Alaska. Most of that time was devoted to training at the park's headquarters in King Salmon, a small community sprawling around a mothballed Air Force base and airport. Compared to most civilized places in the United States, King Salmon held a bare simplicity. There were few stores or restaurants. A single paved road led from the airport to Bristol Bay and the commercial fishing village of Naknek. A handful of dirt roads radiated into the tundra and sparse spruce woodlands, ending where cars and trucks needn't or couldn't go farther. Those first gray overcast days in King Salmon felt wonderfully isolated. I loved it almost immediately but was more than eager to go farther afield and experience a more secluded place—Brooks Camp, the complex of tourist facilities adjacent to Brooks River.

On the morning of my first flight to Brooks Camp (which is only accessible by boat, plane, or a very long, boggy, buggy, and rough cross-country hike), my coworkers and I hauled our clothing, equipment, and months of food to the floatplane docks along Naknek River. We were excited and enthusiastic to begin the adventure, but few of us, I believe, truly understood what we were getting ourselves into. I certainly didn't. Not quite a greenhorn when it came to wild areas, I had never experienced a landscape like this.

Immediately after takeoff, I gazed out the window of our small plane, my eyes transfixed on what many people would describe as nothing. King Salmon's few houses, roads, and infrastructure quickly yielded to tundra and scattered spruce trees. This was land devoid of permanent human habitation. Crosshatching animal trails led to unknown destinations. I saw wildly meandering creeks, too many ponds and lakes to count, and a horizon bounded by unnamed mountains.

After 25 minutes of flying, the pilot landed smoothly on Naknek Lake's calm surface, and we taxied to an empty beach in front of the few scattered buildings that marked Brooks Camp. With the help of fellow staff, I hurriedly unloaded and stashed my gear inside a nearby tent-frame cabin and began to settle in.

Later that evening, Jeanne, my then girlfriend and now wife, and I returned to the beach. I had just finished a winter job at Death Valley National Park, where daily temperatures had already risen above 100°F, but Brooks Camp looked like winter couldn't decide to stay or go. Leaves had not broken bud, thick blankets of snow clung to the mountains, and the underground water pipes to our cabin remained frozen. I walked wide-eyed, trying to take in the totality of the scene—the turquoise color of Naknek Lake, the snowcapped mountains, the pumice-strewn beach, a set of bear prints in the sand—when Jeanne waved her arm toward the horizon and remarked, "This is spectacular."

I don't recall if I responded or not. Doesn't matter, because she was right. I had never looked upon land so empty yet so full.

PART ONE

CREATION AND DISCOVERY

CHAPTER 1

THE VALLEY OF
TEN THOUSAND SMOKES

When gifted an idle moment at the mouth of Brooks River, near driftwood and the tracks of brown bears, I often toss stones in the water simply to watch them float. Anomalous among rocks, the pumice splashes lightly on the water's surface where it remains buoyed like a cork. Although I use it as a source of amusement, this pumice is more than just rock. It floats as symbols of violence and creation—byproducts of an event that catalyzed the creation of one of the world's great national parks.

The first days of June 1912 were unnerving for the residents of Katmai village. When earthquakes began to shake the region on June 1, the rumblings didn't provoke alarm, as earthquakes have always been a fact of life across the Alaska Peninsula. But the quakes grew stronger and more frequent with each of spring's lengthening days.

Dozens of glacially clad and geologically active volcanoes form the backbone of the Aleutian Range, a mountainous terrain sweeping southwest along the Alaska Peninsula. Although none of immediately local volcanoes had erupted within the lifetimes of Katmai's residents—Mount

Katmai, geologists would later discover, had not erupted in at least 8,000 years—they were still wary, and for good reason.

Strategically placed between volcano and sea, Katmai village was formerly a key trading post, home to over 200 people during the period of Russian colonization. By the turn of the 20th century, epidemics and the decline in the sea otter trade lessened Katmai's commercial importance. By 1912, most residents had already migrated to nearby villages, canneries, and other outposts up and down the coast to find seasonal work in the area's fledging salmon industry. The modest seasonal income allowed them to purchase the goods they needed to supplement a largely subsistence life.

So when the earthquakes failed to relent and Earth's unrest continued to build, the last two families at the village left their homes. On June 4, they began to paddle south toward a neighboring village at Puale Bay.

No one would ever return to live at Katmai village again.

On June 6, the largest eruption of the century buried their homes under feet of ash, turning a verdant coastline and prosperous village site into a volcanic wasteland. The eruption also reshaped the landscape in unforeseen ways, inspiring explorers to protect the land's geologic wonders and its potential for life.

For tens of thousands of years, Mount Katmai has formed one of the most prominent landmarks on the northern Alaska Peninsula. Triple-peaked and glacially clad, the 7,000-foot-tall volcano appeared peaceful during the days preceding June 6, 1912. Underneath, however, it stirred with unrest. From a chamber deep underground, magma exploited weaknesses in the bedrock and marched toward the surface. The migrating melt caused the surrounding rock to buckle and fracture, generating earthquakes felt by local residents.

Curiously, instead of pushing upward into Mount Katmai, most of the magma migrated laterally and away from the volcano, traveling 6 miles west before it began to dike abruptly to the surface in the upper Ukak River valley. The magma was made viscous by large amounts of silica and explosive from its high levels of dissolved water, carbon dioxide, sulfur dioxide, and other volatile gases. Given sufficient time to cool deep under Earth's surface, the igneous soup would crystalize into granite, but if it reached the surface, its chemistry and viscosity would make the magma predisposed to erupt violently. Like carbon dioxide in a capped soda bottle, the dissolved gases in magma cannot escape easily as long as pressure from the overlying bedrock remains high enough to contain it. Uncap the bottle though and the gases escape rapidly, often with great force. On the scale of a volcano, rather than a soda bottle, the results can be catastrophic.

Strong earthquakes continued into June 6, but the geologic unrest was not reflected in the sky above. While the Katmai village families paddled away to seek safety elsewhere, the crew of the mail steamer *Dora* enjoyed fine, clear weather as they sailed in Shelikof Strait along the western coast of Kodiak Island. In the early afternoon, around 1 p.m., the day's tranquility was broken by a distant detonation heard over the sound of wind and waves. Looking northwest toward the source of the blast, Captain C. B. McMullen saw a plume of ash rising into the sky. As he wrote in the ship's log, "I took bearings of same, which I made out to be Katmai Volcano, distance about 55 miles away. The smoke spread in the sky, following the vessel, and by 3 p.m. was directly over us, having traveled at the rate of 20 miles an hour."

Blackness began to envelope the *Dora*. The air became hot, sultry, and filled with static electricity. Birds, choking and blinded, dropped helplessly onto the ship's deck.

On the mainland, the seasonal fishing camp at Kaflia Bay was directly downwind of the volcano. At first, children at the camp viewed the rising ash plume with curiosity and they ran up a small bluff to watch it grow. Harry Kaiakokonok was one of the children who met the sight of an erupting volcano with excitement. As he remembered years later, once the plume's scale became apparent, people realized the seriousness of the situation.

"And then one old man from Katmai [village] . . . started hollering and telling people about their water. 'Put away as much water as you can store and reserve it. Wherever ashes come down there will be no water to drink anywhere.'

"Started snowing like that fine pumice coming down . . . Kaflia Bay started to get white gradually. That water used to be blue . . . pretty soon all white and dark, dark came.... Getting darker and darker and darker and darker, and pretty soon pitch black. So black even if you put your hand 2 or 3 inches from your face outside you can't see it."

The crew of the *Dora* and the summer residents at Kaflia Bay were experiencing the first salvo of one of the largest volcanic eruptions ever recorded. A new volcanic vent, later named Novarupta, had exploded in the upper Ukak River valley. In the final moments of its ascent, the surging magma changed from a liquid mush to explosive foam. Lava and gas roared out the earth anywhere from 300 to 1,300 feet per second, fragmenting most of the former magma into microscopic ash particles. The resulting ash plume, under the influences of its own momentum and latent heat, ascended 100,000 feet into the atmosphere. Other parts of the eruption column were too dense to rise far and collapsed into a series of scalding volcanic avalanches. These pyroclastic flows and surges traveled as much as 14 miles from Novarupta, smothering an area twice the size of Manhattan Island under searing ash and pumice, killing any life beneath or adjacent to the pyroclastic sheet.

Around midnight on June 7, Mount Katmai itself began to collapse as the eruption siphoned its magmatic core. Over the next 24 hours, the summit fell inward, generating 14 earthquakes between magnitudes 6 and 7. Thick ash replaced daylight with an inky blackness. In the town of Kodiak, on the northeastern corner of its namesake island—over 100 miles away from the volcano—it was impossible to even see a lantern's light held at arm's length. When daybreak didn't arrive on June 8, Kodiak's residents wondered aloud if they'd meet the same fate as the citizens of Pompeii. Townspeople even took the extreme step of closing saloons, agreeing that every man should keep his mind clear.

When the eruption finally ebbed on June 9, people woke to a land rocked by volcanic change. Although no one would successfully reach Novarupta or Mount Katmai for years, even from a distance the destruction was obvious. The 7,500-foot summit of Mount Katmai had vanished and most of the Pacific coastline had become a gray wasteland. A foot of ash covered an area half again as large as Delaware. A yard of ash fell at Kaflia Bay, where Harry Kaiakokonok and others weathered the harsh conditions before a steamship came to their aid several days after the eruption ceased. Wildlife died from suffocation, burial, and starvation. Waves churned the ash, and pumice smothered and scoured the barnacles, mussels, sea stars, and other intertidal organisms. Porpoises along the Katmai coast floated dead amidst pumice rafts too thick to swim through. Salmon runs collapsed for several years because the young fry couldn't find food to eat and returning adults failed to spawn.

The 1912 Novarupta-Katmai eruption was the largest of the 20th century and the fifth largest in recorded human history. Novarupta unleashed roughly 4 cubic miles of ash and 2.6 cubic miles of pyroclastic flows. In total, this represents 3 cubic miles of underground magma, an output greater than the eruption of Krakatoa in 1883 and 30 times more than the eruption of Mount Saint Helens in 1980. Despite its magnitude, the full extent and significance of the eruption of Novarupta-Katmai would not be understood for many years—and only after a Midwestern professor realized the Katmai area was far more than a volcanic wasteland.

In June 1915, Robert Griggs led a National Geographic Society expedition to Kodiak. Griggs, a botanist at The Ohio State University, was tasked with documenting and exploring vegetative recovery on the island in the wake of the eruption. He first visited the Kodiak Archipelago in 1913 when it appeared, in his words, "bleak and desolate." Only tall shrubs, trees, and sparse patches of vigorous perennials like fireweed and lupine survived above the year-old ash.

When he returned in 1915, Griggs found a wholly different place. Grass grew head high and townsfolk harvested bumper crops of wild berries. The thick, rhyolitic ash provided almost no nutrients to fuel plant growth, as it was mostly silica. Instead of fertilizing the area, it became mulch that suppressed the growth of competing plants and helped to retain soil moisture. As Griggs recalled, "[I] could not . . . believe my eyes. It was not the same Kodiak I had left two years before. . . . I had come to study the revegetation, but I found my problem vanished in an accomplished fact."

With this news and now a few extra days in hand, Griggs set off to the mainland and into the devastated Katmai River valley. The contrast between the reinvigorated Kodiak and the Katmai coastline couldn't have been more striking.

After landing at Katmai Bay, Griggs and two companions found the remains of Katmai village devastated by a catastrophic flood and the rest of the area ravaged by ash and pumice. Almost all trees and shrubs had perished. Meager vegetation survived only where ash had sloughed or blown off the original soil surface. It was utterly different than anything he had ever witnessed, a scene he described as "an entrance to another world."

To travel beyond the wrecked village, the team was forced to slog through thigh-deep quicksand. "The labor involved in such travel cannot be described, but must be experienced to be appreciated," he wrote. They wore their fingertips raw climbing over steep ash-covered slopes and risked drowning while fording dangerously swift river channels in an attempt to reach the base of Mount Katmai, but they were not equipped or afforded time to go farther. Even with the hardships posed by the terrain, Griggs was quite convinced that the area was worthy of more thorough exploration.

The next summer, in July 1916, Griggs returned determined to reach the beheaded Mount Katmai, then thought to be the sole source of the eruption. This time, his small expedition was better prepared for the rigors of quicksand and deep ash. Relaying food and other camping supplies up the Katmai River valley, the group established a base camp near the foot of Observation Mountain, not far from the slopes of the volcano. From there, they climbed Mount Katmai's southern slopes and were the first people ever to look into the 2,000-foot-deep and nearly 2-mile-wide caldera. At the unstable and knife-edged rim, they found glaciers cleaved flush with the precipitous walls where several thousand feet of mountain once stood. Peering into the gaping earth, Griggs had difficulty comprehending the caldera's scale, and he stared amazed at a horseshoe-shaped island of hardened lava in a milky, robin-egg-blue lake in the bowels of the volcano.

Eleven days later, on their second ascent of Mount Katmai, the team thought they glimpsed wisps of steam ascending from a hidden valley across the Aleutian Range divide. Might more geologic wonders lie on the other side of the mountains? Since their position on the caldera rim afforded no means to satisfy their curiosity, Griggs decided to reconnoiter the Katmai

Pass area. But even after climbing to the caldera rim twice, he remained mentally unprepared to view the landscape on the other side of the volcano.

Around 2,600 feet in elevation, Katmai Pass is a relatively accessible notch in the Aleutian Range, used for millennia as a trade and travel route between the Pacific coast and the inland settlements on Naknek Lake and beyond. The pass had a deservedly rough reputation, even before the eruption. It was, and remains, prone to blinding whiteouts in winter and disorienting fog in summer. The narrow topography funnels fearsome windstorms, sometimes strong enough to blow sizeable rocks through the air (a threat even greater today since the pass is covered in pumice). It is a place to move through, not linger, and then only during calm weather.

After the eruption, Katmai Pass and the adjacent travel route lay buried under dozens, perhaps hundreds, of feet of ash and remained vacant of animals and all plants but the hardiest pioneering mosses and algae. When nearby villages were abandoned in 1912, the route's utility nearly vanished. For Griggs, though, the pass offered the easiest and only feasible way through to the Aleutian Range from the Katmai River valley.

July 31, 1916, was a tiresome day for Griggs and his two partners, Donovan Church and Lucius Folsom. Their legs remained fatigued from their second Mount Katmai climb and the ash beds offered little firm ground to stand on. Not far from the highest point in Katmai Pass, Church gave out, "incapacitated by too many flapjacks at breakfast" and waited while Griggs and Folsom continued onward. Griggs's first glimpse through the pass didn't hint of much worth investigating except more ash and pumice, but just as he considered turning back a tiny puff of steam caught his attention. This fumarole, or volcanic gas vent, wasn't particularly large, but the day was damp and chilly so Griggs used it practically, warming his hands in the condensing steam. Shortly afterward he spotted another plume rising from a larger fumarole in the distance. Curiosity hastened Griggs forward and he climbed a small hillock for a better vantage.

> *The sight that flashed into view . . . was one of the most amazing visions ever beheld by mortal eye. The whole valley as far as the eye could reach*

*was full of hundreds, no thousands—literally tens of thousands—of
smokes curling up from its fissured floor. . . . After a careful estimate, we
judged there must be a thousand whose columns exceeded 500 feet. . . .
I tried to "keep my head" and observe carefully, yet I exposed two films
from my one precious roll in trying for pictures that I should've known
were impossible. For a few moments we stood gaping at the awe inspiring
vision before us. . . . It was as though all the steam engines in the world,
assembled together, had popped their safety valves at once and were letting off steam in concert.*

With the day waning and Church still waiting on the other side of Katmai Pass, Griggs and Folsom had little time to explore further, but this was
truly virgin territory. No one had set foot in this valley since the eruption
irreparably altered it. No one had felt the hot earth under their shoe leather
or warmed their hands next to the fumaroles. No one had seen the eruption's epicenter, the steaming dark gray lava dome Griggs would later name
Novarupta. After roughly estimating the number and extent of visible fumaroles, he christened the landscape the Valley of Ten Thousand Smokes.

Griggs didn't return to his base camp until very late in the day. Despite
his fatigue he found sleep impossible, his mind whirling with thoughts
about the valley he had just found. "I had yet only a very inadequate conception of the place we had discovered, but I had seen enough to know that
we had accidentally discovered one of the great wonders of the world. . . . I
recognized at once that the Katmai district must be made a great national
park, accessible to all the people, like the Yellowstone."

The scars of a violent volcanic eruption had sown the seeds for one of
America's largest and wildest national parks.

CHAPTER 2

A NEW PARK

The National Geographic Society greeted the discovery of the Valley of Ten Thousand Smokes enthusiastically and funded another trip in 1917. Ten experts took part in this expedition, including a chemist, zoologist, topographer, botanist, and packer. They gathered the first in-depth observations of the valley, but for all their effort, the 1917 expedition recorded few new scientific discoveries.

Robert Griggs seemed eager to use the expedition as an opportunity to thoroughly expound on the area's wonders. His descriptions, published in the February 1918 edition of *National Geographic Magazine,* became even more florid than the initial recounting of the Valley's discovery. He described himself as "overawed" and in a state where he "could neither think nor act in a normal fashion." The Valley of Ten Thousand Smokes was a "miracle of nature" with sublimity comparable to Haleakala, Crater Lake, and the Grand Canyon. As described by National Park Service (NPS) historian Frank Norris, Griggs became, and for much of the rest of his life remained, the leading publicist and lobbyist for Katmai.

Shortly after the 1917 trip, Griggs convinced the National Geographic Society to lobby Congress and the Department of Interior's fledgling agency, the National Park Service, to protect Katmai as a national park.

But after weathering strong congressional opposition to establish Mount McKinley (now Denali) National Park in February 1917, the NPS was unwilling to engage Congress in an effort to establish another park in Alaska. An alternative option existed, however. The NPS suggested Griggs and the National Geographic Society sidestep Congress and seek national monument status instead. Unlike national parks, which can only be created by an act of Congress, the president, through the authority granted by the 1906 Antiquities Act, can proclaim national monuments to protect historic landmarks, historic and prehistoric structures, and other objects of historic or scientific interest. If a national park wasn't feasible, then a national monument could offer the same level of protection.

Griggs drew the monument's proposed boundaries, but questions lagged about the longevity of the "ten thousand" fumaroles. He was convinced the fumaroles were permanent and the Valley of Ten Thousand Smokes was a formative Yellowstone, but the NPS and the National Geographic Society wanted more proof. In the summer of 1918, Jasper Sayre and Paul Hagelbarger, members of Griggs's 1917 expedition, returned to the Valley to observe the fumaroles more carefully and determined, incorrectly, that activity continued undiminished.

On September 24, 1918, President Woodrow Wilson created Katmai National Monument through presidential proclamation. The monument's trapezium boundaries extended from the head of Naknek Lake south and southeast to the Pacific coast. It included all of the Valley of Ten Thousand Smokes, adjacent volcanoes, and more than 93 miles of coastline. As President Wilson declared, the new monument's natural wonders afforded "a conspicuous object lesson in volcanism . . . [and] inspiration to patriotism and the study of nature."

But this was not the end of Griggs's advocacy. In 1919, with a $35,000 appropriation from the National Geographic Society (a huge sum considering the average income reported to the IRS in 1919 was about $3,700), Griggs returned to the newly declared monument, and his enthrallment with the region began to extend beyond the shadow of Mount Katmai and the fumaroles. While he and most of the other expedition participants focused the core of their work in and around the Valley of Ten Thousand

Smokes, Griggs traveled outside the monument's boundaries to Naknek Lake and Brooks River. At Brooks Falls, he watched thousands of sockeye salmon and "stood for hours, held by the fascination of one of the most wonderful sights afforded by the animal kingdom, as the endless procession of fish kept leaping in the air, up and over the falls."

Alaska's great brown bears were rarely seen during the expeditions, but they captivated Griggs as well. He devoted eight pages of his classic 1922 book, *The Valley of Ten Thousand Smokes*, to anecdotes about bears. He saw no bears at Brooks Falls in 1919, despite the prodigious number of leaping salmon, yet the mere possibility of a bear encounter added trepidation and excitement to his adventures.

Griggs's travels in brown bear country came at a time when grizzly bears were driven nearly to extinction in the contiguous United States. From his experiences and conversations on Kodiak Island, Griggs understood that conflict between bears and people, especially regarding the attempt to establish cattle ranching there, could lead to the demise of bears on the island. "No prophet was needed to foretell the result: the rapid decrease in the number of bears, which will soon face complete extinction unless energetically protected," he wrote.

During the world war, a scarcity in beef led many Alaskans to lobby for repeal of any protections for bears, so the 1918 proclamation tacitly avoided any mention of wildlife and it protected only a modicum of productive wildlife habitat. By the mid-1920s though, wildlife advocates urged the NPS to protect more habitat for bears.

In the fall of 1930, at the request of Assistant to the Secretary of the Interior Ernest Walker Sawyer, Griggs penned a letter explaining why and how brown bears should be protected in Alaska. Fresh off his fifth National Geographic Society–sponsored trip to Alaska, he argued that Katmai should be expanded for its scenery, wilderness values, and perhaps most importantly, to protect habitat for bears and other wildlife. He explained the lakes region west of the volcanoes was also excellent waterfowl habitat and took time to note the spectacle of leaping salmon at Brooks Falls.

The letter was mailed to Ray Wilbur, President Herbert Hoover's secretary of the interior. Griggs also drew boundaries for an expanded Katmai National Monument. With an eye on wildlife habitat, he included the mountains and valleys west of the Valley of Ten Thousand Smokes and the coastline and volcanoes to the northeast. The effort convinced the federal government. On April 24, 1931, President Hoover expanded Katmai National Monument by an additional 1.55 million acres "for the protection of brown bear, moose, and other wild animals."

The enlarged monument, largely based on Griggs's proposed boundaries, now included the core area surrounding the Valley of Ten Thousand Smokes, most of the park's modern coastline, and much of the landscape to the north and west including most of Naknek Lake and the Brooks River area. At nearly 2.5 million acres, Katmai became the largest unit in the national park system.

In 1916, when he first gaped in wonder at the steaming Valley of Ten Thousand Smokes, the pumice under Griggs's boots may have simply represented awe-inspiring geologic change and volcanic violence. Prior to June 6, 1912, it was nothing more than ingredients in a molten soup. A violent eruption transformed it into the foamy rock that fell to earth in a scalding pyroclastic flow. Snowmelt and rain eventually eroded it into Ukak River, and the river beveled its edges against canyon walls before dumping it unceremoniously into Naknek Lake. Wind provided the final push to carry the pumice to Brooks River where waves heaved it on shore. I toss bits of it back into the water and contemplate its meaning. Watching the pumice float, I see more than a geologic story. The rock symbolizes Griggs's advocacy and vision— first for the Valley of Ten Thousand Smokes, then for wildlife like bears and salmon.

The executive and legislative effort to protect Katmai culminated in 1980 when Congress passed the Alaska National Interest Lands Conservation Act. This act established Katmai National Park and Preserve: "To protect habitats for, and populations of, fish and wildlife including, but not limited to, high concentrations of brown/grizzly bears and their denning areas; to maintain unimpaired the water habitat for significant salmon populations; and to protect scenic, geological, cultural and recreational features."

Today, long after the "smokes" vanished, the area retains a raw beauty, one rarely matched in America's national parks, and brown bears and salmon are the park's most well-known inhabitants. Griggs likely never foresaw Brooks Falls crowded with bears (he died in 1963, well before bears fishing at Brooks River was a notable event), but he envisioned Katmai as one of the world's great parks. How right he was.

CHAPTER 3

RAMBLE

Quite often, I'm consumed by an urge to wander, precipitated by nothing more than restlessness or too much time spent indoors. The feeling is especially strong when I'm presented with an opportunity to visit places I might otherwise avoid due to weather, inaccessibility, or in the case of Brooks River, a high risk of bear encounters. So when a calm, sunny, late spring evening coincided with a few spare hours, I found time for a slow ramble; a perfect opportunity to reacquaint myself with the river: how it's changed and what to expect as summer arrives and wanes into fall.

Exiting my cabin I hustle past the visitor center and lodge, then cross the river on the footbridge leading to a one-lane dirt road. The road cuts through a dense boreal forest where acres of wind-thrown spruce trees, compromised by a recent bark beetle outbreak, form a tangled maze of downed logs. Without the thick canopy of spruce needles to intercept sunlight, understory plants have exploded upward to fill the gaps and limit visibility to 25 yards or less. So after a mile of walking, the expansive panorama at the shore of Lake Brooks is a welcoming sight.

Nearly 11 miles long and 2.5 to 3 miles wide, Lake Brooks would be a destination in and of itself in the contiguous 48 states. Yet other than a handful of National Park Service buildings and the remnants of a couple of trappers' cabins, its shoreline remains undeveloped. The water is spectacularly clear, harboring large rainbow trout and water pure enough to drink straight.

This pocket of lakeshore is sometimes crowded with floatplanes, bringing anglers and bear watchers eager for adventure. During this first week of June, however, with bear sightings far and few between and the sport fishing season not yet open, almost no tourists are visiting and the shoreline is empty. As I stand facing the water, the rounded summit of Dumpling Mountain, still holding patches of last winter's snow, dominates the view to the north. To my right, below the Dumpling massif on the lake's northeastern corner, Brooks River begins without fanfare.

The river, at first, creates only a few ripples as it pours over an innocuous ledge of ancient lava. Finding myself drawn to explore the opposite bank, I pause and stare at the cold water. There is no bridge here and it is too deep to wade with my knee-high rubber boots, the ubiquitous summer footwear of coastal Alaska, so I remove them and step in. I walk slowly, barefoot, allowing my feet and lower legs to adjust to the cold.

I stick to the shallower water flowing over the ledge and aim for a rock outcrop buttressing the opposite shore. The first few steps aren't pleasant, and I feel a sharp ache of pain as the blood vessels in my toes constrict, but the day is cloudless and relatively warm, conditions that temper the chill.

As I near the far bank, I owe any remaining sensation in my toes to a shallow shelf of sediment extending several hundred yards into the lake where, on calm summer days, ample sunshine warms the water to tolerable temperatures. This corner of the lake, at least in this moment in time, is also a rare pocket of geologic stability. The shelf plays a large role in maintaining the nearby shoreline by moderating the force of wind-driven waves, while the bedrock ledge I walk upon stabilizes Lake Brooks and Brooks River in a landscape that can otherwise transform rapidly. Not long ago, in the blink of an eye, geologically speaking, Brooks River did not exist.

Thirty thousand years ago, nearly all of Katmai lay buried under a sea of ice. Glaciers from an ice cap centered over Cook Inlet and Shelikof Strait moved west through the entire Naknek Lake watershed. Almost no land was exposed in Katmai except for nunataks, isolated mountains projecting above the ice and snow. Off Alaska's southern coast, ice overrode most of Kodiak Island and extended to the outer edge of the continental shelf, over what is now only open ocean. Glaciers covered 116,000 square miles of the Alaska Peninsula, an area about as large as Arizona.

At the peak of the last ice age, when ice covered as much as 30 percent of Earth's surface, similar scenes were found across the Northern Hemisphere. In North America, ice sheets reached south beyond the present locations of Boston, New York City, Chicago, and Seattle. Glaciers trapped enough water to lower sea levels nearly 400 feet below their present elevation. As a result, some of the world's most valuable fisheries in Bristol Bay and the Bering Sea didn't exist. In their place, the low sea levels exposed Beringia, the subcontinent of a combined Alaska and eastern Siberia. In Katmai, there were no bears or salmon. No forests or lakes. No people. Almost no habitat for the living. Ice was the most extensive and dominant force of change.

The last glacier to entirely fill the area now occupied by Naknek Lake, informally known as the Naknek glacier, reached its greatest extent no sooner than 23,000 years ago. Part of a local advance called the Iliamna stade, it carried ice 60 miles from its source area among Katmai's high volcanic peaks to its terminus near King Salmon. By sliding under the influence of gravity and deforming under its own weight, the Naknek glacier eroded and entrained rock, sand, and anything else by plucking or abrading it away. The glacier's size, extent, and erosive power allowed it to accumulate huge amounts of debris near its terminus. Much of the eroded material, or till, was swept into the glacier's interior where deformation and sliding eventually carry it into the glacier's ablation zone, the area on a glacier where ice is lost and all of the previous winter's snow melts. When the ice stagnated and receded, it dropped the reworked earth in place, creating a terminal moraine, the ridge of till deposited at the farthest reach of an advancing glacier.

Naknek glacier's terminal moraine became the earthen dam for Naknek Lake, the end point for Brooks River and the largest lake wholly contained within a US national park. Immediately after the Naknek glacier began its retreat, the in-filling lake had no established outlet and swelled to unprecedented heights.

Naknek Lake sits currently at a modest 42 feet in elevation, but wave-cut terraces on adjacent mountainsides reach over 180 feet above sea level, indicating the lake was once much deeper and more extensive. At full pool it was, perhaps, a third larger than today. It swallowed half of the Savonoski River floodplain, the lake's main tributary; annexed the basins of Lake Brooks (elevation 68 feet), Lake Coville (elevation 108 feet), and Lake Grosvenor (elevation 108 feet); made Dumpling Mountain into an island; and drowned the future site of Brooks River underneath dozens of feet of frigid water. For thousands of years after the glaciers retreated, the proto-Naknek Lake remained so high that no hint of Brooks River existed.

Only after Naknek Lake reached its post-glacial maximum was it able to spill over the moraine at its west end. During the proceeding millennia, islands merged, rivers lengthened, and lake basins separated as the down cutting of the Naknek River reduced the basin's storage capacity. The rate of withdrawal is not entirely clear, but it likely wasn't smooth. During pauses and slowdowns, waves carved their signatures into mountainsides. Time sensitive, these terraces record the level of the lake when they were formed. All terraces higher than 98 feet are capped with ash from a volcanic eruption 12,000 to 13,000 years ago, indicating the land immediately adjacent to modern Brooks River was still below 30 to 50 feet of water at the time. Five to six thousand years later, the level of Naknek Lake had finally dropped low enough for any part of Brooks River to see the light of day.

Once on the opposite shore, I pull my socks and boots back on. I begin walking downstream across one of the first terraces to be exposed along the infant river. The riverbank is lined with white spruce and Kenai birch, while the ground is enveloped by thick clumps of bluejoint grass. The leaves and grasses are vibrantly green, a hue achieved only during the first few weeks after budburst when plants remain unmarred by insect and fungal attacks, and before they become fatigued by a long summer of photosynthesizing.

A few hundred yards downriver, I detour from the water to explore a large bog. Several acres in size, it's the largest bog in close proximity to the river, although the scene is most striking when my eyes are fixed on the plant life near my feet. The plants here are far less green than the plants on the better-drained soil surrounding it; the bog is filled with the rich rust and yellow-brown hues of sphagnum and speckled with sparse green leaves of the few shrubs that are tolerant of the bog's acidic conditions. Sundews perch on top of the saturated moss, their tiny leaves glistening with sticky secretions to capture unfortunate insects. I nibble on a few of last year's maroon-colored cranberries. They're past their prime with an overripe aftertaste (they've been here for nine months, after all), but the juice bursts with an intense sweet-and-sour flavor I can't resist.

With each step into the bog, my feet sink a little more, and the "land" becomes more liquid than solid. I bounce lightly on the moss to test the firmness of the substrate and see waves ripple through the sphagnum. I'm no longer standing on solid earth, but a floating mat of peat, a quaking bog. A few more steps and the vegetation becomes softer, so much so that I no longer trust it to hold my weight. This is as close to walking on liquid water as I'll ever get, but it's too much like walking on thin ice and I fear plunging through the peat to be swallowed permanently. There's a lot preserved down there and I don't wish to add myself to the collection, so I back off and move toward the surrounding forest.

True bogs are fed by aerial precipitation, not by running water. The tannins and acids released by sphagnum lower the water's pH to levels inhospitable for most plants but create conditions where sphagnum thrives and decomposition is hindered. As more sphagnum grows on the surface, it buries and compacts previous generations to form peat. Wind-blown pollen that settles on the bog is buried in the accumulating layers, so peat isn't just a record of what lived in the bog; it also preserves evidence of what grew around it. Similarly, pollen is also preserved in the oxygen-poor sediments of Katmai's deep, cold lakes. Peat and lake sediments, therefore, are time capsules through which palynologists—those who study pollen grains and spores found in archeological or geological deposits—can interpret the habitat compositions in the past.

In southwest Alaska, vegetation changes have been complex since the end of the last ice age. The retreat of the glaciers left the landscape barren and raw, its unoccupied territory open to any plant with the adaptations to tolerate the climate, rampant erosion, and unconsolidated mess of mud, silt, cobbles, and boulders. According to pollen samples sifted from sediments in Idavain Lake, located about 15 miles north of Brooks River, sedge tundra and grasslands were the first habitat communities to invade. By 12,000 years ago, ground-hugging species of birch began to invade, and around 8,000 years ago, alder swept over the area, forever making bushwhacking in Katmai an arduous experience.

The oldest pollen samples extracted from within this bog are about 5,600 years old. During the next 3,000 years, pollen from birch and heath plants increased, a change interpreted as evidence for a slight cooling in the local climate. With renewed warming during the most recent 2,500 years, alder once again became more and more prominent in the pollen record. The net result is the development of the plant community I experience today.

My walk from the bog back into the forest follows, albeit very roughly, the biome shifts the area experienced since the glaciers retreated. In its center, where the footing was questionable, sedges and moss grow in the bog's most waterlogged places. Just a few feet inland and upland, sphagnum becomes most abundant. Toward the bog's margins, I move through scattered dwarf shrubs, then waist-high bushes, and finally small trees where soils are less peaty.

Back in the trees, moving downstream along the riverbank, the chance of encountering a bear grounds me to the moment and keeps me from musing about plant dispersal for too long. I remain reasonably cautious, walking slowly. No developed trails parallel the riverbank so I follow well-worn bear trails where I can.

The upper river is narrow, cobbled with gravel, and usually less than 100 feet wide. From Lake Brooks, it flows north through riffled shallows before taking a right hook east. A few granitic boulders, deposited by ice and exposed by flowing water, break the surface. Spruce and birch lean precariously over the river where water has undercut their roots. Late spring's vigorously growing grass encroaches on the paths. Although the plant community was different, the first people and bears to arrive here likely walked similar routes.

Around 5,000 years ago, the first semblance of Brooks River formed when Naknek Lake dropped low enough and began to separate from the basin now occupied by Lake Brooks. Nearly all the dry land surrounding Brooks River today was exposed then, but lake levels were still high enough that the early river was merely a wide area of water flowing slowly between the diverging basins. More of a strait than river, the area quickly became an important resource for animals and people.

The oldest confirmed evidence of people on the Alaska Peninsula comes from an hourglass squeeze of land about 75 miles southwest of Katmai. At Ugashik Narrows on the Alaska Peninsula National Wildlife Refuge, 9,000-year-old chipped stone artifacts suggest the first residents were hunters of large animals. Caribou, for example, would've moved efficiently across the open tundra, browsing on lichens in winter and green forbs in the summer. Caribou are good swimmers too, but like most ungulates they often stay high and dry when given the option. Encountering the lakes, they could avoid a long cold swim by crossing at the pinch of ground in between. To hunt efficiently at the narrows, people could let the land funnel the quarry.

A similar dynamic occurred at the Brooks River narrows circa 3,000 BC. A caribou herd moving toward the fledgling river faced a choice: swim across the lakes or follow the land. The first people at Brooks River, like those at Ugashik Narrows, knew this. They followed the migratory herds to the emerging river or established camps here and waited. Archeological excavations have uncovered large stone lances and knives belonging to Brooks River's earliest human inhabitants as well as the caribou bones that prove their hunts were successful.

Curiously, salmon were not a major food source for the river's earliest cultures even though the region's most important fish may have colonized Katmai's lakes soon after they formed. Analyses of sediment cores from Nonvianuk Lake north of Brooks River indicate the presence of salmon as early as 10,000 years ago. The most ancient campsites yet discovered at the river are not immediately adjacent to the water. If salmon were present when the first people arrived, perhaps they weren't abundant enough to target or the strait between the Lake Brooks and Naknek Lake basins was simply too deep and wide to fish successfully.

No matter the reason for the lack of large-scale piscivory, free passage for salmon through Brooks River was short lived. As Naknek Lake continued to drain and erode through the terminal moraine at its outlet, the strait evolved into a river. Approximately 4,000 years ago, the lengthening river uncovered a ridge of sedimentary rock. At first, Naknek Lake remained high enough that a bare ripple tumbled over the hard conglomerate. The wavelet, perhaps unnoticeable by migrating salmon at first, grew year by year and slowly expanded from a short drop into a major barrier. A distinct plunge formed by 3,500 years ago, one high enough to temporarily impede salmon migrating upstream to spawn. Brooks Falls had emerged.

At Brooks River, large-scale salmon harvesting began only after the falls started to form. People of the Arctic Small Tool tradition, who used Brooks River 3,800 to 3,000 years ago and were far more populous than earlier cultures, experienced the transition. Their microblades and other tools bespeak a great interest in terrestrial animals, but their camps are also located on every major terrace directly adjacent to the river at the time, just where you'd expect fisher-people to reside.

Within a few hundred yards of the river, around 900 surface features are believed to be the work of people from several different cultures over the span of nearly 5,000 years. Old beaches, preserved as upland terraces when the lake fell away and the river changed course, were perfect places to build communities near an abundant and predictable food source. Today, the top edges of many terraces are unevenly flat, cratered by the depressions of collapsed homes, communal buildings, and storage pits. Some terraces were occupied temporarily, but others were village and food-gathering sites for centuries. Terraces immediately adjacent to Brooks Falls were utilized so frequently that tools from multiple cultural phases are mixed together. Near the river mouth, Brooks Lodge sits on beach and river terraces that have been used by people for 2,000 years, the hummocky ground under the cabins exhibiting where people built their homes and buried their dead. Walking anywhere along the river is an experience shared by people for thousands of years.

About a half mile downstream of the lake, the bushwhack becomes tedious where I'm forced to navigate a muddy thicket, one that most people—past or present—are smart enough to avoid. Having come this way before, I knew the swamp was there and that crossing it would be worth the effort for what lay ahead. As I push through a tangle of willows I hear the distinctive, low noise of frothy water. Exiting the thicket and emerging onto drier ground, I move through a birch woodland where I see the river suddenly plunge over the ledge of Brooks Falls.

From June 15 to August 15, the area immediately adjacent to the falls, excluding the 10-foot-high deck platforms designed for wildlife watching, becomes a regulatory no-man's-land. The National Park Service closes the area to people to provide bears with greater access to the food they need to survive. With mid-June fast approaching, this may be my last opportunity to explore the bears' haunts, so I take the opportunity to step into the river to get a closer look.

When viewed from the side, the lip of the falls is slightly sinuous. From where I stand upstream, however, it looks cleaved in a straight line, giving it an infinity pool-like appearance. As I approach closer, I feel the river bottom change from rough gravel to smooth bedrock. The footing is slick and I'm reminded how deftly and confidently bears move through the water. They seem to not think about the current's strength, but I lack their mass and four-wheel drive, and I'm not brave (or foolish) enough to walk all the way to the edge. I stop about 5 feet from the lip and pause to absorb the scene.

Downstream, the water tumbles through shallow riffles before it turns and flows out of sight. A rock outcrop bounds the waterfall to my left while an empty wildlife-viewing platform stands on the opposite bank. The scene is quiet and tranquil, a far cry from the feeding frenzy soon to come. Only a couple of weeks remain before the first salmon arrive and dozens of hungry bears descend.

The abundance of bears at Brooks River fluctuates seasonally depending on the availability of salmon, yet their numbers often reach staggering levels. From 2005 through 2010, over 100 individual bears were identified using the 1.5-mile river each year, averaging nearly 70 individual bears in July alone. During the right season, it's not uncommon to see a dozen bears competing for space. From the wildlife-viewing platform at Brooks Falls I've counted as many as 31 bears within my line of sight, and I wasn't counting cubs.

Back out of the water on the north side of the river, I move easily through the trees and grass. So many bears use this area as their main access to the falls that the trails are wide and nearly free of vegetation. Salmon bones— vertebrae, needle-thin ribs, gill plates, and mandibles—lie everywhere. A few skeletons remain somewhat articulated, but most are nothing more than heaps of indigestible vertebrae, the last remnants of bear scat deposited last year.

Under evenly spaced spruce and birch, I continue downstream, glancing at the water from time to time and imagine what it will look like when filled with spawning salmon. Come late August, the riffles downstream of the falls will be peppered with ruby red sockeye competing for nesting habitat and mates. After a few moments of slow walking, inspecting old fish heads and listening to river babble, I enter a dense spruce forest. The recent bark beetle outbreak shaved most of the larger trees from the stand, but the ground generally remains moss covered, typical of a boreal forest floor with only dim, speckled light. I stumble over fallen trees and stair-step down a couple of old beach terraces where the river begins to arc in a long reverse S-curve.

Brooks Falls attracts the bulk of the public's attention, but the lower Brooks River and its outlet are probably more ecologically dynamic. Sometimes confined to one channel, sometimes flowing through several, it meanders sharply on the final leg to Naknek Lake. Grassy meadows predominate in the heavily saturated soils adjacent to each bank. Gravel and pumice beaches provide resting areas for waterfowl, gulls, and bears. Beyond the river mouth, Mount Katolinat's herringboned northeastern ridge rises almost 5,000 feet above Naknek Lake. At the base of a broad meander, I spot Brooks Lodge and its cabins sitting on a terrace wedged between the last bends in the river and Naknek Lake.

For bears, the lower river becomes most important in September and October when the business of reproduction leaves salmon exhausted and weathered. Swept downstream and drifting listlessly in the current, dead and dying fish accumulate in the slack water of the lower river where bears spend weeks scavenging their carcasses. They patrol the water like battleships. The search can reward bears with dozens of fish and tens of thousands of calories per day during the weeks preceding hibernation.

Although I can hardly wait to witness that scene again, I remind myself it is still several months away and there is a lot to experience before then. Having run out of river, I tromp through the remaining marshes and head back to my cabin. I walk past the lodge and visitor center—structures representative of the most recent culture to utilize the river and merely one change in a continuing series of cultural, geological, and biological shifts the river has witnessed. Brooks River has evolved ever since glaciers retreated from the landscape. It has assembled a diverse cast of flora and fauna that changes not only over centuries and millennia but, as in the case of bears and salmon, also over days and seasons.

A river is never exactly the same, not even for a millisecond. Water and sediments are in constant chaotic motion, ever shifting under the influence of gravity and unconsciously seeking the path of least resistance. Erosion from the constant flow strips away rock and sediments lining its banks and bottom. Upon, within, and under it, life is always moving, consuming, reproducing, and dying. We can infinitely revisit a river and witness it infinitely changing.

PART TWO

BROWN BEARS
AND
SALMON

CHAPTER 4

WINTER SLUMBER

"Hey-oh," I call as I look upslope toward the large hole in the mountainside. I approach the bear den on Dumpling Mountain cautiously, arcing toward it through a waist-high willow thicket. With the summer solstice only a few days away, the den is almost certainly vacant, but I don't want to risk surprising anything that may still lurk inside. When nothing stirs from within the den, I move a little closer then pause to announce my presence again. Still nothing. I continue forward, slowly, repeating the process until I'm sure any tenant would've heard me.

A bare dirt platform, the spoils of last fall's excavation, sits outside its slightly elliptic entrance and provides a convenient place for me to shed my pack and take in the view. I had investigated other bear dens on Dumpling before, but those were partially collapsed and at least a couple of winters old. This is the freshest and most well preserved I had yet seen, certainly occupied the previous winter.

I appreciate the aesthetic sensibilities of the den's former owner. Although scenery likely didn't factor into the bear's choice to den here, this is a beautiful spot. Just west of the mountain's rounded summit, nothing obstructs the view except mountain and horizon. Naknek Lake's western basin, surrounded by boreal woodlands and bogs, sprawls across the lowlands. Underfoot, a vibrant springtime green slowly overtakes the brown tundra. Nearly immaculate willow leaves sprout at the end of stout stems, and newly emergent fireweed stalks, leaves tightly clustered, poke a few inches above the soil.

The contrast between bright daylight and the den's dark interior makes it difficult for me to see inside, so I stoop low and crawl in. Immediately, the den's geometry begins to take shape. I move through a cylindrical tunnel, approximately 5 feet long and 3 feet high, to a bulbous sleeping chamber. Although it is a cozy space, only slightly wider and taller than the tunnel, I have no problem squatting in it. Tangles of long, thin roots dangle from an arched ceiling. The interior is dry and a little dusty. Nothing adorns the floor except for a few rocks and some compacted soil. I see no fur, scat, bedding, or other evidence a bear spent months resting inside. It smells of clean earth.

Bears spend up to half of their lives in holes like these. Arriving here the previous November, after the salmon run ended and the black crowberries froze and dropped from the stem, the den's architect used a combination of instinct and experience to dig its winter home. The den was refuge during a season of harsh weather and extreme famine. Here, the bear quietly endured winter without food and water, or even urinating and defecating. It survived by performing some of the most incredible physiological feats of any mammal. For me, the vacant den is one of the best places to contemplate the remarkable hibernating bear.

I imagine the bear that dug the den on Dumpling, walking away from the river in late October after one last meal of spawned-out salmon. Every day for the prior three weeks, salmon became increasingly scarce until the fish carcasses were so picked over that only gill plates, toothy jawbones, and putrid remnants of flesh remained. The bear has been preparing for this inevitability though. Now a fully obese animal—brown bears in the fall are often more than one-third body fat—she carries in her body all the energy and water necessary to survive the next several months.

Compelled by an instinctive urge to find a denning site and guided by knowledge gained through experience, the bear traveled north from the river along the pumice-strewn beach of Naknek Lake. The grass had long since turned brown and the last slivers of leaves hung from the birches as she walked past the shuttered lodge and empty campground. The day was dim and chilly, with temperatures barely rising high enough to break the morning frost. Just as the last light faded from the horizon, the bear moved into the forest and dug a shallow depression in the mountainside's soft duff. A dusting of snow fell overnight, but the bear hardly noticed. She remained more than warm under fur and inches of insulating fat.

The next morning, she continued uphill. The trek from Brooks River to Dumpling's summit is relatively short, easily less than a half-day's hike for a motivated bear. She walked, however, with a slow gait and sleepy gaze, stopping frequently to rest and nap. Upon reaching about 800 feet in elevation, she exited the trees and entered a mosaic of open meadows and alder thickets. The bear found travel easiest along an ascending ridgeline where she could follow a trail formed by the footfalls of others before. Along the way, she may have explored several potential denning sites, testing the suitability of the earth by digging shallow excavations on steep, well-vegetated slopes.

When the bear reached Dumpling's summit, she dropped down the steep west-facing slope to a small notch uphill of a willow thicket. After resting again, the bear began to dig. With her considerable strength and claws measuring 4 inches or more in length, she found the soil easy to work. But her sleepiness prolonged the excavation. Over the course of many days, she rested on the mountainside and rose only to dig. The pattern—short bouts of excavation paired with extended periods of rest—was repeated until the den was sufficiently deep and large enough to accommodate her mass.

After the work was complete, she remained outside the den for several more days, not venturing far or moving much at all, just sleeping more and more. Finally, as the hibernative drowsiness overtook her, she crawled inside and lied down. The bear curled tightly into a ball, tucking nose and paws together. She fell asleep to the sound of wind and falling snow.

On my hike to the bear den, while crossing the tundra on Dumpling's upper slopes, I was greeted by sharp, staccato calls of another hibernator, the arctic ground squirrel. Superficially resembling prairie dogs and always wary of predators, their chatter isn't so much a "Hello" as a "Watch out!" to alert neighbors of danger. If I'm lucky, I'll glimpse one of the grayish-brown and well-camouflaged animals before it dives into its burrow.

Like bears, arctic ground squirrels are tied to summer's bounty. After accumulating extensive fat reserves (sometimes as much as 40 to 50 percent of its body weight), the squirrel retires to a constructed den in late summer. Once inside, it deactivates its ability to produce body heat and shiver normally. Its body temperature drops in conjunction with the den's ambient temperature until the den approaches the freezing temperature of water. The ground squirrel then maintains its body temperature near or even slightly below freezing. In this refrigerated state, its energy needs decrease by about 90 percent as compared to active levels.

Throughout much of the 20th century, many biologists defined mammalian hibernation as a physiological state of reduced metabolism coupled with greatly reduced body temperature. So-called true hibernators were small mammals like ground squirrels that met these narrow parameters. Bears were often excluded because their body temperature remains relatively high during winter. This led scientists to use a host of phrases—such as winter dormancy, winter sleep, and winter denning—that hesitantly tied the winter physiology of bears to hibernation but stopped short of defining it as hibernation. However, with animals as diverse as insects, frogs, snakes, lizards, turtles, birds (common poorwills), primates (certain lemurs and a species of loris), bats, hedgehogs, dormice, ground squirrels, and bears surviving winter in long-term dormant states, hibernation is perhaps more appropriately defined by its adaptive function and duration rather than by body temperature or a specific physiology. Hibernation is a type of prolonged torpor in which an organism survives in a hypothermic state for days, weeks, or months.

The precise triggers that signal bears to prepare a den and begin hibernating are unknown, but hibernation is likely prompted by a combination of factors. Frank and John Craighead proposed some of the earliest scientific explanations during their pioneering grizzly bear studies in Yellowstone National Park. They observed grizzlies entering their dens during fall snowstorms, which led the biologists to speculate that snow and freezing temperatures initiated denning. Since then, several studies on black bears have also correlated climatic effects with den entry. Other studies suggest food availability and the animal's overall nutritional condition are the ultimate drivers, with bears in poorer condition (that is, skinnier) denning later than fatter bears. In this chicken-or-egg argument, both factors make sense. The return of snow and cold weather often coincides with a sharp reduction in food availability.

Although we don't know the exact denning location for any bear currently using the river, we can make some reasonable assumptions based on past studies. In the late 1970s, biologist Will Troyer attempted to track the movements of bears from Brooks River during spring, summer, and fall. He tranquilized and radio-collared 10 bears along the river, but due to collar failures or bears slipping their collars, Troyer was only able to determine the probable den sites of five bears. An 8-year-old male and a 3-year-old female traveled to Mount Kelez, about 6 miles away. A 4-year-old female denned on Mount Katolinat, a 12- to 15-mile journey from the river. Two others traveled much farther. A 3-year-old male probably denned near the headwaters of Ikagluik Creek and a young adult traveled to Wolverine Creek at the base of Kukak and Steller volcanoes. Both of these denning areas are nearly 40 straight-line miles from Brooks River.

In his bear den surveys of the Katmai region, Troyer found that bears sought a Goldilocks zone of conditions for their winter slumber. Well-drained soil helps reduce the risk of the den flooding. Thick vegetation conceals the den entrance, while roots stabilize the den's structure. Troyer found dens in Katmai averaged about 1,300 feet in elevation and most were almost always less than 3,000 feet above sea level. A steep hillside and slightly higher elevation increases the probability the den entrance will be sealed with insulating snow. Because dens are carved into fresh earth, they frequently collapse the following summer, forcing bears to excavate new dens each autumn. Bears in Katmai aren't known to den in permanent features such as caves or rock crevices. The regional geology generally doesn't produce such shelters.

Once a bear locates a good denning site, it returns to it frequently. Females, especially, show fidelity toward denning areas (nearly half of the time on nearby Kodiak, bears dig a new den within one kilometer of their previous den). Although Troyer's studies were not able to ascertain when the bears entered their dens, by looking at other research done in Alaska and North America we can surmise that Katmai's bears enter their dens anytime between mid-October and the end of December. The denning window may be even narrower, as studies from Kodiak Island and the southern Alaska Peninsula documented bears entering dens from November to mid-December. In general, pregnant females and females with cubs enter the den earlier than single females, while adult males are last to enter a den. Although this generalized chronology holds across North America, it is not completely universal. There are always some male bears that den before all females do.

Bears are quite tolerant of cold weather and they are so large and powerful that they needn't flee underground to avoid predation, so why do they den at all? Winter lacks one thing that bears require for survival: food. Brown bears aren't so much avoiding cold as they are avoiding famine. Hibernation is a brown bear's single best wintertime survival strategy.

Their physiological preparation begins weeks before they enter dens. In perhaps the most thorough attempt to understand the drivers of hibernation in wild, free-roaming brown bears, a team of biologists used surgically implanted cardiac monitors to track the heart rate and body temperature of 14 wild brown bears in Sweden. They also recorded the bears' location using GPS collars and gathered ambient temperatures and snow depth information from nearby weather stations. This combination of information allowed them to build the first chronology of the environmental and physiological events before, during, and after hibernation.

In October, as the denning season approached, the bears' overall activity, heart rate, and body temperature began to slowly decline. The drop in activity and heart rate began before body temperature, but each started to decrease more than three weeks prior to bears entering their dens. Heart rate and body temperature declined sharply a few days prior to den entry and continued to drop for three additional weeks after the bear had entered the den. Interestingly, these internal changes seemed to correspond with weather, at least at first. In the fall, the bears' physiological shift coincided with a steady decline in air temperature, and the bears entered a den when air temperatures were at or below freezing. The Scandinavian bears also entered dens later during years with warmer weather. Based on the results, a slow-moving bear in October isn't lazy. It is experiencing a lengthy metabolic slowdown, one that ends several weeks later in a fully hibernative physiology.

With a cloak of snow covering their dens, secured from the worst of Katmai's winter weather, the survival and health of bears depends on their ability to cope with the physiological challenges of hibernation. They must stay warm, hydrated, maintain muscle mass and bone density, and avoid poisoning themselves with their own metabolic wastes.

Arctic ground squirrels deal with the challenges, in part, by exiting their hypothermic state; 10 to 12 times per winter, the squirrel shivers to raise its body temperature back to active levels where it remains for about a day. While at "normal" temperatures, it urinates to rid its body of accumulated waste, and then it goes to sleep. Other small hibernating mammals, like chipmunks or dormice, also warm themselves periodically during hibernation to urinate and defecate, sometimes even to eat and drink depending on the species. These warming cycles are quite costly from an energetics standpoint. In the case of an arctic ground squirrel, periodic warming utilizes about half of the animal's fat reserves during winter, but it appears necessary so that the squirrel can rid itself of poisons and resume normal brain function.

Hibernating bears, in contrast, maintain their health in fundamentally different ways. First, their energy savings seem to derive more from their ability to actively suppress their metabolism rather than through reduced body temperature. In the den, bears are only slightly hypothermic. Their body temperatures are maintained about 10°F lower than in summer, even though they experience a metabolic slowdown approaching that of small mammal hibernators. Theoretically, bears would burn even less fuel and exit the den with more body mass if they behaved like ground squirrels and lowered their body temperatures to near the freezing point of water. A further reduction in body temperature, however, seems precluded by unique aspects of bear biology.

Bears are the only large hibernator. The energetic costs for a bear to follow the ground squirrel model and warm up periodically from a near-freezing body temperature may be too high for an animal weighing anywhere from several hundred to over a thousand pounds when fully grown. Even more remarkably, unlike small mammal hibernators, the hibernating bear does not eat, drink, urinate, or defecate. This, combined with its annual cycle of extreme weight gain followed by months of prolonged starvation and lack of exercise, would create profound health issues for people.

Highly sedentary or immobilized persons—either from lifestyle, illness, trauma, or increased age—experience a wide variety of health complications, many of which are difficult to treat and difficult or impossible to reverse. During prolonged bed rest our muscles atrophy quickly, losing strength and endurance. Bones and connective tissues lose mass and strength, leading to osteoporosis and contracture, respectively. We develop pressure sores. Blood clots can form in our legs that, if they break free, can travel to the lungs or brain, increasing the risk of pulmonary embolism and stroke. Lung capacity decreases and we become more susceptible to infection and pneumonia. Much of the cardiovascular system weakens, and the heart becomes less efficient. After long periods of bed rest, our balance and coordination decline and physical exertion can lead to angina. Walking can be extremely difficult. If we stand suddenly we become susceptible to dangerously low blood pressure levels as the body has trouble adapting normally to an upright posture.

Without food, humans approach fatal levels of starvation in a month, and when we accumulate the same amount of fat as prehibernating bears, our risk of developing heart disease and diabetes increases substantially. No matter our health or fat reserves though, without water we're overcome by dehydration within a few days. If, like bears, we shut off our kidneys in order to stop urinating and conserve water, then our own metabolic wastes would soon poison us.

Bears have solved these issues. Despite being one of the most obese land mammals on Earth and remaining sedentary for half of the year, bears do not develop heart disease, diabetes, muscle atrophy, or osteoporosis. With no exercise, they retain the ability to get up and move about normally throughout the denning cycle. Wounds and broken bones continue to heal, and they don't develop bedsores. Their hearts, beating only 8 to 10 times per minute while hibernating, pump so little blood volume that a human with the same condition would die. They don't rid their body of metabolic waste yet aren't poisoned by it. They breathe only one to two times per minute. The body of a hibernating bear is essentially a closed system.

They need nothing from the outside world except oxygen and emit nothing except water vapor, carbon dioxide, and body heat. Even compared to other mammalian hibernators, bears are metabolic magicians.

Bears survive the hibernation period because they got fat beforehand. Metabolizing body fat produces metabolic water, heat, and carbon dioxide. The carbon dioxide is absorbed into the bloodstream and exhaled normally through the lungs, while the heat and water are used for warmth and hydration. A bear also minimizes its body's demand for water by adhering to strict water-conservation principles. Physical movements are limited, so cells don't become thirsty like they would in a more active mammal. Their kidneys produce little urine, which is soon reabsorbed by the bladder. In this way, fat metabolism produces enough metabolic water to keep bears hydrated. Water lost to the environment is primarily through exhaling. Hibernating bears in captivity will even ignore water provided to them.

Despite their reliance on body fat, hibernating bears still utilize some protein stores, and this presents far different physiological challenges than burning fat. Burning lean tissue produces ammonium. In mammals, the liver converts excess ammonium to urea, which the kidneys filter out of the bloodstream. During summer, a bear produces copious amounts of dilute urine to flush this poison from its body. With kidney function greatly reduced during hibernation, however, it must have an alternative method to prevent poisoning by its own metabolic wastes.

When hibernating, metabolic waste that would normally be flushed from the body by urination diffuses into the intestine. There, with the help of a special suite of gut bacteria, over 99 percent of the urea is converted into usable protein, which the bear reabsorbs and recycles back into its muscle tissue. Bears exit the den with little to no loss of muscle mass or strength, despite a lack of exercise and food.

Urea recycling underpins their wintertime muscle fitness, but this alone may not be enough to maintain muscle health. Even when fed a well-balanced diet, a bedridden person loses over half of her strength over 90 days and over half of her muscle mass after two months. Regaining lost muscle is also very difficult for people, as the rate of recovery is much slower than the rate of loss. The periodic warming and waking cycles of hibernating ground squirrels may play an important role in maintaining their muscle health. Even though bears don't experience the deep torpor and waking cycles of hibernating ground squirrels, black bears rhythmically stimulate their muscles through periodic shivering. Intriguingly, bears might also produce a powerful chemical inhibitor that blocks muscle wasting, and they vary the expression of certain genes associated with muscle cell function during their active and hibernation periods.

Muscle preservation and hydration aren't the only challenges of a starving, nearly immobilized animal. Physical activity and gravity stimulate bone cells to reform, which maintains their strength and stiffness. In humans, prolonged immobilization or rest promotes significant bone loss, and afterward our skeleton can take years to recover.

Captive hibernating bears are inactive for over 98 percent of their hibernation period, yet hibernating bears maintain their bone health without the normally required physical stimulus. Eliminating the need to urinate certainly helps them retain some of the calcium that would otherwise be flushed from the body. Perhaps an increase in parathyroid hormone activity stimulates the kidneys to reabsorb more calcium. Genes that control bone formation mechanisms could become more active. Bears may retain more vitamin D and experience an increase in bone formation cells and markers. Other evidence suggests that bears suppress the normal mechanisms of bone turnover and reformation. The sum of the adaptations prevents osteoporosis.

Bears not only maintain their health while hibernating but also possess the ability to improve it. During winter observations of more than 1,000 radio-collared black bears, researchers in Minnesota documented bears with injuries from gunshots, arrows, bite marks, cuts from radio collars, and unknown origins. The wounds were often inflamed or infected in early winter, but they were typically healed a few months later. When small wounds were created experimentally (the researchers chemically immobilized and cut the bears), the wounds healed after several weeks, complete with new hair follicles and minimal scarring. Bears even expelled insertable cardiac monitors, originally designed for human heart patients, like our skin working out a splinter.

Like so many aspects of their hibernative cycle, how bears do this is not understood. Blood flow, high body temperature, and kidney function are important factors for wound healing in people. Since all are reduced in denning bears, we might expect that their wounds would not heal easily, or perhaps not at all. Unlike a hypothermic person, however, reduced body temperature in hibernating bears is purposeful, so it could have very different physiological consequences for them. A black bear's bouts of periodic shivering, which appear to raise skin surface temperature but not core body temperature, could help increase blood circulation and promote healing. Bears may also possess hormonal mechanisms or other substances that assist with healing that have yet to be isolated and identified.

Katmai's brown bears emerge from the den into a large frozen and dormant land. Like the bear, it has only begun to show signs of reawakening. For bears, hibernation is a form of perseverance. It maximizes the time they can survive unfavorable conditions. As I squat inside the den on Dumpling, I can understand the relative comfort and security this shelter provides, but I can't experience how bears survive here and emerge so healthy. My biology is too different.

What if we could apply some of the tricks of bear physiology to our own? A bear's relatively high body temperature during hibernation suggests the mechanisms they utilize to remain healthy may also work at normal human body temperatures. Understanding how bears rest for months while retaining their ability to stand could help people who suffer traumatic injuries maintain muscle and bone health when they otherwise cannot exercise. It could revolutionize space travel, as astronauts experience disuse osteoporosis even though they exercise vigorously while in space. Studying how bears shut off their kidneys for months at a time could lead to novel ways to solve renal diseases and lengthen the life span of organs used in transplants. During hibernation bears become resistant to insulin, a hormone that regulates blood sugar, but the condition reverses back to normal during their active season. Understanding this process and how bears are able to stay healthy while essentially becoming diabetic for part of the year may lead to novel treatments for diabetes in people. Knowing how brown bears tolerate high cholesterol, obesity, and limited circulation—all without accumulating plaque in their arteries—could help us develop treatments for heart disease, which is currently the leading cause of death in the United States. The metabolic and physiologic feats of bears could help us treat some of humanity's most chronic and frustrating diseases.

In early to mid-spring, as the long hours of daylight return, the bear that dug the den remained insulated by earth and snow. She's shown signs of increasing restlessness though. Her heart rate has been slowly increasing during the last several weeks. As ambient air temperatures stabilize above freezing, she pushes through any remaining snow and into the aboveground world. She remains a little groggy after the long slumber; after all, her heart rate won't stabilize at active levels for a few more weeks, but her time of famine is almost over. Having lost one-quarter to one-third or more of her body mass, the lean animal that emerges looks far different than the chubby giant from several months before. But she is poised to take advantage of summer's plenty once again.

CHAPTER 5

FAMILY

A bear approaches the falls with caution. Having visited the river before, this young mother, known as 273, is familiar with Brooks Falls and its salmon. But protecting, nurturing, and caring for her 6-month-old cub, the first she's ever mothered, presents a new set of challenges and the risk of failure is high.

Considering the family's nutritional demands, 273's hunger pangs must be intense. The cub is in the midst of a tremendous growth spurt, but he's not yet mature enough to survive on solid food alone. Mother's milk remains his primary source of calories, and having subsisted mostly on tender blades of emerging grass since exiting the den, mom is down to the last of her fat reserves.

As the family walks upstream, the cub follows as best he can. At his current size, slightly larger than a terrier, the cub struggles to keep pace. The family climbs on top of a shallowly exposed boulder and pauses. While mother evaluates the scene, the spring cub shoves his way underneath her belly and peers with a nervous curiosity.

The family's springtime travels were solitary. After emerging from their den, they wandered slowly across the landscape, largely avoiding places where other bears are prone to linger. Even so, 273's springtime home range overlapped with several other bears. Along a lakeside trail, they encountered a battered spruce tree, its bark splintered by claws and teeth as high as 8 feet above the ground. The ground below was nearly bare of vegetation from the stomping and grinding action of dinner plate–sized paws. Tufts of dark brown fur were glued to the trunk by oozing pitch. Two-seven-three investigated this place carefully. Inhaling deeply, she used her keen sense of smell to evaluate which bears had been there and how long ago they passed through.

The cub watched his mother closely in these situations. He sniffed the ground and tree too, mimicking his mother's every move, letting the aromas fill his nostrils as she did. The brew of scent indicated a few bears marked the tree recently, but one odor was particularly strong and fresh. It trailed away from the tree in a series of footfalls and a squiggly line of urine-soaked dirt. For reasons she didn't communicate, this scent provoked her wariness. She turned and began walking in a different direction, avoiding the path where the large male wandered.

As the family approaches the falls, the memory of that encounter floods back to the cub. Yet here they are, at a place where the air is not only filled with ursine scent, but the water is swarming with other bears, many of them large and smelling distinctly similar to the odors left on that tree.

Two-seven-three knows the visit carries risk. Would the potential reward be worth it? Mother bears are challenged to not only provide for their own welfare but also for their cubs. Throughout the family's life together, which typically spans two to three years, a mother must nourish and nurture her ravenous cubs as well as provide for her own sustenance. The experiences her cub gains at Brooks Falls are just a few of many that will help teach him how to survive in an unforgiving world.

A brown bear's life begins during the coldest time of year, midwinter, when Katmai is locked in ice and snow. Within her den, a pregnant female gives birth to especially tiny babies. A newborn cub is about the size of a beagle puppy, weighing a scant pound and measuring only 8 to 9 inches long. They are blind, lightly furred, and nearly immobile. Their ears are closed and their muzzles are short with a round, toothless mouth. At birth, cubs are so underdeveloped and small that they cannot maintain their own body heat in the chilly den. About the only thing they can do is scream, which, not unlike human newborns, they employ frequently to gain their mother's attention. It's hard to imagine bears so helpless, but they all start life this way.

Brown bears mate in late spring and early summer, but fertilized eggs do not immediately implant in the uterus. During this process of delayed implantation, embryos undergo a few cell divisions and then enter a state of arrested development while the female goes about her business gaining weight in preparation for winter. Implantation and fetal growth renew close to the time she begins hibernation. After implantation, bear fetuses gestate for six to eight weeks. Birth occurs anytime from early January to late February with most births typically happening closer to the last two weeks of January.

The gestation period is remarkably short for such a large mammal. In general, larger placental mammals have longer gestation periods than smaller mammals and give birth to larger offspring. African elephant calves, for example, gestate for nearly two years and are born bigger than elk calves; elk calves gestate for about eight months and are born bigger than deer fawns; deer fawns gestate for seven months and are born bigger than fox kits; and so on. But bears break the rule by a considerable margin, giving birth to the smallest offspring in comparison to adult female body size of any mammal.

Cubs are only 1/100th the size of small reproducing female black bears and 1/500th or less the size of large adult females in Katmai. In comparison, a 7.5-pound human baby born by a 150-pound woman is 1/20th the size of its mother, meaning that a 10-pound baby is an order of magnitude larger than a bear cub. Additionally, offspring born to large mammals, although highly reliant on their mothers' milk, are generally precocial, meaning they are somewhat mobile soon after birth. Only marsupials give birth to offspring as undersized as bears.

The purposeful prematurity of bear cubs appears to be an adaptation to maximize the use of fat, the one energy source a hibernating mother bear has in surplus. Developing mammal fetuses cannot metabolize free-fatty acids, perhaps because these chemicals do not cross the placenta as readily as sugars and protein. Hibernating bears, though, don't have a surplus of sugar and protein to offer. Thus, as long as an expectant mother tries to sustain fetal growth through her placenta, she needs to draw energy from her own body protein and risk dangerously depleting those reserves. To work around these challenges, bears give birth to small, helpless cubs and let them grow on milk supplies. This permits a mother to switch from placental to mammary nourishment, from providing protein and sugar, which are of limited supply, to providing milk, which is something she can produce in abundance from her own body fat.

The first few weeks of a cub's life are calm and peaceful. Immediately after giving birth, 273 helped her cub find her teats where he began to suckle. Mom moved very little, and perhaps didn't even stand for the next three weeks so as to stay in near-constant contact with her cub and to keep him warm. In an exception to the no-eating-while-hibernating rule, 273 ate the placenta after giving birth and the cub's feces to keep the den clean. The cub's eyes opened after three weeks. His motor skills improved daily, and he began walking somewhere around 45 days old. The cub nursed and rested until he became mobile enough to begin to explore the den. Most often, he suckled and rested, sleeping in a milk coma and wearing a creamy milk mustache.

His overall growth during the first few weeks of life is highly dependent on how much milk he drinks. Brown bear milk is particularly rich and nourishing—about 20 percent fat by volume. On this diet, he grows rapidly. Cubs often weigh 5 pounds when 1 month old and 15 to 25 pounds by 90 days. Not coincidentally, this is about as big as they would be if gestation were an "expected" length for a mammal as large as a bear. In this way, the den acts as a surrogate womb. It provides cubs with a secure place to grow until they are mature enough to leave.

The den is also where cubs can get their first taste of competition. Bears have six teats. Four are located on the mother's chest and two are positioned on her lower abdomen. In Katmai, litter size averages two or three cubs, and ranges from one to four, so the number of teats seems adequate to support all cubs in a litter. But depending on the time of year, teats produce milk at different rates. The two abdominal teats are the most productive while the mother continues to hibernate. As a result, early in the lactation cycle, demand for milk exceeds access in litters of three or more cubs. This demand causes the whole litter to grow slower. In a study of tracking the influence of maternal condition on birth date and growth of newborn cubs, researchers from Washington State University and the University of Wyoming found that at 90 days old, triplet cubs were only 55 percent of the size of twin cubs even though they were raised by mothers of the same body fat content.

Milk represents a significant energetic investment for a mother bear, but since cubs are so small at birth they consume only 9 percent of their first year's milk intake in the den. Once outside the den though, a cub's growth rate and demand for food skyrockets. Brown bear cubs can drink 45 ounces of milk per day in midsummer. At that rate, a litter of three would need more than a gallon each day. To meet the demand, a mother bear increases her milk production fourfold between hibernation and summer.

When hungry, a cub will frequently initiate nursing bouts with loud bawls while nosing and sometimes biting its mother's teats. Mother bears aren't always willing to give in. Outside the den, she may have other things on her mind like food or security. When she feels the family is secure, the mom will lie on her back or sometimes recline in an upright sitting position and allow her cubs to clamor on her chest. Contented cubs vocalize as they suckle, the noise reminiscent of a scaled-up version of a house cat purr combined with a car engine that won't start because of a dead battery. Afterward, the entire family may nap in an ephemeral moment of peace.

For the first four to five months of his life, 273's cub was confined within a cramped and, at best, dimly lit space. With spring's warming temperatures, the den's protective veil of snow thinned and the darkness yielded to a deep blue hue. As the thaw continued, perhaps by mid-spring, a hole in the snow formed at the entrance, giving the cub his first glimpse of the sky. Eventually, he followed his mother outside and, if the winter was snowy, into a scene of blinding whiteness.

Leaving the den must seem like entering another world. Melting snow reveals new curiosities around every corner. Twigs and leaves become play toys. Snowy slopes are playgrounds. Cubs play and explore in these carefree moments, but spring is a dangerous time in which mother must be especially cautious.

Young cubs fresh from the den are not yet fleet of foot, and they cannot outrun or evade predators like larger bears, wolves, and golden eagles. They also have trouble navigating rough terrain, are small enough to become chilled when wet, and can drown in rivers and creeks. To compensate, mother bears with spring cubs remain within their den longer than all other bears. They often won't emerge until May or, more rarely, early June. Extra time in the den provides the cubs more opportunities to grow and gain coordination, as well as to isolate the family from danger. A family may travel little during the first few weeks after emerging, opting to remain near their den site instead of undertaking a risky journey at a time of year when little food is available.

The journey to Brooks River takes a toll on mother bears with spring cubs. As a group they are the skinniest of all bears upon arrival. A close look can reveal protruding hip bones and shoulder blades. Their bellies, instead of drooping low, lie parallel to the ground. Two-seven-three certainly lacked the pudgy plumpness of the previous fall, and her thick fur hid a lean frame.

Two days after they first approached the falls, her hunger brought the family even closer to the cascade. She remained just as cautious as before, her cub even more so, while they stood just downstream from the falls on a small grassy island. With several other bears nearby, the cub followed directly behind his mother and often stood on his hind legs to lean against her, conga-line style. As she moved, he didn't seem to want to lose contact. I remember this scene well, and the behavior immediately endeared this family to many bear watchers. Cuteness aside, the family wasn't in a relaxed mood. My field notes from that evening, scribbled quickly as I watched the family, record a gamut of takeaways: "Very cute. Very stressed. Very vulnerable."

The bear closest to 273 was a large adult male fishing in the jacuzzi, one of the most preferred and productive fishing spots at the falls. After catching a salmon, he walks a short distance to the head of the island and lies down to eat the fish. Two-seven-three pays close attention to this bear, an animal perhaps three times larger than she is, and one who could easily overpower her and kill her cub. The family backs away a few yards but then stalls their retreat, held in place by the enticing scent of fish and the potential to scavenge. Thankfully for the family, the big male is only interested in his salmon. He eats the whole fish minus some entrails before calmly returning to his fishing spot. Two-seven-three was waiting for this opportunity, and before another bear or hungry gull can scavenge the leftovers, she rushes over and gulps down the gill plates and entrails, a modest bite given the risk she took.

Mother bears behave across a wide spectrum as they attempt to balance their movement and foraging strategies with the risks to their cubs. At the falls in July, sometimes as many as two dozen bears vie for space at the same time. While the reward of food here can be great (on a productive day, catch rates can be as high as one fish every few minutes), the risk posed by larger bears is significant, especially for bear families with young cubs. Two-seven-three's caution implied that she perceived danger, yet it wasn't enough to prevent her from visiting the falls. That's not the case with other mothers. Some may avoid the river altogether.

Divot was the first bear I ever saw at Brooks River. The day I arrived in 2007, she was digging shallow holes in the exposed gravel upstream of the river mouth, a habit that supposedly inspired her nickname. She was young then, not even 6 years old, yet already a well-known bear at the river. Divot has a distinct face with small eyes, a lack of a brow ridge, a wide muzzle that tapers straight from her forehead to her nose, and a large early summer shed patch on her forehead. She's easy to pick out in a crowd. She was also brought to Brooks River as a cub by her mother and had displayed a high tolerance for human activity. That's why I was surprised in July 2013 when she didn't arrive.

That August, however, during a time when fishing is typically poor at the river, a female with two spring cubs appeared near the river mouth. I watched the mother from the elevated platform. She was sitting on the bank, staring at the water while her two cubs relaxed alongside. Confused at first, I considered whether this was a bear that had not visited the river before. But she seemed tolerant of people, indicating she had experience with nosy humans. Suddenly, after staring at her face, I realized I was looking at Divot. She was with her first known litter. She had avoided the river all of July, forgoing its fishing opportunities perhaps in order to give her cubs a greater level of protection.

Divot's behavior was not uncommon. Tracking studies of brown bears elsewhere in Alaska have found that some females with young cubs may pass up opportunities to fish for salmon altogether, likely to avoid other bears while their cubs are young and vulnerable. Divot's initial avoidance of the river with spring cubs was short-lived though. She didn't stay away from the river in July 2016 with her second litter, and many other mother bears with spring cubs chose to fish here as well. A few mothers boldly march their cubs to the falls, parking them on the bank or in a tree while they assume their preferred fishing spot. Others use a more hybrid approach, avoiding the falls during their cubs' first summer but then fishing there when the cubs are yearlings. Some come to the river yet never fish at the falls, attempting to make a living in areas where male bears are less likely to congregate and personal space is easier to find. Two-seven-three adopted the latter strategy with her second litter in 2019. Instead of taking her three spring cubs to the falls, she fished and scavenged opportunistically near the river mouth.

While raising her first cub though, 273 was discovering the difficulty of maintaining split focus between finding food and scanning for threats. Her cub was learning too. He did not follow his mother passively from one place to another. By watching her and investigating anything she showed interest in, he absorbed a host of life lessons, especially when they pertained to food.

Watching bear families closely, you can see how eager cubs are to investigate nearly everything their mother shows interest in. While serving as a surrogate mother for orphaned cubs, black bear researcher Benjamin Kilham discovered that his cubs could associate what to eat by smelling food on his breath. As he recalled in a 2010 talk at the College of the Atlantic, "I'd get thirsty and I'd go down on my hands and knees to a mountain stream to get a drink of water, and every time I did this the cubs would rush me and then make an audible sniff like they were expecting some kind of information. I got the idea that they were looking for some kind of chemical cue, maybe about what I was eating so I did a little experiment.

"I'm out on a log landing and I got down on my hands and knees and started browsing on red clover, something I knew the bears hadn't experienced yet and something I knew wouldn't kill me when I chewed on it. When I did this each one of the cubs rushed me and stuck their nose in my mouth and took a long sniff and immediately went out searching for red clover and started eating."

While 273 waited to scavenge fish near the falls, her cub ignored the nearby plants until mother started grazing on them. He immediately took the cue and began grazing himself. I once watched a yearling investigate clay that he would've ignored had his mother not stopped to eat it. The clay is ubiquitous at the river, a 6- to 8-inch-deep layer of weathered ash from the 1912 Novarupta eruption. Cubs can access it nearly anywhere, but this one seemed to do so only because mother did.

When a mother bear passes on her lifetime of discovery and exploration, the lessons can be carried from generation to generation, forming matrilineal cultures around food. The process is adaptive for the highly omnivorous brown bear, especially in a place like Katmai where bears don't have access to human food. In other parts of Alaska and North America though, including the towns and villages just outside Katmai's boundaries, if mother teaches her cubs to turn over dumpsters, remove coolers in a campground, grab dog food out of an unlocked garage, or raid a domestic beehive, then the instinct, which had served them well through most of their evolutionary history, can lead to an early death for the bears at the hands of people protecting their life or property. In areas where bear-human conflict is frequent, bears raised by mothers conditioned to exploit human food are more likely to seek out human foods after they become independent compared to bears that were never introduced to human food.

Once a bear associates a place with food, it never forgets, and a lack of food can make bears ornery and prone to defend what little they have. Two-seven-three wasn't the only bear with unfulfilled hunger pangs the evening she ventured close to the falls. Several other bears prowled the fringes, and the search for food brought one of them toward the island and the family.

Not keen on having her space invaded, 273 lowered her head and faced the intruder. Only a few feet separated them now, and 273's defensiveness increased proportionally. Alone and skinny, the other female appeared hungry, but she was mostly a victim of circumstance. She followed her appetite for fish only to encounter a mother who took no chances protecting her offspring.

As the female approached, 273 growled and positioned herself to attack. When the other bear didn't immediately yield, 273 lunged forward and cuffed the lone female with her paws. They growled and stood face to face for a few more seconds before 273 unleashed a flurry of swats that sufficiently communicated the message to back off. The lone female slowly moved away. Two-seven-three and her cub remained on the island, safe for at least another moment.

Although the brief encounter was relatively mild, the lengths to which mothers are willing to go to protect their offspring are justifiably famous. Mother bears sometimes risk everything to keep their cubs safe.

Grazer was especially defensive when she brought triplets, representing her first litter, to Brooks River in the early summer of 2016. Within a few days of her arrival, I watched her and her family from the riffles platform. Grazer seemed particularly nervous. She huffed and stood frequently even though no other bears were close. Her few attempts to fish were brief and interrupted by the calls of her smallest cub who bawled anytime her mother left her side. During a moment between fishing forays, Grazer turned her attention to another bear approaching from downstream.

Eighty-three was a medium-large adult male and no stranger to physical encounters. Just above his tail he bore a large, soggy wound, and numerous scars pockmarked his face and neck. He appeared unaware of or unconcerned about the family upstream. I'd never seen him show overt aggression toward cubs, but Grazer wasn't taking any chances. As he took a few more paces, she looked directly at him and charged. Just seconds later, after running about 30 yards, she hit him with all her force.

Eighty-three seemed startled by the suddenness of her attack. She raked him with her claws and attempted to bite him around his face and neck. The bears roared at each other, heads held high and mouths agape, poised like a couple of snarling dogs to grab their opponent. Although 83 was much larger, he didn't match Grazer's intensity. She pressed the attack, forcing him into the vegetation as the mauling continued. Their loud and intense roars echoed across the river. Branches snapped as 83 was forced through a clump of willows. He inadvertently backed up toward the cubs, causing Grazer to push the fight. Finally, after nearly 40 seconds of maternal fury, Grazer broke off her attack, perhaps exhausted from the battle or sensing 83 wouldn't approach her cubs further. She ran to the spruce tree where her cubs were sheltered in the canopy. She stood upright and leaned on the tree, huffing, panting, and foaming at the mouth.

Caution and defensiveness seem to be an inherent trait in mother bears, providing a strong survival advantage for a species that regularly experiences high cub mortality. In Katmai, survival rates of first-year cubs are among the lowest ever documented. During a multiyear study of brown bears on Katmai's Pacific coast, only one out of three cubs survived their first year. No bears were radio-collared in the Brooks River area for the study, so the results aren't a direct reflection of the population dynamics in the interior of the park, but the statistic underscores the vulnerability of young offspring in a landscape where the bear population may be at or near carrying capacity. Although survival rates are usually better across the rest of the range of North American brown bears, generally hovering between 50 and 70 percent for the first year, survival for cubs is far from guaranteed.

Infanticide, the killing of dependent offspring by another bear, is one of the biggest threats to cubs. This may be the main reason why mother bears are often ornery, belligerent, and much more likely to attack compared to other classes of bears such as single females and males. Most documented cases of infanticide are caused by adult males, yet females have been observed killing cubs too. Therefore, mother bears often view every bear as a threat, a defensive tendency that they occasionally apply toward humans. According to North American bear attack statistics, mother brown bears are the most dangerous to encounter, especially when they are surprised.

Mothers communicate warnings and their level of stress through body language and vocalizations. Huffing, for instance, tells cubs to be on alert. Cubs react immediately by grouping near their mother or, as Grazer's did, by scrambling to shelter in a tree. Mother bears don't attack without provocation, but sometimes the trigger is so minor and the reaction so quick that, like 83, the recipient isn't even aware of what's going on until it is too late.

Although 273 wasn't able to catch or scavenge many fish during the first few evenings she visited the falls, it wasn't reflective of her success over the rest of that summer. The family made a good living downstream, catching and scavenging salmon into early fall.

On an overcast and chilly late September afternoon, I watched 273 and her cub move slowly through the lower river. The nights had become frosty, and yellowed birch leaves littered the ground. Mom was chubby with a glossy and slightly grizzled fur coat. Her cub's appearance matched closely. He had grown considerably during the last few months and weighed nearly 70 pounds. With hibernation season fast approaching, food remained foremost on their minds, but dead and dying salmon were so plentiful that they also had ample time to explore other pursuits.

On the bank near the bridge, the cub lopes a few yards toward his mother and cuffs her on the side of her head. She reciprocates, swatting gently at his face and neck. The cub, eager to play, takes this as a full invitation to battle. He paws and bites the side of her face. She leans forward, pushing her son backward. Two-seven-three shows remarkable restraint, given that the cub tugs on her cheeks and rakes his paws over her face. At one point, he even places his claws in his mother's mouth. The bout ends when mom decides she's had enough. She stands and walks away. A few seconds later, the cub realizes playtime is over and follows her downstream.

In bears, as it was for 273 and her cub, family life might be a time of stress and sacrifice, but it also contains lots of learning and love. We empathize with the sacrifices bears make to raise their cubs, and from afar we share in their moments of parental joy and tenderness. Mother bear is a teacher who provides lessons in survival, a fierce defender willing to risk severe injury to protect vulnerable offspring, and a partner in play helping her cubs gain coordination, strength, and simply have fun. She shows patience and tolerance when her offspring err, but she will not hesitate to discipline them when they misbehave. Cubs become her students, fellow explorers, and companions. It's almost as if, dare I say, we see a bit of humanity in a bear family.

CHAPTER 6

MATING SEASON

I had always known bear 402 as an experienced mother, yet her behavior toward her cub in early July 2014 stumped me. She was in the midst of raising one yearling who represented, up to that time in her life, her fifth known litter. As 402 fished and traveled, she didn't offer her cub much of anything, certainly not food or protection. She seemed almost absentee in her maternal obligations.

Around the same time, the river's most dominant bear, 856, began to show an uncommon interest in her. His behavior wasn't aggressive. He seemed more curious about 402 than anything, sniffing where she had walked and slowly following her movements through the forest. While 402 avoided 856 for the most part, it wasn't with the urgency typical of a mother who is trying to protect her cub.

For several days, I watched 402's yearling keep pace despite mom's disinterest. At the falls, he bawled from the bank while she fished and ate salmon on the lip. On July 9, the yearling climbed a tree near the waterfall. When 402 left that evening, with 856 not far behind, she did not retrieve him. Only then did I finally understand the circumstances: 402 had entered estrus and emancipated her yearling, her body unconsciously transitioning back to the beginning of her reproductive cycle. Eight-five-six, meanwhile, had a twinkle in his eye.

At first, 402 wanted nothing to do with her suitor. She maintained her distance from 856, usually remaining at least 50 to 100 feet in front of him. His pursuit was unwavering, however, and moments of rest for 402 were infrequent. He approached her nearly every time she stopped and followed wherever she moved. For more than a week, 402 meandered up and down the river corridor and 856 followed single-mindedly.

Just as the salmon run begins, Brooks River becomes one of the rare places where the availability of concentrated food coincides partly with the bears' mating season, a roughly 6- to 8-week period in late spring and early summer. Eight-five-six didn't work hard to locate 402 initially—they both came to the falls around the same time—but he did have to keep track of and court her, a challenge to overcome if he was to eventually secure the opportunity to mate.

Courtship is a conspicuous part of bear life in spring and early summer by which a male bear follows a female who he senses may soon be receptive to mating. The goal for the male is to guard access to the female and habituate her to his presence, waiting for the moment when, if he's lucky, so to speak, she will accept his advances. The female, more often than not, remains initially cautious. For most of the year, and even during the mating season, the male can be dangerous. She needs to grow accustomed to his close proximity and evaluate his true intentions.

Male bears don't extend any olive branches to their prospective mates nor do they prove their worthiness through displays of fitness or gifts of food. They follow. Eight-five-six pursued 402 in a steady, nonaggressive manner, generally keeping her within his line of sight, a task made easy as long as she remained in open areas and he didn't become distracted.

Several days into their courtship, I watched 402 walk to the lip of the falls. Eight-five-six, as usual, was not far behind. He decided to occupy the jacuzzi where he could both fish and keep watch over 402. Within a few moments, he snared a salmon in his jaws and walked a short distance out of the jacuzzi to eat. Just as he turned away, 402 coincidentally decided it was time to leave. She marched off the lip and into a meadow upstream of the falls. Eight-five-six didn't rush through his meal or notice 402's departure, and by the time he finished his prospective mate had been absent for several minutes.

As soon as he noticed, 856 moved out of the river and into the forest, following what appeared to be nearly the same path as his love interest. It seemed as though she might have had a sufficient head start to finally separate herself from 856, if that was her intention. Four-zero-two, however, could neither run nor hide, not from a suitor with a nose like 856.

Bears perceive a world of odor that we can scarcely imagine. Through scent, bears not only detect what to eat and where food is located, but also who's a friendly neighbor and who's a foe. They can sniff out animal carcasses from miles away, track lost cubs through the forest, recognize residual food odor on sealed tin cans, and smell clams burrowed deep within exposed tidal flats. They rely on scent like we rely on vision to develop a mental map of their communities.

Unlike hearing, sight, or touch, the capacity to smell provides bears with the ability to perceive the world beyond the immediate. When 856 travels across a landscape, he smells a rich broth of chemical compounds associated with skin, hair, scat, urine, and footprints, all of which provide a thorough description of preceding events. Deep in his nasal cavity, inhaled air passes over a complex scaffold of paper-thin bones. The bones enlarge the surface area within the nasal cavity, helping to condition incoming air and reduce evaporative water loss. A portion of these bones, the olfactory turbinates, are also studded with proteins specialized for detecting scent.

Roughly speaking, the size and complexity of a species' olfactory turbinates is thought to reflect an organism's demand for the sense of smell, and bears devote an impressively large amount of their nasal cavity to catching scent. Using high-resolution CT scans, Patrick Green and Blaire Van Valkenburgh at the University of California Los Angeles found the olfactory turbinate surface area of one male brown bear to equal about 250 inches^2 (1,600 cm^2), a surface area approaching that of the front page of a newspaper. In comparison, the olfactory turbinate surface area of humans averages a measly 1.4 inches^2 (9 cm^2), which is about the size of a postage stamp.

Once odor is detected, neurons transmit the signal from the nasal cavity to the brain's olfactory bulb for interpretation. There, perhaps not surprisingly, bears have spared no brainpower. Their olfactory bulb is five times larger than a human's, impressively big considering their brain is less than half the size of our own. Our sense of smell is far from inactive or vestigial, but if we could talk to bears and they to us, we would lack the vocabulary to fully understand the world of odor they experience.

Eight-five-six soon located 402 and continued his pursuit. As the courtship approached its one-week anniversary, I watched 856 and 402 come and go from the falls, with 402 pausing infrequently to fish, and I wondered how long this could continue. Eight-five-six possessively guarded his narrow window of opportunity, and he seemed quite prepared to use his brawn to fend off anyone who dared challenge him. In the bear world, size and strength matter.

The distinct physical differences between males and females in addition to the differences between the sexual organs themselves is called sexual dimorphism. In humans, sexual dimorphism is expressed by external genitalia, body size, muscle mass, voice, body hair, metabolism, and hormones among other differences. In other species, it can be expressed with a bit more flare. Males belonging to the birds-of-paradise—a group of passerines living in parts of Indonesia, Papua New Guinea, and Australia—are garishly colored and adorned with feathery ornaments. The males of many birds-of-paradise species must not only look their best but also perform elaborate courtship dances to secure the favor of females. This is a ritualized form of sexual combat in which females choose winners based on who has the healthiest plumage and most perfect dances.

Showmanship and flamboyance aren't able to settle competition for mates in all species though. Among mammals, size-based sexual dimorphism reaches an extreme in southern elephant seals living in sub-Antarctic oceans. Fully grown adult males weigh anywhere from 4,900 to 8,800 pounds—up to six times bigger than adult females. The size difference is probably driven by physical conflict between males for access to mates.

Elephant seals gather annually at rookeries to give birth and mate. Males arrive earlier than females to stake claim on an area of beach. When females arrive, the male defends his harem. Battles between males for these territories can be prolonged and intense. Males with the right combination of size, stamina, and strength are most likely to maintain their territory and so pass on their genes to the next generation.

Male bears don't acquire and maintain harems, and bears do not gather in specific locations for the purpose of mating, but they face selection pressures that promote size-based sexual dimorphism. Mating opportunities are limited, because not all female bears are receptive to mating each year and the few that enter estrus do so for only a short period of time. In the absence of male parental care, a male's reproductive success is proportional to the number of cubs he sires. Under this regime, male bears that have the endurance, size, and strength necessary to maintain access to females have a competitive advantage when it comes to reproductive opportunities.

In adult brown bears, the most obvious difference between the sexes is body size. Being at the upper end of the scale for Katmai's bears, 856 is often twice as big as the females he courts. The difference can be so profound that it's not uncommon for inexperienced observers to mistake courting pairs as a family group, albeit one where the bigger "mom" follows the smaller "cub." The size discrepancy is partly reflective of their different reproductive roles. Cubs are energetically expensive, and female bears slow down or even stop their growth rate once they begin to reproduce. In contrast, males can devote all their energy to themselves and continue to grow quickly after they reach sexual maturity.

A study of brown bears in Sweden found older and larger males have the highest yearly reproductive success, yet male breeding opportunities are limited by the number of reproductively available females. On Alaska's North Slope, an arctic environment where brown bears occupy extremely large home ranges and live at low densities, only about half of adult males successfully breed. It's unclear whether that pattern holds true at Brooks River, but the available evidence indicates it pays to grow large and dominant. Genetic analysis of more than 100 bears at Brooks River from the years 2005 through 2007 assigned 14 paternal relationships to just 4 male bears. Biologists visually observed three of these bears, noting they were among the most dominant and largest on the river. One, the legendary BB, reigned at or near the top of the hierarchy for about 10 years. He mated with six females who later produced offspring, and he is the father of 402. The identity of the fourth male is unknown, indicating that there could have been, at least in that decade, a relatively dominant bear that never visited the river.

Male bears use their size to intimidate other males when competing for access to potential mates. Occasionally, posturing does not sufficiently settle these disputes and a violent fight can erupt. These fights, I presume, are the source of many, if not most, of the fresh wounds we see on males in late spring and early summer. Competition for limited mating opportunities isn't restricted to the dudes, however. Male bears will sometimes approach mother bears and her cubs, which can lead to one of the most well-known and infamous examples of conflict between bears.

On an otherwise benign evening in July 2011, while several other bears fished in the water nearby, I turned my attention to 402 and her three spring cubs as they approached the falls. Four-zero-two didn't enter the river immediately, opting to remain on the bank near the platform. Eight-five-six, meanwhile, sat in the jacuzzi. I watched and photographed the family for several minutes, unaware that my attention would quickly transition from enjoying the cuteness of cubs to watching a life-and-death drama.

Eight-five-six was just entering the prime of his life in 2011, and this was the first year he ascended to the top of the bear hierarchy. No other bears, even the few comparably sized adult males, were willing to challenge him. He was tall and muscular and at this point in the season had yet to begin growing in his new fur coat. A stripe of nearly bare skin ran from his forehead to the middle of his back, a likely product of frequent tree rubbing.

For reasons known only to him, 856 exited his fishing spot and slowly walked toward the family. Everything about his posture showed curiosity, dominance, and even predatory instincts. Holding his head high with his ears up and pointed forward, he stared intently at the family. Four-zero-two was tense. With her cubs huddled near her backside, she faced 856, her head low and ears pressed backward against her skull, a clear indication she was not comfortable with his proximity. She and 856 also yawned frequently, a sign their stress levels were elevated. Several minutes of staring followed before 402 decided to send a more overt message. She bluff charged 856, stopping only a few feet short of making contact. Although 856 wasn't used to being pushed around, he seemed to get the message and walked calmly back to the jacuzzi.

The bears settled into their respective positions—856 fishing below the falls with 402 and cubs sitting on the near bank—until 856 saw one of his rivals walking too close to his vicinity. He trotted to displace the other male, who turned tail and moved away. The effort to affirm his dominance over the other bear brought 856 back within 20 feet of the family, and he began to stare with keen interest at them once again. In the moment, I remember remaining unsure of his true intention, but as the minutes passed, I became increasingly convinced he wanted access to the cubs.

Unlike me, 402 recognized his intent. She moved to meet him head-on and gave a low growl. This blocked 856's route to the shore, but it didn't break his concentration. He continued to stand no more than 15 feet from the family, directing his gaze straight at them.

Four-zero-two gave another yawn then, quite suddenly, lowered her head and charged. This was no bluff. In a split second, she contacted 856, clawing and biting at his face and neck. Eight-five-six was prepared though. With the skill of a judo fighter, he deflected 402's attack and used his superior size and strength to throw 402 to the ground, pinning her upside down to the river bottom. Eight-five-six bit her right shoulder and neck and appeared poised to inflict more damage, but he took a step back and let 402 go almost as quickly as he tackled her.

Released from his grasp, 402 returned to the bank to retrieve her cubs, which were not where she left them. Seeing their mother tackled, they turned and ran downstream. The smallest of the litter took shelter under the platform where I stood. The other two paused to my right in a patch of beaten-down grass. Not seeing her smallest cub initially, 402 ran to the pair of cubs farther away. When the runt appeared from underneath the platform to follow its mother, 856 galloped toward it. There was no longer any doubt of his intention. He was in full predatory mode, his gaze seemingly looking through 402 to her cubs, trying to find a way to them.

The cubs were scattered in different places. One remained almost below me, while the other two were in the grass several yards to my right, making it harder for 402 to protect them all. As soon as 856 saw a direct route to one, he began moving that way, forcing 402 to intercept and bellow intense, startling roars within a foot of his face. Caught in the moment, and seeing how vulnerable the smallest cub appeared, I found myself talking out loud to no one in particular. "He's going to kill that cub."

When 402's path was partly blocked by a willow tree, 856 spotted an opening to the two cubs farthest from me. He chased. Four-zero-two, two cubs, and 856 disappeared into the grass behind the platform. As they moved out of sight, the smallest of her litter remained below me, unsure of where its mother went or what to do next.

For 10 minutes or more (I lost track of time), the lone cub moved back and forth in front of the platform, bawling loudly. Try as I might to remain emotionally detached from the bears, I couldn't help but feel empathy for it. It was alone and frightened, searching in vain for its mother. Fear showed on its face and it carried across the forest in its cries. It didn't take 856 long to continue the hunt. He returned and immediately began tracking the cub, nose to the ground, following its scent trail into the tall grass upstream of the platform. I didn't see what happened next. I only heard the scream—a growling cry of fright the moment 856 found and killed the cub.

While infanticide can provoke strong feelings of moral outrage in people, it is relatively common in mammals and appears to have evolved independently multiple times. It's observed in primates, carnivores, and rodents; and to a lesser extent in hares, deer, at least one bat species, hippos, tree shrews, seals and sea lions, killer whales, dolphins, and horses.

It's unclear why bears sometimes commit infanticide, although the behavior, especially when attributed to male bears, is commonly explained through a hypothesis of sexually selected infanticide (SSI), an adaptive male mating strategy in which males kill unrelated dependent offspring to increase opportunities to sire their own offspring. Brown bears, however, fall outside the norm of mammals with SSI in several ways. SSI is found most often in social mammals with females that lack an annual breeding cycle. In these species, the loss of an infant can trigger the mother to enter estrus at any time of the year. Although bears can be social and sometimes even enjoy the company of other bears, excluding the relationship between a mother and her cubs, they neither live in permanent social groups nor do they reproduce all year. For SSI to hold true in brown bears, males should not kill their own offspring, mother's defensiveness should pose little risk to the male, the death of the cub should shorten the interbirth interval of the mother, and the male should obtain more breeding opportunities with the mother. That's a lot of shoulds, yet there is some support for this hypothesis.

Male libido certainly plays a role in some cases of SSI. Among a population of Scandinavian brown bears, immigrant males who are presumed to be unfamiliar with resident females were the most likely to kill cubs. The same study found most cubs are killed before or during the breeding season, when testosterone levels peak in males. Female bears can also enter estrus within a few days of losing their cubs.

If 856's true intent was to create an opportunity to mate with 402, then he didn't succeed, at least not that evening. Four-zero-two's other cubs survived the encounter.[*] Even if he had succeeded and 402 had entered estrus, he would've had to guard access to her. Given his size and rank in the hierarchy, the chances were good he'd be able to do that, but access is never guaranteed. Another bigger and stronger male could appear at any time. Then again, instinct might be driven more often by probability rather than guarantees. Most brown bears live and evolved in low-density populations where encounters between bears are far less common than at Katmai. A male with a home range that overlaps with only a few other females, and who only has to compete with a few other males, might be able to increase his odds of siring offspring through infanticide. Perhaps the instinct to kill cubs under certain circumstances is ingrained in certain bears. When those bears are reproductively successful, the genes encoded with that instinct have a higher probability of being passed on.

However, many researchers reject SSI in bears, or at least admit that infanticide does not always occur to increase male mating opportunities. Evidence of infanticidal bears siring offspring with victimized females is largely lacking. Using DNA and forensic evidence, another study on brown

---

[*] While 856 didn't kill all of 402's cubs that evening, her other two cubs didn't survive to weaning. The cause of their disappearance is unknown. Therefore, 856 partly contributed to the loss of 402's litter in 2011. She was single in 2012 and came back to the river in 2013 with three new cubs.

bears in Sweden attempted to confirm whether male bears that sired litters after a confirmed infanticide committed the infanticide. In each case the fathers of the new litters were not confirmed to have killed the cubs. The fathers were only confirmed to be the first male to accompany the female after she entered estrus, which to me suggests that SSI might work on a population level, but it may not necessarily be a highly rewarding strategy for any one individual male. Infanticide is also not restricted to the mating season nor is it always premeditated. Sometimes cubs become unfortunate victims of circumstances, killed opportunistically when they are in the wrong place at the wrong time.

One thing we know for certain is that infanticide is not limited to male bears. Female bears will sometimes kill cubs, although with much less frequency than males. Hunger too, I don't doubt, often motivates bears to attack cubs. Bears are conditioned to chase and eat vulnerable, small, and furry animals, whether it's a ground squirrel, beaver, or bear cub, even when salmon are abundant. Lastly, while infanticide happens, it's unclear how common it actually is. Studies on cub survival rates rarely record anything more than the presence or absence of offspring (that is, "This mom had three cubs, now two months later she has two"). Since 2000, all but two recorded cub deaths at Brooks River were caused by males, but far more cubs failed to return from unknown causes. Across a vast landscape like Katmai, and most places where brown bears live, the cause of a cub's disappearance most often goes unrecorded.

A clean and simple explanation for infanticide in brown bears may not be possible, given the intelligence and individuality expressed across the species, as well as the complicated circumstances in which it happens. Eight-five-six's urge to kill 402's cub in 2011 wasn't shared by the other males at the falls that evening. During the 10 minutes or so when the cub was alone before 856's return, several other adult males completely ignored the cub even though any one of them could've easily captured and killed it.

Whatever the causes and motivations may be, infanticide occurs often enough to influence the behavior of female bears. Besides a mother's defensiveness, one particularly important counterstrategy is simple avoidance. Many mothers segregate their families from habitats where males are likely to be found, forgoing the opportunity to feed on salmon or other rich food sources to forage in less productive habitats. The effort to protect their cubs, however, might begin long before mother bears even give birth.

During the bear mating season, single females normally cycle through multiple estrous periods. Each cycle appears to be functionally equivalent and can last anywhere from a few days to almost three weeks. A female can mate with multiple males during the same estrous cycle. Since male bears play no role in rearing offspring, it's unlikely that they know which cubs are theirs, but they may recognize females they copulated with previously. Mate recognition has been proposed as one way male bears could potentially avoid killing their own offspring. Although there are examples from Brooks River that contradict the idea (856, for example, mated with 402 in 2010, raising the possibility that he killed his own offspring in 2011), this makes evolutionary sense. You don't want to kill cubs of females you mated with as that risks killing your own offspring. Female promiscuity may be a way to confuse paternity and reduce the risk of SSI.

Bears have evolved a mechanism to overcome the risk of infrequent or unsuccessful mating attempts as well. Induced ovulation is a process by which females of some mammal species release eggs after behavioral, hormonal, or physical stimulation. It offers reproductive assurance for both sexes. Males are assured that eggs are fertilized and females can express some pre- or postcopulatory choice. In such a process, ovulation won't occur if she isn't, well, properly stimulated. Stimulation in this sense could be sexual or it could be based on some other behavioral or physical trait. For example, a study on captive Asiatic black bears found that mere exposure to males caused females to ovulate. Induced ovulation also eliminates the need for males and females to meet during a fixed ovulation period, and it allows females to conceive quickly after they lose a litter.

Female bears utilize one additional strategy to optimize their reproductive success. Delayed implantation allows her body to unconsciously track its readiness to bear young and do so when it is most energetically advantageous. Because cubs are born in the den when the mother must support the family entirely on her fat reserves, female bears with too little body fat are unlikely to give birth. In fact, at Washington State University, a study on captive brown bears found females who began hibernating with less than

20 percent body fat did not give birth. Delayed implantation also allows females to avoid giving birth to cubs at different times or developmental stages. Cubs are born at the same time even though they could have been conceived weeks apart.

Bear courtship is a far cry from anything people might consider romantic. Male bears make no significant (or any) effort to attract females—no displays of flamboyant plumage, no gifts of food, no songs to advertise prowess or protect territory, no dances to publicize fitness. He only offers a slow, steady pursuit. For their own part, female bears aren't passive during the mating process. They utilize their own strategies to ensure reproductive success.

Late in the evening on July 20, 11 days after I first noted the courtship, 856 and 402 consummated their brief relationship. I didn't witness it, but several park visitors watched the coupling near the falls. Mated pairs may lounge, travel, and even play together for a short period of time, but it's not uncommon for them to part ways fairly quickly. After they mated, I did not see 856 paying any more attention to 402 that year. So late in the bears' mating season, this was likely their last courtship experience for the year. It was time for both to begin focusing on other life tasks.

Although it's certainly possible that 402 mated with another male, 402 returned to Brooks River in 2015 with three spring cubs, adding yet another chapter to this pair's multifaceted story. Their relationship or to put it more accurately, brief associations, are full of plot twists that would make any reality TV producer drool. Brown bears do not form lifelong bonds, but that doesn't mean their sex life isn't without complications. This is never truer than during the mating season, a time marked by persistence, competition, and danger, when both males and females have something to gain and lose.

CHAPTER 7

SUBADULTHOOD

On an evening with 14 bears in and around Brooks Falls, 2 are hesitant to enter the water. They are the same size (relatively small), the same shape (lanky), and the same color (light brown). Even their large, forward drooping ears are almost identical. Nine-zero-nine and 910 are twins freshly emancipated from their mother, and this might be their first experience at the falls without a bodyguard.

I watch the pair pause at the top of the steep muddy slope leading to the far pool. The salmon run is only beginning and the young sisters are at an age of rapid growth. They are thin and hungry. Yet, they hesitate to approach any closer. The twins stand on their hind legs, trying to get a better view, trying to decide if they can risk moving into the water. Larger bears seem to be everywhere—standing on the lip of the falls, sitting in the jacuzzi, patrolling the downstream island, occupying the far pool, and scanning the marginal fishing spots in between. I can see no bears approaching or threatening them, but the scene apparently provides many red flags. The sisters drop back down on all four paws and bound away into the forest. Such is life for bears in their subadult years, a life stage of awkward ursine adolescence.

Since bears live without the support of community or extended family, bear cubs have much to gain and little to lose by staying with their mother as long as they can. One more year with mom is one more year of protection and guidance, an opportunity to grow larger and become better prepared for an eventual life of independence. A mother bear understands this, but her interpretation of the situation, at least from a reproductive standpoint, is slightly different. Mother bears must balance the needs of their offspring with their own already low reproductive rates. A fine line exists between emancipating your kids too early and letting them live at home for too long.

Let's say a female bear becomes reproductively mature at 5 years old. She conceives that summer and has her first litter the next winter as a 6-year-old. She weans these cubs at the beginning of their third summer when she is 8. She's single that summer, conceives another litter, and gives birth around her ninth birthday. This cycle continues until the end of her life. She lives to be 25, quite aged but not abnormally old for a wild bear. Barring complete litter loss, her minimum interval between litters is three years. During the first 10 years of her life, she'll have completely raised and weaned only one litter, and none of those cubs will have reached reproductive maturity themselves. At this rate, she can raise only seven litters within her lifetime. Keeping cubs for just one additional summer each decreases her lifetime litter total to five.

Katmai's brown bears typically experience lengthy intervals between litters. Three decades of observations at McNeil River, just north of Katmai, found the interbirth interval of brown bears typically ranged between 3.5 and 4.8 years. On Katmai's Pacific coast in the early 1990s, it was 5.8 years. Combined with the relatively low survival rates of cubs, mother bears that experience repeated hardships raising offspring may struggle to replace themselves over their whole reproductive lifetimes.

Since a mother bear's decision to keep or emancipate her cubs is a balancing act played through the work of natural selection, it's only fitting that the age at which brown bears separate from their mothers varies among populations and especially among individuals. In Sweden, brown bears generally separate from their mothers as yearlings at 2.5 years old. In the Yellowstone ecosystem, they also separate most commonly at 2.5 years old. In Katmai, the age at separation almost always occurs when bears reach their third or fourth summer, at either 2.5 years old or 3.5 years old.

Bear families usually separate just as the mating season ramps up. Emancipation can be gradual or sudden, passive or aggressive. Most often though, a family breakup seems to be instigated by the combination of a mother's increasing readiness to breed and the presence of an adult male who intrudes on the family. Mother stops offering protection, and she may even become intolerant of her cubs while showing increasing tolerance for courting males. The cubs suddenly find themselves in a situation they don't want to occupy, and the transition to independence may be shocking for them. Up to this point in their lives, mother has been their teacher, provider, and guardian. Without mother, subadult bears must immediately begin to find their way through the world, no matter how sudden the family separation process may be. Their journey can keep them close to home or lead into undiscovered territory.

Given the abundance of food at Brooks River, it's not surprising that many subadult bears that first experienced this place as cubs decide to return after they are emancipated. For 909 and 910, using at least part of their mother's home range brings familiarity, a reasonable idea where and when to find food, what the hazards of the habitat might be, and who the competitors are. Yet many young bears never return, instead seeking survival and reproductive opportunities elsewhere. Dispersal can bring bears into inferior habitats and expose them to unfamiliar hazards, but it also offers opportunity, a chance to homestead and sow their seeds far and wide.

Subadult bears disperse and establish their home range during a gradual, yearslong process. In the Flathead River drainage of extreme southeast British Columbia and adjacent northern Montana, a tracking study of 33 young grizzly bears revealed how subadults slowly shifted their home ranges. Researchers found no evidence of subadults dispersing away from their natal home range in one discrete movement. It appeared that the young bears dispersed in pulses, perhaps moving a little farther while returning to familiar terrain in between bouts of exploration.

Whether a bear shares part of its home range with its mother is greatly influenced by its sex. Young males tend to disperse beyond their mother's home range while females are much more philopatric, that is they tend to stay closer to home. Male subadult bears tracked in the Flathead River study dispersed about 19 miles from their mother's home range, on average, while females dispersed less than 6 miles. Working on the central Alaska Peninsula in the 1970s, Alaska Department of Fish and Game biologists Leland Glenn and Leo Miller found subadult males dispersed a mean average distance of 30 miles, or about twice that of females in the same area. This pattern, especially regarding the tendency of males to disperse farther and have larger home ranges than females, has far-reaching consequences, not only for their individual success but also for the genetic diversity of their species.

Although North American brown, grizzly, and Kodiak bears belong to the same species, *Ursus arctos*, bear taxonomy underwent many revisions before scientists reached this conclusion. The most commonly held differences are largely based on geography and diet. Grizzly bears, it is often said, inhabit inland areas; whereas brown bears occupy areas where they can feed on coastal food resources like salmon. Kodiak bears are like brown bears only bigger, with additional differences attributed to their skull morphology and geographic isolation. I unquestioningly repeated this trope for many years. The distinctions seem simple enough. However, the difference between brown, grizzly, and Kodiak bears is more complicated than the geographic associations we've pigeonholed them into.

During the Pleistocene's last 100,000 years, brown bears immigrated and emigrated across much of the Northern Hemisphere as climate and habitat allowed. At their peak distribution, they ranged from the British Isles south to North Africa and east across northern and central Asia to western and central North America. Even today, with their range greatly reduced, *Ursus arctos* is one of the most widely distributed mammal species on Earth. Yet, not until the middle 20th century did anything resembling scientific consensus emerge about the number of brown bear species in North America.

Working long before the knowledge of DNA and the tools to analyze it, taxonomists in the 19th and early 20th centuries utilized physical, morphological, and behavioral characteristics to classify living and extinct organisms. Air-breathing, warm-blooded, milk-producing animals with hair were classified as mammals; but air-breathing, warm-blooded, and egg-laying animals with feathers were classified as birds. These are greatly simplified examples, of course. Such tidy and clear distinctions became more difficult to resolve at the species level, especially in cases of hybridization or when taxonomic distinctiveness is based on subtle physical differences, as was the case with brown bears.

The number of described brown bear species peaked in 1918 with the publication of Clinton Hart Merriam's *Review of the Grizzly and Big Brown Bears of North America (Genus Ursus)* in which Merriam proposed over 80 (not a typo) species and subspecies in North America. Merriam's classifications of brown and grizzly bears were nuanced, which he based on differences in skull morphology and tooth dentition, characteristics he examined in painstaking detail. On southeast Alaska's Admiralty Island alone, he classified five distinct species. In the Katmai region, Merriam described two species: *Ursus gyas* for the Alaska Peninsula and *Ursus middendorffi* for Kodiak Island. He went on to classify more bear species in the Cook Inlet area and the Kenai Peninsula.

With increasing knowledge of bear behavior and biology, subsequent taxonomists considered nearly all Merriam's species and subspecies as individual variants of *Ursus arctos*. Yet, in the mid-1980s as many as nine extant or extinct subspecies of *U. arctos* were recognized in North America. Biologists have since whittled down that list even further. Currently, the only names for North American brown bear subspecies still widely used are *U. a. horribilis*, the grizzly bear, and *U. a. middendorffi*, the Kodiak bear. Recently, however, even these classifications have come under question. Given access to the same tools and information as modern taxonomists, Merriam may have discovered grizzly and brown bears can't be so easily divided by differences in skull morphology and tooth shape.

DNA analysis has opened a revolutionary window into evolution and ancestry, but not all DNA tells the same story. Among mammals, the nuclear DNA residing in a cell's nucleus is a recombination of genes from both parents. In contrast, mitochondrial DNA (mtDNA) is inherited through the female line only, and its analysis has become a particularly useful marker to trace female ancestry in mammals.

MtDNA resides in the mitochondrion, the organelle that powers respiration and energy consumption within a cell. Because sperm do not have mitochondria and do not alter the egg's mitochondria when fertilization occurs, the mother's egg provides the mitochondria that will be copied from cell to cell through the offspring's entire life. My cells still contain my mother's mtDNA, just as you carry your mother's version.

Curious as to what insights this type of DNA would reveal about brown bears, biologists in the 1990s began to analyze mtDNA from different populations. The results revealed no genetic divide between brown and grizzly bears based on an animal's relationship to the Pacific coast, nor did it support the status of Kodiak or grizzly bears as separate subspecies or any other historical subspecies in North America for that matter. The only classification that held was at the species level: *Ursus arctos*. The mtDNA analysis did, however, reveal a varied history of brown bear migration into North America.

Biologists currently identify three clades of North American brown bears based on their mtDNA. Like an extended family, each clade is a group of animals that share a common ancestor. One clade resides on mainland Alaska, the Kodiak Archipelago, and northwest Canada. Another makes their home on the Alexander Archipelago (Admiralty, Baranof, and Chichagof islands or ABC islands) in southeast Alaska. The third inhabits southwestern Canada and the western United States. The mtDNA evidence suggests each bear clade is descended from a different founding population of females, which due to their tendency to remain near their mother's home range, have mixed little even as habitat barriers in North America disappeared.

According to fossil and mtDNA evidence, sometime around 70,000 years ago, the first wave of brown bears crossed Beringia and entered North America. Over tens of thousands of years and during a gap between large-scale glaciations, a few of these initial migrants ventured south into what is now southern Canada, the western United States, and possibly the coastal islands off Alaska. When ice sheets began to advance again, these bears became isolated south of the glacial front and became the mainland bears that now occupy the contiguous 48 states, Alberta, and British Columbia.

A little more recently, around the time of the last glacial maximum, two waves of closely related brown bears invaded Beringia from Asia. The first arrived around 21,000 years ago and traveled as far as eastern Alaska and northwest Canada but did not colonize the rest of North America, perhaps because of the continued presence of the continental ice sheet farther south and east. Just before rising seas at the end of the last ice age swamped the land bridge between Asia and North America, a second group of these bears dispersed from Asia into the landscape we now call Alaska. Katmai's bears are descended from this last immigration, making them relative newcomers to the continent.

While highly informative, mtDNA cannot trace genes spread exclusively by male brown bears, so it underrepresents the role of males in genetic diversity. Males carry one bit of DNA that females don't: the Y chromosome. Because it can only be passed from father to son, the Y chromosome is an important marker to trace paternal gene flow and diversity, and with brown bears the Y chromosome tells a far different story than mtDNA.

While mtDNA shows particularly strong clade differentiation across the entire range of *Ursus arctos*, geographic variation in the Y chromosome is much shallower. Brown bears from populations as separate as Norway and Alaska, for example, carry some highly similar genetic markers in their Y chromosomes. Overall, brown bear Y chromosome DNA shows no deep genetic divergence within Eurasian or North American brown bears.

These insights have revealed a few taxonomic conundrums. Kodiak bears immigrated to the Kodiak Archipelago around 12,000 years ago. Their DNA suggests the founders established a single inbreeding population that now numbers about 3,000 individuals. Based on their skull morphology, ecology, and isolation, they are still recognized as an endemic subspecies (*U. a. middendorffi*), but their mtDNA suggests their evolutionary relationship remains too close to bears from Siberia, western Alaska, and the Alaska Peninsula to be separated on a genetic basis.

Unlike Kodiak, bears of the ABC islands are more genetically distinct, but in a most peculiar way. Their mtDNA is closely aligned with polar bears while their Y chromosome DNA is brown bear. The reason for this genetic diversity remains a point of speculation, but perhaps sometime near the end of the last ice age, polar bears occupied the sea ice adjacent to the ABC islands. Under the warming climate of the time, sea ice became less abundant and surviving polar bears were forced to spend more and more time on land, eventually becoming trapped permanently by open water. At the same time, ice was also rapidly shrinking on land-fast glaciers, opening opportunities for brown bears to exploit new territory along the coast. As the area became more amenable to brown bears, the earliest colonizers would have been predominantly dispersing subadult males. They established home ranges and began to interbreed with the remaining female polar bears. Additional male brown bears arrived on the islands and backcrossed with the hybrids, while the mainland females stood pat. The trysts preserved the maternal polar bear mtDNA and the paternal brown bear Y chromosome DNA. With each new generation the nuclear DNA recombined to include an increasingly higher percentage of brown bear DNA until nearly all the polar bear DNA was subsumed.

The ABC bears, perhaps more than any other group, illustrate how the contrasting dispersal patterns of subadult male and female bears influence bear genetic diversity. Female brown bears, due to their philopatry, differentiate a population's genetics over time. Male bears homogenize it by spreading their seed far and wide.

So far in their young lives, 909 and 910 followed the typical pattern of dispersal for female bears. Without tranquilizing and fitting them with tracking collars, we have no idea where they travel when away from the river, but their return meant at least part of their home range overlaps with their mother's. Their familiarity with the river was an advantage. They knew what it offered, both in terms of opportunity and danger.

The twins encountered their mother here too, but unlike her gangly and lanky former cubs, Beadnose was filling in rapidly on a diet of a dozen or more salmon per day. One evening while the twins hover in the shallow water on the near side of the falls, 910 sees Beadnose fishing on the lip above. Slowly, she climbs to the top of the falls and approaches her mother. It's early in the summer, meaning they've only been separated for two months at most, and they undoubtedly recognize each other, but the family reunion isn't cordial. Beadnose cocks a sideways glance toward her former cub, and then pivots to chase 910 away. Nine-one-zero turns as quickly as her mother charges and flees upstream.

Beadnose's reaction wasn't solely in defense of her personal space. She tolerated the presence of a different bear fishing on her left flank when 910 approached. The charge, then, may have been a warning to reaffirm the family's separation. It wouldn't be the last time. Later in the summer, when Beadnose was near peak weight, she rushed one of her twins at the river mouth. I could not discern any overt reason for her agonistic reaction. Beadnose is normally quite tolerant of other bears, and there didn't appear to be any food or space issues to haggle over, so her charge indicated it was to remind her former cub to stay away. Learning curves and hardships abound in a subadult's world, and some of those are even brought about by a mother.

Although mother bears pass on a considerable amount of knowledge to their offspring, some tasks can only be mastered through practice. Fishing was difficult for the twins that first summer apart from mother. They lacked the skills of the more experienced adults as well as the body mass that would allow them to consistently compete for space. But a record number of salmon returned to Bristol Bay in 2018, and over 2 million of them entered the Naknek watershed. Salmon were so thick at times that even the smallest, least experienced bears were able to run through the water and catch one, albeit with some effort. In 2019, with that good year of experience to lean on, the twins were eager to enhance their fishing skills.

On June 19, 2019, amidst the first sizeable waves of incoming salmon, 909 returns to the falls. She's hungry and wants to secure a meal, and the lip is open. She approaches with caution and stands several feet back from the edge. Salmon clear the falls and strike the water in front of her. Nine-zero-nine gives chase, but she's poorly positioned to catch the fish as they sprint upstream. A half hour passes without any success.

However, the falls is relatively empty of bears, which provides 909 with the perfect opportunity to hone her skills. After 45 minutes, she's still caught no salmon. Yet, 909 shows a great deal of patience for a young and hungry bear. Not all are so willing to practice for so long before they lose motivation and try another spot.

With the passing moments, she gains more confidence in her footing and creeps closer to the edge of the lip. Just then another young bear arrives and walks upstream toward the falls. Evoking her behavior from the prior spring, 909 turns and bolts away.

A few nights later, her tribulations continue. Several other bears use the falls this evening, and 909 is kept constantly on the move, either because she is overtly displaced or is trying to avoid the other bears. On the lip, Grazer is having a good night though. In total, I see her catch and eat most of nine salmon. Nine-zero-nine dances from place to place, depending on the availability of Grazer's leftovers.

After Grazer departs for the evening, 909 moves toward the lip but again seems to not understand where exactly to stand. Unsure and hesitant, she retreats upon the approach of a third bear. A little later and still without fish, 909 is displaced from the island downstream of the falls. She displays a frustration-like response when she runs to the near bank. She growls, and pounds on a willow. The other bear pays no attention.

On June 25, she's back at it again, motivated by hunger and the memories of her mother catching salmon on the lip. Now confident enough to stand on the edge, 909 has done everything except catch a fish.

The lip is a precarious spot and she intuits that a wrong move could send her over the edge. Although salmon land near her feet, she restricts her movements and misses several fish that come within reach. She stays focused on her effort despite the difficulty. Finally, her patience pays off. An unfortunate salmon lands at the base of her front paws. She lunges, downward-dog style, to pin the fish in her jaws. With her catch, she turns and trots to the near bank, disappearing into the grass to eat her fish out of sight.

Nine-zero-nine watched her mother perform this feat dozens, perhaps hundreds, of times. After accomplishing it on her own, she has set herself on a trajectory to receive a lifetime of salmon meals.

Subadulthood is a multiyear saga that, biologically speaking, ends as a brown bear reaches sexual maturity. However, it's defined just as much by a young bear's journey of independence, discovery, and learning.

During the rest of the summer, 909 and 910 visited the falls frequently. With growing experience and confidence, they quickly gained the skills necessary to catch salmon with regularity. They evaluated encounters with other bears carefully before deciding to remain or depart. Their relationship was changing too. Their bond loosened and they spent less time traveling together. Emancipated from their mother two years ago, they were now emancipating from each other. Their time of strife was far from over, yet they had become increasingly prepared to face the challenges of adulthood.

CHAPTER 8

LIVING LARGE

I'm watching a giant among bears. While there are bears that stand taller at the shoulder and measure longer from head to tail, the barrel-shaped 747 is the most massive bear I've ever seen. He pushes the upper size limit for adult males, approaching 1,000 pounds in late June, the season when bears are at their skinniest. I shake my head in near disbelief, thinking about how fat he might become by October.

On June 24, 2019, 747 seems eager to work on his figure. Over a couple of hours in the jacuzzi, he snares five salmon during an otherwise unproductive evening. His catch total may have climbed much higher had he not faced a formidable competitor. With head held high, ears oriented forward, and eyes focused directly on his target, 856 enters the river and signals his confidence and intent to challenge 747's fishing spot.

It's a bold move under the circumstances. Seven-four-seven is not easily intimidated and no rule states he must yield his fishing spot. The stage seems set for a climactic fight. Yet, a nonviolent result is almost guaranteed. After years of interactions, 856 is counting on body language and precedent to convey his message to 747. Both bears recognize the motives of the other and both know their place in the hierarchy, a system of resource allocation that helps bears survive a very unfair world.

Through careful observations of domestic chickens, Norwegian zoologist and comparative psychologist Thorleif Schjelderup-Ebbe introduced the idea of a pecking order into the science of animal behavior in the early 1920s. It's since become part of English-language lexicon, referring to a system of dominance and hierarchy where individuals, whether chickens in a barnyard or people in a corporate office, are not equal and lower ranking or subordinate individuals have access to fewer or inferior resources. Although bears are not a prototypically social species, they live in environments where resources are limited and they interact with enough individuals of their kind to have evolved behaviors and physical characteristics that dictate and maintain their own unique form of a pecking order. A friend of mine who spends several weeks each summer inserting himself into the Brooks River bear hierarchy by volunteering his time to haze[*] bears away from the buildings at Brooks Camp, considers the bear hierarchy akin to an armistice, an uneasy truce between individuals who could easily war with one another but only at great cost.

A bear's relative level of dominance can be predicted by its age and size. When bears are much different in size, then size alone usually determines status. As a result, adults are dominant over subadults, and adult males are typically dominant over adult females. During encounters between bears of near-equal size, disposition and fighting skills play an especially important role in determining rank. Within limits, assertiveness, defensiveness, and aggressiveness can allow smaller bears to attain a higher rank than their size would otherwise allow. During their studies of bear social behavior at McNeil River, Derek Stonorov and Allen Stokes described one bear family—a particularly aggressive mother with three large and aggressive cubs—who could back down all bears except the most dominant male. A similar situation occurred at Brooks River with Grazer in 2016 and 2020 while she raised separate litters of first-year cubs. Significantly smaller than

---

[*] Hazing, in this context, is a form of aversive conditioning with the goal to protect Brooks Camp's buildings and other infrastructure from bears. Rangers use a variety of techniques, typically body posture and voice, to make bears feel uncomfortable near the lodge and visitor center until they leave the near vicinity.

the adult males, Grazer's ferocity when defending her young cubs forced most males to yield space.

The hierarchy at Brooks River ebbs and flows depending on the suite of bears occupying the area at any given time. Yet, its top tier has been remarkably consistent for nearly a decade. Since he ascended to the top of the hierarchy in 2011, 856 has rarely been challenged.

From 2011 through 2019, I attempted to note every interaction I witnessed between bears at Brooks Falls. Anytime I saw a bear displace another, act submissive toward an aggressor, or purposely avoid another bear, I recorded the identity of the interacting bears and the outcome. Bears that "won" an encounter were considered to be more dominant. Winners displaced others from food, fishing spots, and access to estrous females, or forced other bears to act submissively when challenged. If a bear avoided the approach of another bear, then I scored the deferring bear as subordinate as well. I also noted other ways in which bears interacted, such as courtship, copulation, play, and fish stealing.

I attempted to record the outcome of every interaction I saw, but some interactions were less meaningful than others because I was not able to conclusively identify every bear. My observations can't be considered a continuous sample either. I recorded no interactions in 2012 or 2017 when I was working in Yellowstone and North Cascades national parks, respectively. Even with those limitations, the data reveals some intriguing results about the nature of the bear's hierarchy and its advantages for dominant bears.

In total, I recorded 1,745 interactions during 436 hours of bear watching (Table 1). Avoidance interactions—when a subordinate bear preemptively yielded space or passively deferred upon the approach of another bear—were the most numerous encounters. They occurred in almost 46 percent of all interactions. Forced submission encounters were the next most common, totaling about 40 percent. Other types of interactions were uncommon or rare. Stealing and courting accounted for 6.5 and 3 percent of interactions, respectively. During 1.5 percent of encounters I could discern no clear winner. All other interactions (play, mating, begging, and others) totaled well less than 1 percent apiece.

Table 1: Bear interactions recorded at Brooks Falls during portions of 2011, 2013–2016, and 2018–2019. Total number of interactions was 1,745.

Type of Interaction	Number of Interactions	% of Total Interactions
Avoidance (Passive Deferral)	799	45.8%
Dominant > Subordinate (Forced Submission)	701	40.2%
Steal (Successful or Attempted)	114	6.5%
Courting	62	3.6%
Dominance Unclear	27	1.5%
Play	13	0.7%
Mating (Copulation Observed)	11	0.6%
Begging	7	0.4%
Other	11	0.6%

Analyzing the data on the level of individual bears indicates that the hierarchy is relatively stable within a given year. Once bears establish their rank in early summer, they tend to remain dominant and submissive to the same cohort for the rest of the year. I recorded few instances when two bears reversed their subordinate or dominant positions in the same year.

Throughout my observational period, no bear commanded the same level of respect as 856 and no other bear interacted as much with other bears. His dominance was overwhelming at times. Of the 1,700-plus interactions I witnessed, 856 was involved in 595 of them, almost one-third of my observations. Yet, this could simply indicate he was present at the falls more often than most others, so the reaction of other bears toward 856 is perhaps more telling. In almost half of 856's interactions, he displaced a subordinate bear by direct confrontation or forced a subordinate bear to act submissive. The rest of the time, bears simply avoided him. His approach would cause almost stampede-like chain reactions as bears scattered out of his path. I observed him losing only two encounters,* both with particularly defensive mothers.

Seven-four-seven was also quite dominant during the same time span. He was involved in 320 interactions where I scored him as the winner, but in 99 other instances 747 was the subordinate bear. Perhaps not surprisingly, 856 was involved in 85 of 747's losses, and not once did I see 747 challenge 856, despite 747 appearing more massive.

Eight-five-six and 747 have known each other for many years. Their acquaintance began in the mid-2000s when they were both young adults trying to establish their niche at the falls. By the summer of 2011, 747 was already deferring to 856 and his subordination was reinforced in 2012 when rangers reported that 856 defeated 747 in an intense fight, one that supposedly took 747 days to recover from.

Eight-five-six's behavior can seem excessive. Why expend so much time and energy challenging other bears when you could be fishing or pursuing mating opportunities instead? I suspect the reason is partly instinctual (in other words, that's how he is programmed to behave) and partly reinforced through learning. Each time 856 challenges another bear and successfully asserts his dominance, the subordinate bear is less likely to stand its ground the next time.

Statistically, this is reflected by a great number of interactions where 856 remained dominant yet didn't have to do anything except walk toward another bear. Half of 856's winning interactions were avoidance interactions, encounters when bears preemptively moved out of his way, costing 856 nothing except the energy of walking. Subordinate bears—whether from a lack of size, age, experience, or disposition—understood that challenging him was fraught with risk, and they most often chose to avoid it.

---

* In 2017, a year when I didn't formally record observations, 856 was largely absent from the river. When he was seen in midsummer, he seemed injured, limping on one of his rear legs. Temporarily disabled, 856 yielded space to bears he had held dominance over in prior years. I thought that perhaps this might have signaled the end of 856's reign, but the next summer, appearing to be fully healed and just as large as ever, 856 regained his place at the top of the hierarchy. His behavior was identical to that which he displayed between 2011 and 2016. Even so, the lack of data from 2017 biases the results of my observations in favor of a more dominant 856.

Eight-five-six was rewarded with more fishing opportunities, more frequent stream visits, less risk of predation, and less time spent being vigilant.

Subordinate bears aren't total losers in these scenarios though. As 856 walks through the river on this late June evening, 747 sees the threat coming and begins a preemptive retreat toward the downstream island. As the bears close within 30 feet, 747 stops and turns to face 856 who also pauses his advance. The two stare at each other until 856 resumes his original course and enters the jacuzzi. Seven-four-seven quietly exits the river. He abandoned the fishing spot but maintained his health and security by knowing and abiding by a cardinal rule of bear conduct—yield space to those who you know are more dominant.

Although 856 works hard to maintain his status, dominance appears to have its limits. It may not provide much advantage where food is too widely dispersed to defend, or when food is so abundant that there is little need to compete for it. But, under other circumstances, it's easy to conceive how 856's dominance would be greatly advantageous at singular food sources like a moose carcass, when he's pursuing a mating opportunity, or when salmon numbers are low and fishing is productive at only one or two locations.

It's sometimes hard to watch the behavior of large, dominant males and not feel some sympathy for their "victims." Eight-five-six moves through the river with an aura of high confidence, knowing that few if any bears will challenge him or even stand in his way. Displaced bears are often smaller and hungrier than he, yet 856 expresses no sympathy. In fact, he often doesn't acknowledge the presence of any bears except the few within his size class, of which there are typically only four or five each summer. Using his strength and power to intimidate, 856 forces other bears to yield food or space, and he'll use physical violence when he doesn't immediately get his way. When he wants something, he takes it, behaving not unlike a schoolyard bully.

When 856, or any other bear for that matter, displaces a subordinate bear, his behavior fits the dictionary definition of bully: someone who uses superior strength or influence to intimidate another, which typically means forcing the victim to do what the bully wants. When describing bears, I don't use the term *bully* casually. Until writing this, I've never publicly described a bear as a bully. Used either as a noun (he is a bully) or verb (he bullies), the word is culturally loaded and carries a heavy stigma. By calling 856 a bully, I therefore risk judging his behavior by human standards, implying his bullying is wrong or bad. It smacks of the worst kind of anthropomorphism.

The thing about it is, bears don't live within or have any conception of our codes of conduct. As the famed primatologist and ethologist Frans de Waal states in his book *Are We Smart Enough to Know How Smart Animals Are?*, "Saying that ants have 'queens,' 'soldiers,' and 'slaves' is mere anthropomorphic shorthand. We should attach no more significance to it than we do when we name a hurricane after a person or curse our computer as if it had free will." So when I describe 856 as a bully, it's along de Waal's line of reasoning; bully is a descriptive term instead of judgmental construct. Anthropocentric terms can be used to describe the behavior of nonhumans as long as we decouple the words from their cultural context. Bears and other nonhumans are organisms whose minds and rules of social engagement exist outside of humanity's ethical and moral realm. They should be judged on their own terms, not our own, and since we currently lack a full understanding of what those terms might be we should refrain from judging.

Dominant and subordinate bears may behave differently, but their places in the hierarchy are not genetically fixed positions. While few bears possess the genetic attributes to grow as large as 856, low-ranking and subordinate bears are fully capable of assuming a position of dominance under the right circumstances. The past and present of the bear hierarchy portends its future.

In 2007, when I first had the opportunity to observe 856 and 747, they were young adults with more tolerant demeanors. I often watched them fish the jacuzzi and other productive locations when the opportunity became available, but they were also clearly outmuscled and victimized by larger males who displaced them and sometimes stole their fish. At the time, one bear was particularly famous for his unflinching dominance.

I clearly remember the first time I saw BB. On a sunny afternoon in late June 2007, I stood on the platform at the riffles, enjoying a quiet moment in between managing groups of people waiting their turn to visit the falls. Glancing upstream, I saw a large, darkly furred bear enter the far pool. He was a head taller than most, had narrowly set eyes, a muzzle that evenly tapered from his snout to his forehead, and ivory-colored claws. His nickname, I would later learn, was inspired by his tendency to shed large patches of fur on his rump, giving him a "bald butt." As I watched through my binoculars I thought to myself, "Who is this giant?"

I wasn't the first person to notice BB's commanding presence. Park staff noted him as the river's most dominant bear as early as 1997. A decade is a long time to remain at the top of the hierarchy though. In 2006, the park's bear monitoring staff documented the arrival of Norman, a very large adult male who had never been observed before. But judging from the wounds and scars on his face and neck, it was evident he was a veteran of conflict. Unlike BB, who visited the falls often during the day, Norman was cryptic, generally arriving at the falls late in the evening or after the wildlife-viewing platforms had closed to the public. Because he was rarely observed, in most instances his influence on the cohort of bears at the river can only be inferred. Judging by his size alone, though, Norman commanded respect.

In a comment buried in their observational database, bear monitoring staff noted Norman "displaced" BB in 2006, but the displacement must not have been convincing because BB challenged Norman the next June. Video recorded by park biologists conducting an overnight observation session showed BB precipitating the interaction through a direct and unambiguous approach. Norman did not back down. Both bears held their head high and growled as the distance between them shrunk. In a flash, they stood on their hind legs and brawled, claws raking their opponent's shoulders and upper arms, jaws and teeth clamped on their opponent's faces. The minute-long fight ended with Norman pinning BB on his back in the shallow water next to the riverbank. BB threw his jaws open in a bite-threat as Norman lorded over him. As the combatants separated, BB regained his footing only to watch the victorious Norman walk away and mark a nearby tree, a further insult to BB's status.

Because of his size and reputation, BB still ranked extremely high in the hierarchy, but he became an infrequent presence at the river after that evening. He was hardly seen at all in 2008 and only once in 2009, the last year we observed him.

BB's example is not the only one that may presage 856's fate. As they age, some bears adapt to and persevere through the increased competition. In 2007, Otis was one of the largest adult males at the river, and he was often able to gain access to his most preferred fishing spots in the far pool or jacuzzi by displacing smaller bears like 747 and 856. As those bears matured and grew into the prime of their lives, however, Otis aged. Within a few years, the dominant-subordinate roles reversed, and all without fighting. By 2019, Otis was in his mid-20s and ranked near the bottom tier of adult males, a position he'll probably retain until he's too weak to compete at all.

The hierarchy ebbs and flows as bears like Otis age and youngsters gain size and strength. Still, 747 and 856 were so large in 2019 that I did not expect other bears to challenge either of them. As bears often do, though, they proved my expectations wrong.

On the evening of July 2, few salmon hover in the water at the falls, perhaps adding to the air of orneriness filling the river. Bears posture with each other and frequently change fishing locations as they try to find success. I cannot know whether 747 is hungry and cranky when he arrives, or if he is still well nourished and energetic from his previous meals, but whatever he feels he immediately takes issue with the presence of a new arrival.

Sixty-eight is a tall, large-bodied bear with a long muzzle and a forehead of neatly parted fur. He's used the river for most of his known life, having been first identified in 2007, but until 2015 we had only seen him in late summer. During September and October, 68 was willing to assert his dominance over many of the large males at the falls, but he also kept a wary eye on 856 and 747, yielding space to them when necessary.

As 68 moves into the middle of the river, 747 leaves his fishing spot in the jacuzzi and provokes a direct confrontation. He approaches 68 with confidence, holding his head high and positioning his ears forward as he stares directly at his opponent. Sixty-eight, meanwhile, assumes a more defensive posture by lowering his head and averting his gaze. Neither vocalizes as the gap between them shrinks to a few yards. They stand broadside, sizing up the other before 747 decides to end the encounter and move to the island downriver.

I'm left with a feeling that their differences remain unsettled. I've just begun a live, play-by-play-style broadcast on the Brooks Falls webcam and there's a lot to keep track of, especially while attempting to sound somewhat intelligent to thousands of people on the Internet, but I soon ignore much of the behavior of the other bears to focus on 747 as he approaches 68 once again, this time in the far pool.

Sixty-eight seems more intent on fishing than confrontation, but 747's renewed proximity forces 68 to pay attention. Having reached the far wall, 747 stands on his hind legs and begins to rub his back on the rocks and pull low-hanging branches over his head and face. It's a visual and olfactory display intended to communicate dominance. Sixty-eight once again stands and watches. After 747 finishes his display, he and 68 part ways and settle into separate fishing spots.

These posturing bouts are often enough to determine dominance between two similarly sized bears, but this was not one of those instances. A little over 10 minutes later, apparently unsatisfied with his fishing success in the far pool, 68 decides to try another spot. As confidently as 856 would have done, 68 moves directly toward the jacuzzi. The only issue is that 747 occupies it.

Perhaps emboldened by his earlier posturing and 68's deference, 747 is not intimidated by the newcomer's approach. He moves into 68's path. Sixty-eight tries to dodge the maneuver and turns toward a more direct route to the jacuzzi. Seven-four-seven finds this unacceptable and blocks the challenger's path once again. Sixty-eight pushes the challenge, bellowing a deep growl in 747's face. Just feet apart now, with neither willing to yield, the bears stand and lunge forward. In a split second, they are locked in battle.

The bears maul each other on the edge of the jacuzzi. Both direct their attacks toward their opponent's face and neck. They lean forward, trying to use their strength to wrestle the other to the ground. While 747 is more massive, 68 may be more agile. He quickly gains an advantage by grabbing the right side of 747's neck in his jaws. Seven-four-seven tries to counter but loses his leverage and is pushed onto his back.

In the chaos, 68 eventually locks his jaws on the left side of 747's head. A pained look comes across 747's face. Sixty-eight pushes him sideways then down onto the river gravel. Seven-four-seven is almost completely submerged. Only his face projects above the water. He bellows as 68 holds him down in the water, continuing to hold the side of 747's head firmly in his canines.

When 68 releases his grasp, 747 twists upright to defend himself but he seems spent. Sixty-eight stands over him, ready to push the attack further. Seven-four-seven declines, however, and walks ever so slowly downstream, blood dripping from his mouth. Victorious, 68 settles into the jacuzzi.

Fights of this intensity represent only a small fraction of bear interactions at the river, and I hesitated to write about this and the BB-Norman fight because they are so uncommon. The importance of these fights is undeniable though. Winning a fight can secure access to an estrous female and provide a rare mating opportunity. When the reward is a singular food resource, winning confrontations can mean the difference between barely surviving the winter and emerging in the spring with ample fat reserves. Fights can be defining moments for the hierarchy and perhaps a bear's very life.

Seven-four-seven did not challenge 68 the rest of the summer, but 856 was not as shy. The day after the brawl, I try to leave the platform complex at the falls and find that the trail is occupied by 856 who is busy rubbing his back on a tree near the exit gate. After he moves a sufficient distance down the trail, I exit the ramp with about 10 other people and inspect the tree where he left his mark. The bark is damp 6 to 7 feet off the ground where the wet fur of his shoulder blades contacted the tree, while the ground beneath is soaked with salmon-scented urine.

Eight-five-six didn't appear to be in a hurry on the trail, so we move slowly as a group. Around a bend, we catch a glimpse of 856. He's focused on a comparatively sized male who is the right size and shape to be 68. We wait until they continue down the trail and disappear into the trees. Upon reaching the road at the end of the trail, neither bear is in sight. So we walk on with more than a little uneasiness, not knowing which direction they went.

Along the entire Brooks Falls trail, 856 had been signaling his dominance through urination and tree marking. Intricate squiggles of urine dampened the crushed gravel surface, and we had walked past a freshly uprooted 6-foot-tall spruce tree, a casualty of the bear's posturing.

Communication plays an important role in the hierarchy's establishment and maintenance, but the purpose of marking behavior in bears remained mostly speculative throughout the 20th century. After his long-term observations of grizzlies in Mount McKinley (now Denali) National Park, Adolph Murie supposed bears rubbed on trees or rocks to massage themselves. Other observers hypothesized that bears marked trees to sharpen their claws, for personal hygiene reasons, or in response to biting insects. Bears of almost all age classes mark trees, and watching them do so suggests they sometimes enjoy it. Recent studies, however, have found that marking is a form of social communication, which bears clearly understand even if we don't.

Bears release oily secretions from glands in the skin of their back, head, and the pads of their paws. They possess anal glands similar to dogs, and their urine, I suspect, also contains chemical cocktails that communicate sex, social rank, and reproductive status.

Specialized marking behaviors allow bears to distribute these odors across their home ranges. Males are prone to stomp and grind their hind feet with an exaggerated, stiff-legged gait known as cowboy walking. When performed with gusto, you can almost hear the jangle of spurs. Along all human and ursine travel routes near Brooks River, trees bear the brunt of physical and chemical marking. Bears strip and gouge wood by clawing and biting as high as they can reach, sometimes 9 feet above the ground. Through rubbing their backs, flanks, and rumps, they ingrain the bark and splintered wood with tufts of fur and skin oils. Tree marking and cowboy walking happen during all active seasons, but the behaviors peak during the mating season and are performed far more often by males than females.

Marking is a signpost written in the language of scent. It advertises where you've been, who you are, whether you are male or female, your relative level of dominance, and your reproductive status. It can be both a warning for competitors and the ursine equivalent of a Tinder profile.

The next evening 68 arrives at the top of the falls. Eight-five-six leaves his fishing spot near the far pool to confront 68, stopping only 10 feet from his rival. They lower and sway their heads slowly. Neither vocalizes. A moment passes before 856 turns and walks back to his fishing spot.

Sixty-eight watches 856 intently, then ventures down the slope adjacent to the fish ladder. Now at the foot of the jacuzzi, 68 lunges forward into the froth. Eight-five-six glares across the river, paying close attention to 68's movements and decides another confrontation is necessary. Sixty-eight sees 856's approach and avoids the aggressor by climbing to the top of the falls. Eight-five-six follows partway but doesn't seem motivated to push the challenge further. His dominance reaffirmed, he stops and turns back to fish in the jacuzzi.

With 856 settled into the jacuzzi, 68 circles to the far pool. Meanwhile, 747 has been napping upstream, half submerged in the water, for an hour. After waking, he pauses to consider his limited options. His toughest competitors occupy both sides of the falls, so his next moves will have to be made with caution. He creeps down the rocks and settles, for the time being, into a neutral fishing spot. Neither 68 nor 856 react. In my notebook, I don't score 747 as a winner or loser but I must give him some credit for threading the needle, something not easy to do when you are as large as he.

The rise and reign of bears such as 856, 747, and 68 is ephemeral. One day, perhaps much sooner than these bears expect, they will face a younger and stronger competitor who is not only willing to stand up to their challenges but also has the strength and skill to displace the longtime, top-ranking bears. Younger bears are always waiting in the wings, motivated by the real and perceived advantages of dominance. They only require opportunity. For as long as they can, though, the river's most dominant bears will hold their rank and every advantage it gives them.

CHAPTER 9

HUNGER

Partly eaten salmon carcasses litter the riverbank and ring the downstream island. Each second, several salmon launch out of the water in their attempt to leap the falls. Only the giant 747 is fishing when I arrive to observe, but it's clearly been a very good day for hungry bears.

During the peak of the salmon migration, bears rarely fish alone and 747 is soon joined by an even more experienced bear. Reaching the far bank, Otis promptly lays down in the river, letting the water cool his flanks. For several minutes he doesn't move except to place his face under the water to casually search for fish. With drooping eyelids and a downwardly nodding head, Otis appears groggy, enough so that my wife and I joke he might fall asleep in the water. Rather than a nap, Otis apparently has something else on his mind. He shakes off his sleepiness and moves slowly toward one of his most preferred fishing spots, the jacuzzi.

A borderline adult when he was first identified in 2001, Otis has become one of the oldest and most skilled bears using the falls. Tall and lean, with blond early summer fur and a floppy right ear, he stands out among the consort of adult males at the river. Otis understands he cannot challenge 747 for the jacuzzi, so he waits downstream. When 747 moves into the forest, perhaps to rest and digest his earnings, Otis fills the vacancy. Settling into the plunge pool, he sits statuesque, facing upstream with only his head, shoulders, and upper back exposed above water. The jacuzzi offers no visibility to see the salmon in the water, but Otis makes no effort to place himself in a different position. He has no need. He knows exactly what he is doing.

When a salmon bumps into his body, disoriented by the churning water or forced there by another fish, Otis snaps into action. His reflexes are quick and precise. Pinning the fish to the river gravel or his body, he plunges his muzzle into the water to secure his catch.

I watch, impressed and curious, as his catch rate grows quickly, from 1 to 5 to 10 to 15 before 747 returns and retakes the jacuzzi. The elder bear gives a modest growl but easily yields. No matter, though. Otis sees opportunity elsewhere. He moves to the far pool and resumes fishing. With his back against the rock wall, he sits on his haunches, an Eeyore-like pose that likely has no reflection on his mood.

Otis's catch rate slows only slightly at this new location. Soon, it climbs to 20 then 25, then beyond 30. When I leave the falls that evening, I'm left awed by the capacity of his stomach. Otis caught and ate most of 35 salmon in about five hours. The webcam audience continues to track his success rate after I depart, observing Otis eating another seven salmon before he retires for the night. In total, he ate all or most of 42 fish—the most salmon I've ever observed a bear eat in a single sitting. From a human perspective, his effort may seem gluttonous. From a bear's perspective, though, it is a mark of success. Perhaps nothing engages bears more than the pursuit of food.

A bear fishing for salmon has become an almost clichéd representation of the species, yet most bear populations survive without much or any fish on the menu, or without much meat at all. They utilize instead an extremely varied set of foods to meet their dietary demands. Omnivory enables bears to occupy a diverse range of habitats.

A casual list of brown bear foods from any one area includes dozens of species. A more comprehensive inventory would comprise hundreds. In Yellowstone, grizzly bears usurp elk and bison carcasses from wolves, climb mountains to feast on moths in barren scree, use their sense of smell to locate underground truffles, search meadows for seeds carefully cached by rodents, smash open the cones of whitebark pine to extract the fat-rich nuts, and raid underground ant colonies, lapping up larvae and futilely defending adults just as readily as we dig a spoon into a bowl of ice cream. They are quite capable of living a mostly vegetarian lifestyle too, merely supplementing their diet with animal proteins when given the opportunity. Grizzlies in the northern Rocky Mountains include some 200 plants in their diet and gain 90 percent of their annual energy from plant matter. Early in the growing season, they'll swallow mouthfuls of green forbs and till subalpine meadows seeking roots and tubers. In late summer, they vacuum thousands of blueberries off the stem at rates that exceed the most skillful bare-handed human pickers.

The diet of bears on the Alaska Peninsula is no less varied, although it relies on a different suite of foods. They eat carrion, bird eggs, birds, voles, ground squirrels, moose, caribou, other bears, and beavers. They graze on herbaceous plants such as seacoast angelica, seaside plantain, cow parsnip, grasses, and sedges. Late summer is typically berry season in Katmai when bear scat turns black, blue, and maroon with the remnants of blueberries, crowberries, lingonberries, elderberries, highbush cranberry, watermelon berry, and currants. On the coast of the park, virtually any animal is on the menu including sea otters, harbor seals, dead whales, clams, mussels, barnacles, and beach fleas. They relish fish, especially salmon of course, yet their own vomit and human feces aren't too taboo to cross off the menu. If bears were as widespread across the planet as humans, then the diversity of their diet might exceed our own.

Salmon are, on average, the richest and most nutritious food for Katmai's bears, and bears will go to great effort to catch them. Most bears that fish at Brooks Falls are regulars like Otis who come back year after year. Others are newly emancipated subadults, looking to find a niche without the aid of their mother's protection or guidance. A few are transients that depart about as quickly as they come, perhaps intimidated by the crowds of people or the competition posed by other bears. Most rare though, is the arrival of a fully mature adult, one with no prior history at the falls, who decides to stay. Watching these bears try to fish the falls and navigate its sleuth of bears illustrates how powerful a motivator hunger can be and how well bears adapt to new situations.

On a rainy evening in mid-July 2015, I watch a patchy-furred bear emerge from the trees and bound toward the waterfall. His muzzle is short and blocky, a large wound mars his right flank, and his body lacks the bulk of the other adults who had spent the last three weeks fishing here. Most noticeably, his left ear is about half the size of his right. It's Lefty, a bear that until this day had only been seen regularly in late summer and fall, and one I never had the opportunity to watch before.

Lefty's behavior that evening strongly suggested he had no significant experience fishing the falls or interacting with its gathering of bears. The season was also young enough that Brooks River was still the only place to catch fish, so Lefty arrived hungry. He dashes from place to place, distracted by every fish that catches his glance. He confronts almost every bear without regard to their place in the hierarchy. He moves from the lip of the falls to the far pool, where he encounters an older, nearly 27-year-old female, 410, and promptly steals her salmon. Motivated by the success, he tries the same move with 856, who is not intimidated by the newcomer's growling approach. When Lefty reaches in for the steal, 856 drops his catch then thrashes and attacks the thief. Neither bear gets the salmon, and Lefty has learned some bears at the falls are not easy victims. But the failure doesn't stop his spree. Continuing on, he returns to 410's vicinity and steals another of her salmon, then one from Otis, and yet another from 410.

He eats with vigor, consuming each salmon in a few large gulps. Yet the few fish he's gathered so far aren't nearly enough to satisfy him. He moves to the lip again where an adult female had just finished eating her catch. He trades blows with her and then forces her to slide over the edge of the waterfall.

Lefty has the lip to himself, but he seems unsure what to do next. He weaves his head, pantomiming the movement of the salmon swirling in the pool below, and might have been able to catch a few of the jumping salmon if he could have stood still, but he couldn't. Looking down on the fish, he bobs his head upward once, twice, then leaps off the waterfall into the pool below. Although unsuccessful, it's a belly flop for the ages.

On July 20, I again watch Lefty walk to the lip. He places his front paws on the cusp of the falls and . . . waits there patiently. Within a minute of arriving, he's rewarded. He snaps his jaws shut on a leaping salmon.

His focused routine developed quickly after his initial arrival, just five days removed from his incessant attempts to steal fish and his frantic belly flop. Ever since, Lefty has remained a skilled and proficient angler on the lip, albeit with a continued look of excitement and expectation.

Although his subsequent behavior has never matched his display in 2015, Lefty still offers a stark contrast to Otis who maintains a calm, focused demeanor, no matter his hunger level. The significances of their differences extend beyond their mannerisms. Their ability to exploit salmon at different locations allow both bears to make a living in an area where space is not always easy to come by.

Each species occupies a niche, a role or position in an ecological community. Niches are influenced by a species' adaptations, competition with other species, predation, habitat, and climate. Brown bears occupy such a wide diversity of habitats, from the arctic coastal plain to temperate rainforests to (formerly) the mixed-grass prairies of the Great Plains and the desert mountains of the Southwest and northern Mexico, in large part because of their ability to live as large-bodied generalist omnivores.

Not every bear within a given ecosystem relies on the same food sources or foraging locations though. Different bears are able to exist within the same habitats, all the while occupying the same broad niche, because of their individuality. Niches apply at the level of the individual just as much as the species.

On the east side of the park, sandwiched between the volcanic crest of the Aleutian Range and the stormy waters of Shelikof Strait, Katmai's Pacific coast includes over 400 miles of intricately carved fjords and rugged headlands. Although marine debris is an increasingly worrisome issue and tar from the 1989 Exxon Valdez oil spill still fouls some of the cobbled beaches, the Katmai coast is nonetheless a wild and productive environment that supports bears living within one of the densest populations anywhere on Earth. While a lot of food is available on the Katmai coast, tremendous numbers of bears live there in no small part because they are clever enough to exploit all the foods the coast offers.

During a three-year-long tracking and dietary study of bears on Katmai's coast, biologists from the National Park Service and the US Geological Survey noticed a GPS-collared bear, 085,[*] and her pair of 2.5-year-old cubs, were spending a lot of time on offshore islands. Ninagiak and Shakun islands are relatively small and grass-covered. They are not places where a bear, let alone one raising two large and ravenous offspring, would be expected to make a living. Nor are they casually and easily visited places. Shakun, for example, is separated from the mainland by 2.5 miles of water, so the family's prolonged presence on the islands was a bit baffling. Grant Hilderbrand, one of the lead biologists for the project, later recalled, "We were definitely pondering, why is she spending all summer on these islands? It did seem like an odd place and once we got out there and physically saw it, then we were really wondering. There's nothing out there except for just grass and rock."

While investigating one of the islands that 085 occupied, Hilderbrand found some unusually textured bear scat filled with mammal remains. He also located the bones and skulls of harbor seals scattered in the grass. The remnants appeared to have been cached—they didn't seem to be dead animals that had washed ashore. The following day, he observed 085 and her cubs swimming offshore of the island toward a patch of rocks where seals were resting, perhaps in an attempt to trap the seals in shallow water. Could the family really be hunting marine mammals regularly on these islands?

The following spring, park biologists installed motion sensor and time-lapse cameras on Shukan Island. Whether 085 visited the island is not known (her tracking collar was removed the previous fall), but the cameras documented that some bears continued to visit the islands. Although the cameras didn't capture direct evidence of bears killing harbor seals, they did photograph bears successfully hunting sea otters that had hauled-out to rest on an exposed rocky reef.

While sea otters, harbor seals, and other marine mammals are abundant all along Katmai's coast, there aren't enough accessible haul-outs to give many bears this opportunity. The niche, however, apparently exists for the few bears that learn to exploit it, providing an example of how bears,

---

[*] Bear numbers for this study do not correspond with those from the Brooks River bear monitoring program.

on a population scale, partition themselves within a shared space. Bears in Katmai are everything from majority pescetarians to berry aficionados to carrion connoisseurs to sea otter hunters.

The gathering of bears at Brooks Falls reflects this partitioning on a micro scale. All bears at the falls focus on salmon, but rarely does a bear's personal fishing strategy completely overlap with another. Each bear specializes in a slightly different way to catch fish. Otis uses the jacuzzi and far pool. If those aren't available, he waits patiently for the more dominant males to vacate his preferred fishing spots. Grazer fishes the far pool, lip, and riffles. Lefty fishes the lip almost as much as 402, but 402 also dives in the jacuzzi on rare occasions and makes greater use of the lower river. Eight-five-six and 747 ignore the lip and dominate access to the jacuzzi and the far pool. Popeye fishes near the jacuzzi, in the far pool, and on the lip, but he'll also steal fish. The subadults mostly hover on the fringes, moving anywhere to take advantage of space and opportunity. Others rarely or never visit the falls, utilizing instead the less productive riffles and lower river areas. Each individual decides how, where, and when to fish depending on its physical abilities and the challenges posed by competition. By learning how to separate themselves in time, space, and technique, far more bears can occupy the falls and the river as a whole than if they all tried to fish in the same way or at the same time.

The exceptional amount of food available to Katmai's bears and the relative ease in which bears can acquire it allows them to quickly gain body mass during the active seasons. As part of the same study that discovered bears hunting seals and sea otters, biologists documented one female gaining an incredible 140 pounds (or 3.4 pounds per day) over about 40 days between late May and early July, in spite of caring for three yearlings and at a time of year before salmon are available. For bears feeding on salmon at Brooks River, especially the adult males who are not burdened with the energetic costs of raising cubs, weight gains are at least as equally impressive. To maximize their mass gain, though, bears make many choices about the quality of their calories.

I've spent many afternoons picking tiny blueberries from the ground-hugging *Vaccinium uliginosum* on Dumpling Mountain. These were hands-

and-knees efforts, as this species of blueberry grows only a few inches high on the mountain and its berries, most of which are a $1/4$-inch or less in diameter, are widely spaced on the stem. After one such trip, I became curious to know how many berries would constitute a gallon. Back at my cabin in two separate tallies, I counted 276 and 286 berries per cup, respectively, for an average of 281 per cup or 4,496 berries per gallon. Although I neglected to weigh the batch, a pint of commercial blueberries weighs about three-quarters of a pound. Scaling up, this equals about 6 pounds per gallon. As blueberries contain about 1,600 calories per pound, I estimate I picked about 9,600 calories.

Eating this amount of berries is easily achievable for a brown bear. When fed an unlimited amount of berries, bears can eat up to a third of their body weight per day. In one trial at Washington State University, a bear ate 200 pounds of berries in a single day, an amount equivalent to 184,000 half-gram blueberries. Feeding on berries to complete satiation probably isn't a realistic scenario for a wild bear, however.

One of the primary challenges a bear faces when trying to make a living is the rate of harvest, an action constrained by the time necessary to search for and locate food, the time needed to take a bite, and the amount of food that can be eaten with each bite. Many brown bear populations utilize berries as their main source of calories in late summer and fall, but berries are distributed unevenly across the landscape. Limits on harvest rates reduce a bear's total calorie intake when eating dispersed foods such as berries. From a purely energetics standpoint, especially when considering the time and energy needed to access and eat berries, berry picking doesn't compare to salmon fishing.

Seasonality, the physical features of a landscape, chance, and competition further limit foraging efficiency for many bear foods. Moose and caribou calves might only be available as a food source for a couple of weeks per year, after which the young ungulates are too swift for bears to hunt them successfully. Bears on the coast can only access and locate clams during the narrow window of time around low tide. Large animal carcasses, whether whale, moose, or caribou, are too uncommon and dispersed to be regularly encountered. And, when they do appear, a foraging bear might find that it has already been claimed by a more dominant bear.

Brown bears are much better suited to make a living off plants than the typical member of the carnivore order. Their molars are slightly flattened, which helps them better chew roughage. Long front claws act like buckets on an excavator, allowing brown bears to quickly and easily till the earth when seeking edible roots and tubers. Their lips are somewhat dexterous too, making them an important tool for skillfully stripping berries from shrubs.

Yet, bears are also a bit of a dietary chimera. Brown bears live as an omnivore but their ability to make a living off plants is constrained by their carnivore-like digestive tract. In many mammal herbivores, chambered stomachs and ceca function as fermentation and composting tanks where specially adapted bacteria aid in the digestion of cellulous and fibrous plant matter. It is a symbiosis that provides the bacteria with a home and helps the animal extract far more energy from plants than it would be able to do alone. Bears lack those anatomical adaptations. While a brown bear's digestive tract is slightly elongated in proportion to obligate carnivores like wolves and lynx, and it contains its own unique suite of gut fauna, their digestive tract remains unspecialized for extracting energy from fibrous plants.

One of the most sought-after plant foods for bears in Katmai is Lyngbye's sedge, a grass-like plant that grows in coastal salt marshes. When its first tender blades emerge from the wet ground in late spring, this sedge contains about 2,000 calories per pound. Most of the sedge's energy is trapped as indigestible fiber, however. Bears can only digest about 29 percent of its dry weight. The larger the bear, the more difficult it becomes to make a living on this diet.

As part of her master's thesis research on brown bears at Brooks River, Tamara Olson calculated that resting adult male bears in Katmai needed anywhere from 3,100 to 7,100 calories per day just to break even. When active, their metabolic rates climb to nearly 9,500 calories per day. In feeding trials of captive grizzly bears at Washington State University, Karyn Rode found that bears weighing more than about 350 pounds had difficulty meeting their energy requirements on clover and grass because of the combination of the bears' large absolute energy requirements and relatively small bite size. In contrast, bears that weighed less than 250 pounds were able to gain body mass on herbaceous plants, because of their somewhat low daily energy requirements and proportionally larger bite sizes.

For bears as large as Otis, Lefty, and 747, grass and sedge are starvation diets, so it's no wonder they seek salmon so enthusiastically. From a bear's perspective, salmon are dense, highly digestible bundles of energy. Just days removed from the ocean, a newly arriving sockeye at Brooks River offers bears an impressive 4,500 calories of digestible energy. Even the biggest adult males can easily meet their energy requirements by consuming just a couple of salmon per day in early summer. Each additional fish is gravy. If Otis only consumed half of each fish during his marathon fishing session (and to me it looked like he was eating proportionally more), then he still ate an incredible 90,000 calories.

When you are trying to gain weight, it pays to optimize the type of calories you ingest. Walking downstream after one of his innumerable catches, 747 moves to water just shallow enough where he can eat his salmon comfortably. The fish, very much alive at this moment, struggles to free itself but can't overcome 747's strength. As he kneels and then lies prone on his stomach, 747 positions his catch with his forepaws, placing it belly-down in the gravel. He leans forward, bites hard at the base of the neck, and begins to methodically skin the fish from head to tail. Torn skin dangles from his mouth like long, wet lasagna noodles. After eating the skin, he turns over the fish and opens the belly. Skeins of bright red-orange eggs spill onto the gravel. Gulls and magpies gather round, looking to pounce on any scraps that drift away. The salmon eggs, however, are far too valuable to leave to the birds. Seven-four-seven daintily retrieves each skein with his long claws and slurps them down. Finally, he focuses his attention on the salmon's head. Biting around the brain case, he cleaves a concave gap. After swallowing the brain, he stands slowly, pinning the carcass possessively with one paw. Seven-four-seven has so thoroughly cleaned the salmon that it would need little additional prep before I could cook it on my stove. He has no remaining interest in the carcass though, and turns away to resume fishing in the jacuzzi. The birds swarm on it.

Seven-four-seven repeats the process many times over the next few hours, consuming only the skin, brain, and eggs of each catch. His methodology may seem wasteful and counterintuitive. Why leave food on the table, especially the highly digestible protein of salmon fillets, with the clock tick-ing toward winter? To gain body mass most quickly, bears are faced with a multivariable choice. They need to select the highest calorie foods available, the most digestible and calorie-rich parts of those foods, and foods that provide the correct ratio of nutrients to maximize weight gain.

Seven-four-seven isn't shy about eating the entirety of a fish when he has the stomach capacity to spare, but on days when he is well fed, he becomes more selective, foregoing much of his catch to maximize the quality of his calories. Like a miner looking for the most valuable hard rock ore, 747 high-grades the most energy-rich and digestible parts of his food.

The overall energy content of a salmon is patchily distributed throughout its body. Fat is particularly concentrated in the eggs, skin, and brain. Eggs are also numerous, commonly comprising 20 percent of a mature female salmon's pre-spawning weight, and at spawning, salmon eggs contain almost twice as many calories as salmon flesh. Unlike the fat stored in a salmon's muscle or viscera, which dissipates through the rigors of upstream migration and spawning, the fat in a salmon's brain presumably needs to stay in place to help keep the salmon clearheaded. The energy content of the salmon brain, therefore, may not decline as precipitously as other parts of their body, and the brain is sometimes the only part of the fish that well-fed bears will eat. I was unable to locate published statistics on the calorie and fat content of salmon skin. However, at Brooks Falls high-grading bears usually eat the skin, so I suspect it is preferentially selected for its calorie or nutrient content rather than simply being part of the most efficient strategy to eat the fish.

Along with mining the most calorie-rich parts of foods, bears seek a variety of foods to best optimize weight gain. At Washington State University, Joy Erlenbach found that when given a choice among foods that offered primarily protein (Chinook salmon or lean beef), carbohydrates (apples or bread), or fat (beef or pork fat or salmon oil), bears do not feed indiscriminately. They self-selected a diet that contained about 17 percent protein. The rest was a combination of carbs and fat. This ratio provided bears with two important benefits: It prioritized the accumulation of fat and allowed the bears to maintain or even increase their muscle mass.

For wild bears, the consequences of the sugar-fat-protein ratio are manyfold. High-protein diets are good for their muscle mass but not for their fat reserves. For coastal brown bears, springtime foods such as sedge, other vegetation, and carrion are typically high in protein but low in fat and sugar. Consequently, mass gain in the spring is mostly lean tissue. In the fall, when many foods are rich in fat and sugar, mass gain is mostly fat.

Two female bears from Katmai's coast demonstrate these changes. Tracked as part of the same study that led to the discovery of bears actively hunting seals and sea otters, bear 105 weighed 187 pounds in late May with 2 percent of body fat. Through the rest of the spring, she gained about a pound per day, and she weighed 225 pounds in early July with a body fat content of 7 percent. The other female, bear 035, tells a similar story. From May to July, she increased her mass from 242 to 332 pounds, and her body fat content increased from 13 to 20 percent. By October, bear 105 topped out at 357 pounds, while bear 035 reached 471 pounds. However, with the opportunity to eat fatty salmon and sugary berries, the bears substantially increased the rate at which they accumulated fat. Just before they entered their dens, bear 105 had 38 percent body fat, and bear 035 had 39 percent body fat.

With berries providing sugar and salmon providing fat and protein, Katmai's bears can easily meet their macronutrient requirements. Katmai's habitats may provide bears with their ultimate diet.

As the fall equinox approaches, with the first touches of frost on Dumpling Mountain's alpine tundra, Otis sits on his haunches in the far pool. The sum of his summer of effort has paid off. The outline of his hips and ribs has disappeared under inches of fat. The diameter of his neck has surpassed that of his head. When he stands, his belly hangs low enough to almost touch the foot-deep water. But he's not done yet.

As he's gained weight over the last few weeks, his meals have become less fulfilling. Even as he increased the amount of time spent searching for food and the number of calories he consumed, he cannot sate the pang of hunger. Unaware of why or how, the hunger has become insatiable and his fishing has taken on an increased urgency.

A variety of hormones help to regulate hunger and appetite in mammals. Ghrelin, for example, comes and goes depending on how full your stomach may be. An empty stomach releases ghrelin to stimulate hunger. A full stomach reduces ghrelin production, which communicates to the brain, "That's enough for now." The hormone leptin is produced by fat cells. Normally, a long-term increase in leptin suppresses appetite and increases the body's metabolic rate. Resistance to leptin's effects, however, can create a rare disorder in humans known as hyperphagia.

Simply defined, hyperphagia means excessive or extreme eating. Unlike feelings of normal hunger, even those feelings provoked by starvation or physical activity, hyperphagia won't go away with more food. People who suffer from hyperphagia describe the urge to eat as overwhelming. They experience preoccupation with food, food seeking, impaired satiety, mental distress, eating in the absence of hunger, and binge eating. For bears, though, animals who must become obese in order to survive winter, hyperphagia is not a disorder. It is adaptive.

Bears become hyperphagic in late summer and early fall as their brains become resistant to leptin's effects. Hyperphagia prioritizes eating over other life tasks so that bears can build their fat reserves in the final weeks before they begin to hibernate.

As the sockeye dwindle in late summer, a small run of coho salmon enters the river. Larger and certainly fresher than the almost fatally starved sockeye, they have become Otis's main targets. He focuses an unwavering gaze on the water in front of him. With the quickness and precision he displayed in early summer, he flashes into action. A splash of water later, Otis pulls his face from the river to reveal a 10-pound coho in his jaws. Otis uses a paw to pin the still squirming fish to his opposite forearm and begins to devour it. Methodically, he eats almost the whole fish in a few minutes, and when he's done he drops the remaining entrails and mandibles into the water. A few seconds later, he resumes his Eeyore-like posture, ready for another meal.

Over the course of spring, summer, and fall, a bear's journey focuses largely on locating and exploiting the most energetic and nutritious foods available. They must eat a year's worth of food in fewer than six months simply to survive, and as a result they experience hunger in profoundly different ways than people. Gluttony is no sin when your life depends on it.

CHAPTER 10

ODYSSEY

On a free evening in early June, I trudge a few hundred yards upstream from the river mouth to a small channel shortcutting the lower river's meandering, reverse S-curve. I stop at a knee-deep pool to admire tiny fish that have just begun a remarkable journey. A journey, I might add, that few will complete.

Salmon fry, hundreds of them, swirl in the pocket below, working their tails vigorously to remain in place and resist the modest current. Most are no more than an inch-and-a-half long, pale-brown, and freckled with spots. Each has huge eyes compared to the size of its head, and they are ever watchful for the river's myriad predators and for bits of food invisible to my eye. I wonder what it must be like to see the world from their perspective, a dichotomous experience where, at this age, only weeks removed from the gravel nests where they hatched, everything is new and nearly everything is dangerous.

Today they've found a safe haven—no trout lurk in this particular spot—but they'll soon venture into much more foreboding waters where predators will extract a heavy toll. Over the next several years, they will attempt a truly epic journey, a once-in-a-lifetime round trip that climaxes with a fatal return. Very few will succeed. Yet, they will all try, undeterred by obstacles and hazards they cannot know until they experience them. Sockeye salmon are a quintessential example of determination in the face of tremendous challenge.

With bears retired to their dens and buildings shuttered and empty, winter at Brooks River offers a stark contrast from summer. A veneer of thin, crusty snow blankets the forest and marsh. Ice covers the slower moving portions of the river. Migratory animals departed long ago, leaving the river to its few year-round residents. Moose browse willow and wolves visit in search of moose. An otter family or a porcupine might shelter underneath a cabin or two. Small groups of chickadees call onomatopoeically, while redpolls trill as they pick seeds from alder catkins. A snow bunting, having descended from the volcanic slopes, chirps as it searches for food on the wind-scoured beach.

Near the falls, buried several inches within the river gravel, new life stirs. Larval salmon twitch inside pea-sized eggs. Their lives began the previous year when their mother spawned them into a nest she constructed using only her tail. Eyespots and rudimentary bodies slowly developed. Now, several weeks past the winter solstice, with the sun rising a little higher each day, the larvae are ready to hatch.

To escape the membranous shell, the baby salmon convulse with a whiplash-like motion. Free of the egg, the larval salmon, otherwise known as alevins, resemble little of the adult fish they may come to be. Fragility defines them. Alevins are unable to swim, defend themselves, or even remain upright without support. Weighted by a large yolk sac attached to their abdomens, about the most they can do is wiggle.

Until their yolk sack is nearly or completely absorbed, alevins are averse to light and actively move away from it. Immediately after hatching, they display an attraction to solid objects and bury themselves farther into the gravel where they remain for several more weeks. The world above their gravel home is harsh, filled with hazards and predators that they are not prepared to cope with or avoid, at least not yet.

Alevins represent the luckiest of their generation so far, and having survived this long is no easy feat. Most eggs never reach this stage. Spawning in fast-moving water is a somewhat haphazard affair for their parents, and many eggs are swept from the security of their mother's nest before they are buried. Eggs displaced from the nest are certain to die. Predators such as rainbow trout and arctic char relish them as one of their most important late-summer foods. Any uneaten eggs are at the mercy of the downstream current. If the bruising they receive from striking rocks doesn't kill them, then other hazards will. When exposed to freezing temperatures, ice ruptures their cell membranes. Still other eggs suffocate in poorly oxygenated water or are consumed by fungus.

Like a bear's den, the gravel nest provided safety and security, but the fish can't survive there indefinitely. The yolk is a finite energy source intended only to jumpstart their growth. Starvation becomes a significant threat once the yolk is exhausted. In order to survive, alevins emerge into the water column, a hazardous world where the young fish must avoid predation and begin to feed if they are to have a chance to migrate to sea.

Climbing upward through the gravel, the young salmon position themselves to enter the water column. On a circadian scale, the timing of emergence is optimized to reduce the risks of predation. They emerge en masse during the darkest hours of night. With luck, the lack of visibility will cloak at least some from predators, and their large numbers lessen the chance that any one fish will be eaten.

Once in the water column, the fry, as they are called in their first free-swimming life stage, move to the surface where they gulp air to fill their swim bladder. They then become neutrally buoyant for the first time in their lives. Having achieved this first goal, instinct implores them to move toward their rearing areas.

Sockeye have a wider variety of juvenile-rearing strategies than other species of Pacific salmon. Some populations remain in streams and rivers, while others travel almost immediately to sea. The vast majority of sockeye, however, rear in lakes for one to two years before continuing onward. This makes sockeye unique compared to other Pacific salmon species, and it makes the Katmai and Bristol Bay landscapes, with its interconnected series of pristine lakes, a perfect habitat for the young fish.

A sockeye fry's first weeks of life are timed to take advantage of a waning winter and the growing spring. In Naknek Lake or Lake Brooks, fry encounter a cold and richly oxygenated environment that is also highly seasonal. Productivity is scarce in winter when ice cover, near-freezing water temperatures, and limited daylight hinder or stop the growth of plankton. Biological productivity grows through spring upon ice breakup and peaks in summer, not long after the young fish move to their lacustrine homes.

Because the timing and rate of plankton production can vary annually, most sockeye fry arrive in lakes before the peak of plankton growth in summer. Warmer water and increasing daylight simulate the photosynthetic phytoplankton at the base of the food chain, which, in turn, feed the millimeter-scale crustaceans the fry so prefer to eat—*Daphnia* and *Bosmina* water fleas and one-eyed copepods of the genus *Cyclops*. These foods are motile but nonevasive, easy targets for the inch-long fish.

Fry must grow and avoid becoming prey, two goals not completely compatible. Still too small to easily fight the current or evade predators, their journey through creeks, rivers, and lakes is fraught with risk. In the weeks preceding the summer solstice, fry utilize small eddies and slack water as refuge, attempting to hide from the Bristol Bay area's famed rainbow trout. Not all are successful. The rainbows, looking for their first substantial meals since the previous fall, and ravenous from their springtime spawning efforts, fill their stomachs with the tiny fry. Where rivers empty into lakes, lake trout drift in wait, ready to ambush the salmon fry as they begin to feel the current slacken.

Compelled by the instincts that allowed their parents to survive the same life stage, the fry attempt to strike a balance between finding food and not becoming food. In lakes, they soon adopt a diurnal rhythm, residing deeper during the day and migrating upward to feed toward twilight. Feeding at the surface during the day would presumably help them locate prey more easily—sockeye are visual hunters, readily taking prey that is not only the right size but easiest to see—yet it would also make them more visible to fish and avian predators. The safest place is at the bottom of the lake, but at those depths there is little food to eat. The daily migration is a compromise between safety and hunger, one that allows young salmon to take advantage of an "antipredator window" when enough light remains for them to feed and the risk of predation is reduced.

Around the time the tiny fry become conspicuous in the river, their older brethren start a new and equally risky transition. Beginning in May, as the serenades of sparrows and robins fill the forest and the first tender blades of grass emerge from the recently thawed earth, yearling and 2-year-old sockeye gather in schools to migrate, as salmon biologist Thomas Quinn describes, "to a distant and totally new environment, whose conditions they cannot know until they get there." The changes salmon undergo to survive this journey and their life at sea may come naturally, but the process shouldn't be construed as easy as or less dangerous than anything they've experienced so far.

As a smolt, a juvenile salmon undergoes the physiological and physical changes necessary to survive the transition from a freshwater to a saltwater existence. Its freckly parr marks and greenish-brown back is replaced with a sheen of polished silver. It develops teeth on its tongue and gums to help it catch larger prey.

Whether to leave as a yearling or a 2-year-old is an individual choice in sockeye. Unlike chum and pink salmon that have no significant freshwater residency and become smolt almost immediately after emerging from their gravel nests, sockeye begin the smolting process at variable ages and body sizes. Sockeyes that migrate to the sea in their first year are fish that grew fast and reached a size in which they are better equipped to handle the rigors of sea life. Those that stay another year in fresh water may be able to grow larger than the yearlings, but they are no closer to completing their life's journey.

Collecting in schools at lake outlets, the smolt turn and swim rapidly downstream. Those in Lake Brooks plunge through Brooks River, tumbling over the falls without hesitation, sticking to the fastest sections of the river as much as possible and swimming faster than the current where the flow is uniform and quiet. Quickness lessens their vulnerability, as does migrating at night. In Brooks River, smolt out-migration usually peaks near midnight, with well over 90 percent migrating during the window between 11 p.m. and 4 a.m.

I can't ever recall standing along the river and spotting a school of smolts on my own. Their progress is announced by those who feed on them.

Predators know the smolts are coming. They've learned to expect it, and they watch for it. When they discover a school, the scene is frantic. Arctic terns, having just returned from as far as the waters surrounding Antarctica, fill the air with hoarse, chattering cries. They are joined by Bonaparte's gulls and glaucous-winged gulls, all of which bombard the school from above. Armadas of merganser ducks and rainbow trout give chase. At the river mouth, the smolts are ambushed by arctic char and lake trout that have waited patiently for the feast. The water's surface ripples with fleeing sockeye as the attackers give chase. Slivers of silver flash at the surface only to disappear down trout gullets and feathered throats.

Having survived Brooks River, smolts swim ever closer to the ocean. They travel west across Naknek Lake through improving water clarity as the lake's glacial flour is diluted. Into the lake's outlet, the smolts continue their harried migration. Halfway through Naknek River, 45 miles from Brooks and after dodging some of the largest rainbow trout found anywhere, giants that measure over 30 inches long and weigh 10 pounds, smolt notice the current slacken again. They've reached tidewater. If they are to survive the ocean though, they must adapt their bodies to water conditions that are typically fatal to freshwater fish. Salmon constantly fight a battle forced upon them by the chemistry of the water they live within.

Our bodies are good at telling us when we need salt and when we don't. If salt concentrations grow a little high, we feel thirsty. If they are too low, we crave salty foods or simply a nourishing meal. Properly balancing your body's salt content is trickier when you exist in a salt-depleted solution. Salt concentrations in salmon blood are about the same as our own, hovering around 10 parts salt per 1,000 parts water. Fresh water, however, averages less than 1 part salt per 1,000 parts water, a concentration far too low to support proper muscle and nerve activity. Without a means to sequester salt from fresh water and keep it from escaping into the environment, osmotic forces would pull salt from the salmon's bodies and excess water would flood inward as the solutions between the two environments equalize. Left unchecked, the once salty-blooded salmon would experience cells turgid and swollen beyond tolerance, as well as impaired nerve and muscle function. If these impacts fail to kill the fish outright, a predator would soon take advantage of its weakened condition.

For a salmon to breathe, their gills must be quite permeable to gas exchange. But this permeability can also allow other molecules to cross the cell barrier. With osmosis constantly threatening to pull salt ions from their bodies, and normal cellular function requiring a ready supply of salt, freshwater fish must prevent the salt from crossing the gill membranes while scavenging it from the environment at the same time. To accomplish this feat in fresh water, salmon are equipped with specialized cells and molecular pumps on the gill membranes. These act like border guards to regulate the traffic through the cell membrane. When activated by cellular energy, the pumps gather salt ions from the water and release them into the blood. Once the salt is in the body of a fish, the fish is loath to give the salt back to the environment. It won't drink water (enough is absorbed through the gills) and the intestines reduce water absorption. Cells along the gut lining also house their own pumps to catch salt from water and food, while the kidneys and bladder work to recycle salt back into the body before it is lost through urination.

In the ocean, though, salmon encounter the reverse issue. Seawater generally contains dissolved salts at concentrations around 33 parts per thousand. Unregulated osmosis in this habitat would therefore pull salt into the salmon's bodies and push water out until the solutions reached equilibrium. The fish would dehydrate and die while surrounded by water.

To survive life at sea, a salmon's salt pumps reverse during smolting. At the gill membranes, the pipeline of ion exchange reverses, while the number and size of the cells housing the molecular salt pumps increase. Salmon begin to drink water while the intestinal lining uses its salt pumps to create localized areas where salt concentrations exist at levels higher than seawater. The resulting osmotic pressure between the salty areas and the interior of the intestine causes water to flow from the digestive tract into the fish's blood. To sequester water further, they pee very little and what urine is produced is highly concentrated.

Proceeding downstream and exiting Naknek River, the sockeye move into a broad estuary fed by the combined waters of Bristol Bay's largest rivers. Visibility is poor in the muddy water and the currents move in ways the fish have never experienced before. The farther the fish swim into Bristol Bay, the stronger the pang of salt becomes on their tongues. To add to the challenges, new hazards await in this place. Some 2,000 beluga whales live in Bristol Bay and a few hundred of them remain in the upper bay during late spring. Unlike the trout and birds, which took the lives of many smolts before they reached the sea, the belugas do not need to restrict their hunts to daylight hours or to water with good visibility. From a bulbous melon, a mass of waxy material in their forehead, the white whales emit piercing clicks and whistles. The sounds travel unimpeded through the turbid water until they encounter an object and return to the singer. A whale's lower jaw receives and amplifies the sound, allowing a beluga to not only know what objects lie before it but also the density, direction, and rate of travel. Echo-locating like bats on a moonless night, the belugas feast on millions of outgoing smolts per year.

If wilderness can be a feeling, I've felt it most strongly while standing at the edge of the ocean. Its oxygen is inaccessible to my lungs; its salt concentrations a poison for my body. Without life-supporting technology, whether a boat, ship, submersible vehicle, or life raft made of sticks and twine, I cannot survive the ocean much easier than the surface of Mars. Perhaps not surprisingly, we know less about the lives of salmon in the ocean than at any other life stage.

Through the mid-20th century, the marine travels of salmon were essentially unknown. We knew salmon went to the sea and came back to spawn, but little else. And even today, observing and tracking the fish remains a challenging endeavor. Stomach contents tell us what they eat but not necessarily about their hunting behavior. Growth rings on scales record how long salmon spend in fresh water versus salt water, but not where they went in between. Tags and catch locations provide some basic information on where salmon go but not necessarily how they get there. Surgically implanted acoustic transmitters can signal where a salmon is but it requires a vast network of hydrophones to receive the sound, and as such is feasible only in limited locations. All in all, our knowledge of their sea life is the sum result of pieces of a vast puzzle that fisheries biologists are still in the process of assembling.

For the survivors of the journey so far, their time at sea will come to represent a phase of rapid growth and long migrations. Their first summer of ocean life is spent mostly in the Bering Sea while swimming over 500 miles along the arc of the Alaska Peninsula to the Aleutian Islands. Throughout autumn and winter, the fish move south through the gaps between the Aleutians, perhaps motivated by the lowering of sea surface temperatures and the reduced food supply that accompany winter in northern oceans. South of the volcanic arc, the salmon migrate counterclockwise in an elongated oval through the North Pacific. By April and May, Bristol Bay salmon can be found as far south as 43°N, the same latitude as southern Oregon, and spread along a band stretching from 167°E, which is closer to Asia than anywhere else, to 140°W, about 800 miles offshore of the US West Coast. In total, this is a longitudinal spread of more than 2,500 miles.

Upon the return of summer, the salmon that remain far to the west migrate north while those in the east move westward along the south side of the Alaska Peninsula and Aleutians. Portions of each geographical group swing into the Bering Sea before the migration roughly repeats during the salmons' second year in the ocean. This will be the last year at sea for most Bristol Bay salmon, as long as they find enough food to support their growth and achieve their reproductive size. A salmon gets one chance to spawn and could die from predation at any time, so once its body determines it is ready for the journey to fresh water, there's little sense remaining in the sea. But first, they must find their way back through the vastness of the North Pacific.

A salmon's ability to navigate the sea seems remarkable to me, especially as someone who's learned from experience that he lacks a sense of dead reckoning. Salmon travel thousands of miles through the open ocean only to return, years later, to their natal watersheds, and all without landmarks pointing the way. They know where they are, where they want to go, how to get there, and how long the journey will take.

Changes in day length appear to trigger migration in ocean-going salmon. By possessing a celestial calendar of sorts, one synchronized by day length, they can recognize when to migrate. The relative position of the sun also helps determine latitude. But the sun isn't visible between sunrise and sunset or on overcast days. For salmon to find their way more precisely, they utilize a sense that ties the Earth's magnetic field with their very cells.

Earth is a giant magnet whose magnetic field is generated by the planet's molten outer core. Magnetic field lines, or vectors, emanate from the southern magnetic pole and reenter the Earth in the Northern Hemisphere. No matter where you are, some magnetic vectors intersect your location, but their angles of inclination differ considerably. At the magnetic equator, the dip is shallow, nearly parallel to the ground. The closer you get to the magnetic poles though, the steeper the angle becomes until, at the poles, it is perpendicular to the ground. As such, the magnetic field's intensity and direction vary predictably, creating a signature that is specific to each location on the planet. For animals that possess magnetoreception, a sixth sense once thought preposterous by biologists and physicists, the magnetic field becomes a compass to set and maintain direction while its intensity and inclination provide a map.

The ability of living organisms to detect and use Earth's magnetic field is best understood in migratory birds. In captive settings, the urge to move in migratory directions is so strong that caged birds will consistently orient the direction they would otherwise be migrating. By altering the magnetic field around cages containing European robins, making south feel like north for example, biologist Wolfgang Wiltschko found the birds had a strong preference for their seasonally appropriate migratory direction. Subsequent laboratory experiments on sea turtles and salmon revealed similar results. Navigationally naïve salmon (that is, those raised in hatcheries or labs and have never migrated) will bias their swimming in a particular direction when they encounter magnetic conditions resembling certain regions along their natural migratory route. This has also been demonstrated in landlocked Atlantic salmon many generations removed from their anadromous ancestors.

How animals sense and interpret magnetic field information remains mysterious. To sense the world, our nose and eyes must make contact with the environment outside our bodies. Magnetic fields, however, pass unimpeded through biological tissue, so there's nothing to suggest that magnetoreceptors need be centralized, large, or connected in any way with the external environment. Biologists, in their search for a physical magnetoreceptor, are looking for submicroscopic structures that could be scattered anywhere within an animal.

The search has led to the discovery of three promising mechanisms.

In electromagnetic induction, an electrically conductive object moving through a magnetic field creates a constant voltage that changes with speed and direction. A circuit forms and current flows if the body passes through a conductive medium like water. Sharks could perceive magnetism in this manner due to their ability to sense changes in electric currents.

Electromagnetic induction seems an unlikely mechanism for some long-distance migrants though. Sea turtles travel across thousands of miles of ocean only to return and lay their eggs on the same beach where they had hatched. Yet, they lack the electroreceptors sharks utilize so well. Birds (excluding penguins) migrate through air, but air doesn't normally conduct electricity so they too likely rely on other mechanisms.

A second hypothesis involves a process on an atomic level. Chemical magnetoreception begins when one molecule gives an electron to another molecule, leaving each with an unpaired electron. Interactions with the magnetic field can then cause the unpaired electrons to change their orbit like a wobbling spinning top. Since sunlight can induce the electron transfers, perhaps the eyes are a location where this process can take place. The eyes of some migratory birds may possess cells with molecules that react in this way. If changes to the magnetic field cause a chemical reaction in a bird's eye, for example, then perhaps birds can see magnetic fields.

Lastly, some organisms may house magnetic minerals within their cells. In certain species of bacteria, magnetite crystals cause the bacteria to physically rotate and align with the magnetic field. Magnetite crystals have also been found in the bills of migratory songbirds as well as in the noses of rainbow trout, Chinook salmon, and sockeye salmon.

So far, the magnetite hypothesis seems to be the most likely explanation for guiding the travels of ocean-going salmon, although the mystery of how it functions remains. In birds and fish, magnetite crystals are incredibly small, about 50 nanometers (50 *billionths* of a meter) in diameter, so observing changes to them or their effects on cells is extremely challenging. Magnetite crystals exist in a salmon's ethmoid bone—a bone at the root of the nose through which the olfactory nerves pass. A study of different life stages of sockeye salmon indicated an orderly production of magnetite in the front part of the skull. When examined more closely, the crystallography implied that the magnetite grows under precise biological control.

As the crystals try to align with the magnetic field, they might stimulate the nervous system in some yet-unknown way. Its presence and function led biologists Kenneth Lohmann, Nathan Putman, and Catherine Lohmann to hypothesize that salmon are able to geomagnetically imprint on the magnetic field of their natal watershed and later use this information to find their way home.

A salmon's compass, combined with its inherited map, guides the fish to areas where it is likely to find conditions favorable for growth and survival. From both lab experiments and observations at sea, we know that salmon swim in certain directions and go to certain areas of the ocean depending on their age and the time of year. Based on those observations, Nathan Putman used a computer model to simulate the magnetic navigational path of Chinook salmon. He found that if they followed their inherited magnetic map, they would remain in and return to portions of the North Pacific where water temperatures are suitable for their physiology as cold-water fish. While ocean conditions vary considerably, the magnetic map guides fish along routes that, on average, take them to areas where waters are favorable for growth and survival. The ability to navigate the sea and find their way home is as engrained in their genome as the instinct to eat when hungry.

A salmon's life is an odyssey fraught with danger. Most eggs never hatch and most fry never become smolt. If you survive long enough to journey to sea, you are unlikely to return. The burden and challenges of anadromy are reflected in the mortality rate of sockeye, which equals or exceeds 75 percent at most juvenile life stages. If the journey to sea and back is so risky, why make it at all, especially if your species possesses another survival strategy?

On a map, Naknek Lake resembles a gnarled, inverted crab claw, the claw's pincers opening eastward to form its Iliuk Arm and North Arm. Toward the isolated end of the North Arm, beyond the small clearing where trapper Roy Fure built his hand-hewn cabin almost a century ago, and hidden behind the granitic knolls that pimple the lake surface, a broad marsh extends into the trackless wilderness. In spring and early summer, when the lake basin has yet to swell with precipitation and glacial melt, the marsh remains dry. By August, though, especially in wet years, a thin sheet of water flows through the sedge, only rarely dropping into defined drainage channels. Farther inland, the marsh becomes dimpled with small lakes and ponds that have no surface connection to Naknek Lake. One, nicknamed Jo-Jo, harbors salmon that haven't experienced the sea for generations.

When the fitness cost of going to sea exceeds the cost of remaining in fresh water, sockeye can evolve populations that forego anadromy. Kokanee are sockeye that remain in fresh water their entire lives. Three kokanee populations reside in Katmai. Two live in separate small lakes just inland from the Pacific coast, and one lives in Jo-Jo. Despite the abundance of sockeye in the region, these are the only kokanee populations in southwest Alaska.

Kokanee usually remain planktivores, and they grow slower than sockeye due to their smaller and less caloric foods. Kokanee also reproduce at smaller sizes and produce fewer eggs per female. Still, freshwater residency isn't without its advantages. Kokanee needn't undertake a risky and uncertain journey to the sea and back. They also deal with fewer predator species and smaller-sized predators.

Reproductive fitness is not measured by Olympian feats, such as how fast or efficiently you can swim or how strong your muscles grow. Fitness is the probability of surviving to reproduce at any age combined with an individual's fecundity at that age. At Jo-Jo, the cost of migrating to sea is insurmountable, so fish have no other choice. It's not so simple elsewhere. Most kokanee populations coexist with sea-run sockeye. Anadromy allows sockeye to survive in fresh water at high densities during life stages when the habitat can support them. It pawns, in a sense, the responsibility of rearing the fish to large size on the ocean where food and space are less constrained. Anadromous salmon risk death on the journey but grow much faster, grow larger, and produce more eggs compared to kokanee salmon. Each strategy plays a numbers game; a species-wide, lifelong bet to win the game of survival and reproduction.

Salmon aren't marooned or shipwrecked by spiteful gods nor are they seduced by singing sirens like Odysseus, but they arguably endure even greater trials. Every stage of their life is filled with significant risk, and few survive the journey. Predators pursue sockeye from almost the moment they emerge from the gravel. They must dead reckon across thousands of miles of open ocean. They see their brethren fall ill or get devoured. The odds of surviving are so low that the ones that do make it can almost seem

like the chosen ones. In a sense, they are. Chosen not by divine intervention but by their navigational instincts, ability to find prey, skill in avoiding
predators, and chance.

In Bristol Bay, the return of the sockeye is celebrated as much as any
other holiday, secular or otherwise. The pulse of the area's culture and ecosystem beats with these fish, and for those salmon that survive to return,
reaching their spawning grounds may be their biggest challenge yet.

CHAPTER 11

SPAWN

During the weeks following the spring equinox, the small town of King Salmon undergoes a rebirth. As the river sheds its cloak of ice, thousands of tundra swans and even more ducks descend from the skies to revel in the newly open water. Sandhill cranes and white-fronted geese bugle from flocks high in the air, and the first white-crowned sparrows sing their trill from the shrub thickets. Where the soils thaw early, a few select willow buds break free of their protective scales. Initially soft like rabbit's fur, they expand and mature into petal-less male flowers hanging heavy with yellow pollen. Emerging bumblebee queens, appearing even before mosquitoes, seek them out as one of their first reliable sources of food.

Like the flocks of returning birds and awakening bees, waves of humanity descend upon the region. The boatyard along Naknek River thrums with noise as boat captains, crew, and mechanics ready their vessels for the water. At the airport, traffic increases steadily, bringing supplies and a workforce that frequently overwhelms the tiny passenger terminal. An inordinate number of people wear rubber boots and noticeably more men than women exit the planes. Experienced hands react with a calm excitement as they enter the terminal to greet coworkers and friends, while some of the greener arrivals look as though they aren't sure if they've made a mistake or not.

As people and wildlife converge on the Alaska Peninsula, near-mature sockeye are spread across thousands of miles of the North Pacific and Bering Sea. Triggered and guided by instinct, they swim 30 to 50 miles per day during the final weeks of their oceanic odyssey, soon to arrive tens of millions strong in Bristol Bay.

Days before the summer solstice, the first sockeye enter fresh water. The flow of migrants increases with each day until it crescendos in early July. It's a remarkably precise arrival window given the disparate places sockeye start from and the distances they must cover to return. Eighty percent of the annual sockeye run passes through Bristol Bay within two weeks, a wave of salmon unlike any other on the planet. While the days tick through our calendars, in Bristol Bay it is the return of salmon by which the season is measured.

In outer Bristol Bay, the sockeye show little segregation. Fish that spawn in different watersheds continue to school and travel together. They experience the same conditions at sea, yet must respond in different ways to reach their final destination. As they near their natal watersheds, salmon actively navigate toward their home river, ignoring the cues guiding the rest of the fish in other directions. They break away to Ugashik and Egegik at the southern end of the bay. Others branch north into the Togiak and Nushagak, or they go eastward toward homes far up the Naknek, Alagnak, and Kvichak watersheds.

On the final landward approach, something threatens to stop their forward momentum. A fleet of flat-bowed fishing boats, nearly 1,900 strong, patrols the inner bay, drifting gillnets behind them. From the tundra-covered bluffs bordering the water, people string hundreds of additional nets perpendicular to the shoreline. The monofilament netting is nearly invisible to the fish and woven to accommodate a sockeye's head but not its body.

Only a mile from Naknek River, a boat lounges at the surface, waiting for fish to arrive. A school of salmon turns in its direction, drawn by the scent of home mixing in the current. Striking the net, salmon twitch in the water as the plastic strands wrap behind their gill plates. The hard polystyrene floats that buoy the net dip farther into the water under the weight of fish. Suddenly, the salmon feel themselves lifted into the air as the net is reeled onto the stern of a boat. A small crew clad in rubber overalls, their hands thickened with muscle built by the labor, picks the salmon out of the net one by one. In Bristol Bay, the majority of the returning salmon will meet their fate this way. The rest escape by chance, not skill.

For more than a week I had ventured to the falls each evening, watching bears come and go, wondering when the first big wave of salmon would arrive. Throughout most of June 2019, few salmon had entered the Naknek watershed and fewer had been captured in the fishery. Then on June 23 over 50,000 fish passed the metal scaffold counting tower on Naknek River. The 24th of June added another 36,000 to the mix. By June 25, the first large waves of salmon entered Brooks River. I enjoy the scene while standing beneath warm and sunny skies, watching the river fill with fish.

To gauge the relative number of salmon at the falls, I count leaping fish during several one-minute intervals. The numbers slowly tick upward—84, 146, 94, 200—indicating the current wave has not yet crested. For the few bears that are here, the feast is almost overwhelming. Holly stands on the far side where salmon toss and turn in the shallow water. Easily catching one bright silver sockeye, she barely starts to eat it when another struggles in the current and crashes into her feet. She stops eating the first to grab the second, and then another is swept into her paws. She moves to grab it and consequently loses her second catch. Holly sees so many vulnerable prey that she seems unable to cope with the abundance, her head jerking left then right. Fish are everywhere and the run is just beginning. I found myself marveling, as I often do, at the remarkableness of the salmons' journey and their determination to complete it even in the face of such tremendous odds.

Salmon begin the final stages of their journey on a flood tide. The surging water reverses the flow in the lower half of Naknek River, helping to propel the fish swiftly upstream past the narrow graveled beaches and grassy bluffs at the river mouth, beyond Naknek's canneries, dormitories, and boatyards. Soon the pang of salt disappears and for the first time in years, they taste the plain sweetness of fresh water.

Upstream of King Salmon the tide loses momentum and is overtaken by the downstream current. The salmon feel the transition but are primed for the effort. Where the river gradient steepens and the current strengthens, the sockeye shift closer to the riverbanks and deeper toward the bottom where the current is less forceful. Their forward movement is purposeful and direct. Through the river and into Naknek Lake, the salmon know where they want to go.

We've known for centuries that salmon go home to their place of birth. In *The Compleat Angler*, first published in 1653, Izaak Walton and Charles Cotton note that "by tying a ribbon, or some known tape or thread, in the tail of young salmons, which have been taken in weirs as they have swimmed towards the salt water, and then by taking a part of them again with the known mark at the same place at their return from the sea . . . has inclined many to think, that every salmon usually returns to the same river in which it was bred." We know now the process is even more remarkable. Not only do most salmon return to the same river or stream where they were reared but also to the same section of river, even the same gravel bar where they hatched. Their magnetic map and compass remain important navigational assets to guide them through Katmai's lakes, but from the edge of the sea onward, it's the smell of home that offers the most guidance.

Odors have a powerful ability to evoke memory. Consider how a scent can transport you through time and space, back to places and experiences long since passed. Catch the aroma of a particular food and suddenly your mind wanders to your grandmother's kitchen, or perhaps a hint of a certain perfume elicits the emotions once experienced with a lost love. When I catch the scent of wet leaves no matter the setting—I can be in a wooded desert canyon of southeast New Mexico, an alder thicket on the Alaska Peninsula, or an apple orchard in Washington State—memories of my childhood autumns in western Pennsylvania flash to mind. With the waft of earthy vegetative dampness, I once again see the leaf pile's collage of reds, browns, and yellows on the lawn, feel the warm autumn sun filtering through the tree branches, and experience the moment just before I leap into the stack. In salmon, odors of "childhood" are even more powerful, evoking far more than nostalgia. Odors are waypoints that guide them to their places of birth.

For salmon to navigate by their sense of smell, water bodies must differ in chemical characteristics. Salmon must be able to distinguish the differences and learn the distinctions prior to entering the sea. The memory of the odors must then remain with the fish through their ocean migration. Finally, the fish must respond to them upon returning to fresh water.

Salmon have a particular talent for sensing and remembering odor. At certain life stages—emergence from the gravel and migration to sea, for example—salmon imprint on the odors in the water, mapping them for future use. It was long assumed the scent-detecting tissue in a salmon's nose captured the odor's info while the brain's olfactory bulb stored the memory until it was needed on the upstream migration. The process has proven to be more complex though. A salmon's olfactory cells have their own form of memory. Exposure to a chemical in the water sensitizes the olfactory cells to the odor. Afterward, the fish can detect the odor at concentrations much lower than the original level of exposure. The memory of the odor is retained for years even though the original scent-detecting cells die and are replaced by newer cells never exposed to it.

One can understand how useful this might be on a homeward journey when the odor of your spawning site is diluted and mixed with waters from many sources. For the distinctions to be meaningful for the fish, and for it to become useful in their homeward migration, salmon need to learn the sequential order of scents. Exposure to odor alone is apparently insufficient for salmon to imprint on a home location and then return to it. Exposure must be coupled with migration. This enables salmon to recall the right odors in the right sequence on their homeward journey.

Precise homing is remarkable, yet at first glance it may not seem particularly advantageous when you pass suitable spawning sites along the way. Salmon that spawn in tributaries of Lake Brooks, for example, could feasibly spawn in Brooks River. Salmon that spawn upstream of Brooks Falls ignore prime spawning habitat downstream of the falls. A sockeye could save considerable time, energy, and risk by "choosing" to spawn at the first suitable habitat they encounter instead of pushing onward to more distant locations.

Yet, although salmon know what constitutes good spawning and rearing habitat, they only have proof it exists in one place: the site where they were born. A returning salmon has its own existence as evidence that its natal area provides the conditions necessary for successful reproduction and juvenile survival. Homing to your natal site means you are likely to find the right nesting conditions. It means you and your offspring are unlikely to encounter impassible barriers. It means that your eggs will incubate at the appropriate rate and your offspring, like you, will possess the instincts necessary to find a suitable rearing area and evade the predators lurking in the ecosystem.

Homing is a powerful instinct, but I envision something greater than chemical reactions happening in the minds of the fish as they follow their sense of smell upstream. Perhaps the odors evoke a feeling of something that is right and good in the fish; memories of where they came from, where they belong, and where they must go. It evokes a sense of home.

The homing instinct compels nearly all salmon to return to their places of birth, but the power of home is not universal. A small percentage of salmon take a chance elsewhere. Strays bet against the odds in an effort to spawn somewhere different than where they were born.

On its face, straying seems highly risky. Strays cannot know what conditions they will experience, and wandering in this way can easily lead to reproductive dead ends. However, by accessing newly available territory, strays experience little competition for breeding and rearing habitat. It allows them to colonize new areas when habitat becomes available, and it provides them with a fighting chance to reproduce when disasters such as landslides and volcanic eruptions prevent access to their natal site. Most current salmon populations are founded by strays, so when straying pays off, it can pay off big.

As the glaciers receded from the Naknek basin tens of thousands of years ago, a few sockeye took a chance. Instead of returning to their natal site, they migrated farther than their predecessors had ever gone before. They knew what to look for—a vision of the ideal spawning site being embedded in their genetic code—and they took the risk to find it. These founders strayed into the cold, spring-fed tributaries of Lake Brooks or the emerging river at its outlet. Maybe few or none were successful at first, dying without spawning or spawning in marginal areas where their eggs or offspring could not survive. Some found success though. Thousands of generations later, their genes are now spread among the hundreds of thousands of salmon that return to Brooks River each year.

As salmon move upstream through Naknek River, the potpourri of glacial flour and traces of volcanic ash becomes stronger as they bypass each successive tributary. In Naknek Lake, the odor of home directs a few into North Arm to spawn in Idavain Creek and the nameless rivulets draining into Bay of Islands. The majority, however, sometimes over 2 million strong, continue east. Just a couple of miles shy of Iliuk Arm, where fingers of a breached glacial moraine gate the coldest and deepest part of Naknek Lake, they find Brooks River. Those born farther up the watershed continue their journey into Iliuk Arm and beyond, but about 20 percent of the Naknek escapement turns into Brooks River.

Salmon continue to flood the river as I watch spellbound. The fish queue in the shallows outside the jacuzzi, looking for the space and opportunity to surmount the falls. Five to ten leap out of the water every second, and I stop counting the number of jumping fish because there are too many to count accurately.

Collectively, the leaps look haphazard and awkward. Fish shoot out of the water in nearly every direction. Some break the surface perpendicular to the water's surface, gaining height but not the direction necessary to crest the cascade. Others aim too far left or right and plunge back into the water, having gained no ground. Still more angle too low and hit the falls too soon. The falling water either shoves them back down or they crash into the rocks. An unlucky few concuss themselves in this way. I see their limp bodies drift downstream, the livelier salmon parting ways to let the stunned fish drift by. They will either regain their composure and try again or they will soon be scavenged by a hungry bear.

During the four 1-minute counts I conduct this evening, I see 2, 4, 0, and 10 fish make the leap, while a total of 521 fish tried the jump during the same intervals. This translates into a lowly 3 percent success rate. More typically, jumping success is a bit better, but not by much. From 2013 to 2019, I conducted 499 1-minute counts of leaping salmon at the falls. During each

count I tallied jumpers and successful jumpers to determine what their success rate might be. Out of 18,598 jumping salmon just 1,159 fish, a mere 6.2
percent, made the leap. Bears, not surprisingly, lowered the salmons' overall
success rate. About 5.1 and 4.7 percent of jumps were successful with bears
in the jacuzzi or standing on the lip, respectively. When bears were in both
places at the same time, the success rate plunged to 2.6 percent.

Their lack of success is a combination of inexperience and difficulty.
The falls is unlike any obstacle they've faced so far. As smolt, they tumbled
over it but then reoriented to the flow of the current and kept going downstream. They didn't have the luxury of investigating further. Years later,
now moving upstream, they must fight to the base of the falls and probe
the barrier with only the knowledge that somewhere above is where they
came from.

I got a sense of how disorienting the currents at the falls can be while
exploring the water on a warm day in early June. I had come after my work
shift ended, eager to enjoy a quick half hour of wandering in the water.
Attempting to see the falls from the perspective of a bear hunting salmon,
I entered the jacuzzi from downstream. The waterfall looked intimidat-
ing, a solid 6 feet or more tall, and the jacuzzi roiled with a foam. Working
upstream, I felt the gravel drop away to an unknown depth precisely at the
spot where bears sit to fish. I tried moving farther toward the falls but the
strength of the downward rushing water was too great. I couldn't keep my
footing or stay in one place.

Curious to get even closer (a thought that has led to the undoing of
many young men over the history of humanity), I decided on an alternative
route, this one following the base of the falls. Hugging the wall, I reached
the edge of the lip, where the water cascades freely to the plunge pool below.
I still couldn't see much within the water, so acting on an impulse I let go of
the wall and hopped in. It was far deeper than I expected. How deep I cannot say because my feet didn't touch bottom. The current tumbled me like a
rag in a washing machine. After what seemed like 10 seconds, but was probably no more than 2, I was spit out into the graveled shallows.

A 6.2 percent success rate demonstrates the overall odds of jumping
success are quite low, but the statistic is also a bit misleading. Salmon aren't
limited to just one jump. They can try as many times as health, energy, and

predation permit. Through determination and strength, they try again and again until they get it right. I emerged uninjured from my tumbling in the jacuzzi, and with a greatly reinforced respect for a salmon's athleticism in the face of such conditions. Over the course of the run, several hundred thousand fish make the leap, and those that make the jump exemplify beauty, grace, and strength.

Starting deep within the jacuzzi, they utilize the circulating hydraulic to accelerate upward. Through the air, following a parabolic trajectory, their bodies reflect sunlight like polished silver. Above the falls, they strike the water swimming, their tails pumping rapidly from side to side. For half a second, the current's opposing force holds them in place, working to sweep them back over the falls. Resisting with a burst of strength and speed, the salmon sprint forward to leave the falls behind, perhaps their last major obstacle before reaching their spawning grounds.

As bears come and go, additional waves of salmon arrive. The water is so full of fish that the slightest uncertainty causes localized panic, and the water boils as salmon flee real or envisioned predators or fight to stay in the water and not be forced onto the bank. So many salmon fill the river at the base of the falls that the water attains the hue of their scales.

This evening, 747 lumbers away after catching and eating 10 fish in about 30 minutes. Two-eight-four, a female with a large shoulder hump, thin neck, and ragged goatee, keeps catching fish and then dropping them, like she wants to eat but is too full. A young subadult does the same before she leaves. Soon enough, only 856 remains to exploit the bounty, not because he chased the others away but because no one else is hungry.

Moments such as these seem counterintuitive. Shouldn't more bears utilize the falls when there are more fish available? Over weekly or monthly time scales, more bears do use the falls when the salmon are running. The number of bears at Brooks River is greatest in July, during the peak of the salmon migration, and again in September through October when spawning activity is greatest and dead salmon are easy to scavenge. On a finer scale, though, especially day to day and hour to hour, the abundance of bears at the falls is highly variable and highly influenced by salmon abundance.

Predators have a greater chance of success when there are more prey, but predators also remain constrained by handling time—the rate they can catch their food as well as the time needed to eat and digest it. Prey levels, therefore, can reach a threshold, a saturation point, beyond which predation rates cannot keep up. When food overwhelms the capacity of a predator population to consume it, then the predators become swamped.

Predator swamping is exemplified by the periodic emergence of cicadas. In eastern and central North America, larval cicadas of many different species spend years underground, slowly feeding on plant juices before they emerge en masse. Adult cicadas have no defense against predators. They are weak fliers, apparently taste fine, and with their loud buzzing calls can be quite conspicuous. Individual insects gain safety only through sheer abundance.

In May 1985, more than 1 million cicadas emerged from the earth in a 40-acre site in northwest Arkansas. About 50 percent of the cicadas emerged during four consecutive nights. Birds ate as much as 40 percent of the cicadas at low densities, but when cicada densities were more than 9,700 individuals per acre, birds ate only about 15 percent. So many cicadas inhabited the forest that they overwhelmed the local bird population's ability to eat them all, giving most cicadas the opportunity to reproduce.

When we envision salmon runs at Brooks River like cicadas, it becomes easier to understand why fewer bears would use the falls during times with lots of salmon. The sheer amount of fish overwhelms the capacity of the local bear population (defined in this context as the bears actively using the river on that day) to eat them. Individual bears gorge for short bouts, sometimes catching and consuming dozens of fish, but thousands more salmon remain alive and thriving.

Like nearly everything in nature, the predator-prey relationship between bears and salmon is more complicated though. Salmon abundance varies considerably in any given stream from year to year and even day to day. In the Wood River watershed, on the north side of Bristol Bay, Thomas Quinn and colleagues found the average bear predation rates varied significantly across different streams. Predation rates were greatest in small, shallow streams where fishing is easier, and they found the rates lowest in wider and deeper streams where salmon can evade bears more easily. Happy Creek, a medium-sized stream 20 feet wide and 12 inches deep, for example, had the highest average annual salmon abundance during the study period (about 11,300 per year), but bears killed only 21 percent of the fish annually. In contrast, bears killed 77 percent of salmon per year in "A" Creek, a small stream only 4.6 feet wide and 4 inches deep.

Even in streams where bears ate the most salmon, Quinn found predation rates eventually reached asymptote. Comparing salmon abundance and predation rates, he found the number of salmon killed by bears initially increases sharply but then plateaus as fish abundance exceeds the bears' capacity to catch, eat, and digest them. Through predator swamping, individual prey will be sacrificed so that most will live, as though salmon and cicadas subscribe to Spock's cold, yet arguably flawed logic: the needs of the many outweigh the needs of the few, or the one.

Almost two months past the summer solstice, most sockeye have reached their spawning grounds and are busy with the final act of their lives. Standing at the riffles on a mid-August afternoon, looking down at the river with the bright late summer sun warming my back, ruby-colored sockeye sparkle in the water.

We tend to think of salmon caught in the Bristol Bay fishery as adults, but those fish as well as many of the earliest arrivals at Brooks River are incapable of reproduction. They remain physically immature, having yet to undergo their own version of puberty. Upon entry to fresh water, testes and eggs begin to enlarge and mature, making the fishes reproductively capable for the first and only time in their lives.

Dramatic changes also happen externally. Salmon fresh from the ocean retain their fusiform shape and keep it through most of their upstream journey to reduce drag and increase swimming efficiency. But almost as soon as the run begins, some fish at the river show hints of change. Among the schools of bright silver salmon stacking against the falls, one swims with pink-tinged flanks. A bear catches another with a conspicuously protruding snout. Upon the final approach to its spawning grounds, a salmon's skin thickens as its scales are resorbed. Gums recede. Front teeth grow into fangs. Jawlines elongate and curve at the end like slip-joint pliers. The fish's body compresses laterally and its backbone arches upward to create a prominent hump. Most strikingly, its original color, ocean-silver, is replaced. The salmon's head and face turn green while its body grows crimson. In full spawning regalia, a sockeye becomes a grotesque beauty, while their flesh becomes as white and pale as the inside of a frozen fish stick, a stark contrast to the pink filet that salmon are so prized for.

Sockeye acquire carotenoids from their oceanic prey and sequester them in muscle tissue that colors their flesh. Upon reentry into fresh water, carotenoids are released by the muscle into the bloodstream where they may act as antioxidants and help limit damage to soft tissues and DNA caused by free radical molecules.

But what to do with the pigments in the bloodstream? It could be excreted harmlessly into the environment, but their release from muscle also makes them available to be used in other ways. In a parsimonious strategy, salmon transfer the newly available carotenoids to their skin. The bright red skin of a fully mature sockeye can then serve as a nuptial signal, and on the spawning grounds a salmon needs every advantage.

Their physical transformation complete, the fish are now equipped with weaponry to battle in the final, and most important, fight of their lives. Elongated jaws armed with prominent teeth are meant to slice and puncture. Chasing and fighting are routine on the spawning grounds as males search for mates and females establish and defend nesting territory. Like bears jostling for fishing spots, salmon use body size and posturing to intimidate and dissuade competitors, and a size-based social hierarchy develops with larger fish holding serve.

Because of their longer jaws and more exaggerated hump, male salmon are sometimes perceived as more aggressive than females. On the spawning grounds, though, females are the fiercer sex. Once she's chosen and committed to a spawning site, known as a redd, she repeatedly and aggressively chases away other females and undesirable males. It's an extra effort that can pay big dividends for her overall reproductive success. Finding and protecting a good nesting site, where eggs are safe and experience the proper incubation conditions, is extremely important. Measuring salmon mortality from egg to adult, the great majority die prior to or during incubation. Indeed, only about 13 percent survive long enough to hatch. When demand for good nesting sites exceeds supply, a displaced female risks losing not only her territory but also the success of any eggs she's already laid if another female prepares a nest in the same place. Plus, she won't be able to try again. While a male sockeye's reproductive success depends on delivering millions of sperm to eggs, a female's is capped by the number of eggs in her body, a few thousand at most.

From the riffles platform, I watch fish hover in the current. Their movements appear random at first, but soon a discernable pattern of courtship and competition emerges. One large female lurks in the water between a saturated, partly submerged log and microwave-sized boulder. She intuits the physics of water and employs it to assist preparing her nest. Facing upstream, holding steady in the current, she turns on her side and flexes her body and tail to fan the gravel with a series of rapid, rhythmic, and vigorous movements. The work forces sand and silt into the water column where the current winnows it away. She repeats the process many times, deepening her nest while at the same time ridding it of small particles that if left in place would restrict the flow of oxygen around her eggs. On the downstream side of the growing depression, the denser and larger gravel forms a crescent-shaped tailspin.

She maintains a small territory around her nest and her intolerance of other females is especially apparent. Any who approach are quickly chased away. She's a bit more tolerant of males, allowing most to hover nearby, especially one particularly large male that is waiting not so patiently for the spawning event.

He's not a recent arrival to the riffles. The skin at the base of his tail has begun to yellow, revealing he's seen his share of battles. He remains within a foot of his prospective mate as she alternates between digging and resting. Perhaps he's one of the more dominant males in the vicinity. If so, he may be able to court multiple females during his time on the spawning grounds.

The male frequently approaches her flanks, ever hopeful she's ready to spawn, until a rival of near-equal size swims into his line of sight. He moves to meet the intruder and positions himself parallel with the other male. The newcomer is not initially intimidated, and they engage in a battle of postures. Jaws raised, both males swim slowly upstream, side by side and eye to eye. The exact cues that determine dominance remain a mystery to me. From my vantage, I cannot see why the contest is resolved, but the posturing soon pays off for the defending male. The intruder breaks away and continues upstream in search of another opportunity.

Back at the female's side, the male gives a slight quiver, a sign that might encourage the female to continue preparing her nest and release her eggs. She's not quite ready though. Her nest needs more preparation and she begins digging again. This is where I leave them as I depart for the day, courting and competing in the fight of their lives.

At a time unbeknownst to me but right for the salmon, when the female has determined her nest is sufficiently prepared, she lowers her tail into the redd. The male quivers again and she releases a stream of eggs. The male sends a cloud of milt into the water. Within a few seconds, the spawning event is over. The eggs settle to the bottom of the nest and the female gently buries them by fanning the gravel with her tail. If she has any remaining eggs, she'll dig another nest directly upstream of the first. If not, she'll stay at her redd as long as her energy allows, protecting it from all females that contemplate choosing it for themselves.

At the end of summer, successful salmon are battered remnants of their former selves. White fungus frosts patches of skin. Formerly bold crimson flanks fade to dull pink. The tail fins of females are especially ragged. Digging has worn them threadbare until they are little more than cartilaginous rays and a modicum of connective tissue. Internally, their muscle and fat stores are exhausted. Infection is rampant.

The effort, sacrifice, and ultimate success of salmon becomes even more incredible when we consider that spawning salmon are starved salmon. Once they enter fresh water, salmon cease feeding, meaning that every ounce of energy necessary to sustain weeks and even months of effort must already be contained in their bodies.

Bristol Bay's sockeye travel nowhere near as far as salmon that spawn in the headwaters of the Columbia, Fraser, or Yukon rivers (some of the latter swim over 2,000 miles upstream to reach their spawning site), yet like those other stocks they will exhaust nearly all their energy reserves by the time they spawn. To reach Pick Creek, a headwater stream of the Wood River, sockeye salmon swim about 61 miles and gain 72 feet of elevation, about the same distance and elevation that sockeye travel to reach Lake Brooks from the outlet of Naknek River. By analyzing the body tissues of salmon that traveled to Pick Creek, Andrew Hendry and Ole Berg found the sockeye had almost completely exhausted their fat reserves by the time they finished spawning. At the beginning of their upstream migration, having just entered fresh water, Pick Creek sockeye contained about 6.7 percent fat (excluding eggs) and 21 percent protein. Per gram of flesh, they contained 1.6 calories. At death, though, the fish had almost no body fat (0.1 percent), little protein (4.4 percent), and few calories (0.7 per gram). When accounting for the loss of body mass and the energy invested in the eggs before entering fresh water, Hendry and Berg calculated that the total energy cost of reproduction between freshwater entry and death was 74 percent of a female's initial energy stores. At the end, she has nothing left to give.

On a late summer day, with glossy-furred bears cruising the lower river, chaperoned by gulls looking to scavenge leftovers, I see a tattered female salmon drifting downstream. Her skin is mangled and worn by the battle she just fought and won. The end seems tragic for such a formerly powerful fish, one that possessed endurance beyond human capacity and overcame tremendous odds. From her perspective, though, she is triumphant. Her journey ends in death but guarantees life for the next generation.

CHAPTER 12

KEYSTONE

On a September morning, Holly approaches the river mouth after a long night's sleep. She's been a seminal part of my Brooks River experiences. Holly introduced me to the patience of a mother bear while she successfully raised an injured yearling in 2007. She showed a great adaptability and maternal devotion when she adopted a lone yearling in 2014. Yet during years when she's not raising cubs, it's her body shape that catches the most attention.

There are little bears and large bears, skinny bears and chubby bears. But few get as fat as Holly. Standing at the edge of the water, she seems to have no neck, just a head and stubby legs projecting from a keg-shaped body. When she enters the water, she floats effortlessly, buoyed by a life jacket of ample body fat.

In the river mouth, Holly doesn't need long to find a meal. Her head dips forward and her front paws reach for a lifeless salmon lying on the submerged gravel. It's another couple thousand calories to add to her glorious shape. With her grizzled blond fur, she's become a toasted marshmallow of a bear.

Her figure was the result of focused effort and good fortune. She'll fish at the falls as well as tolerate the presence of people at the river mouth, which allows her to venture into habitat that some bears won't exploit. Years of ample salmon runs have coincided with her adult life. Recent Bristol Bay salmon runs have been exceptional. More than 4 million salmon escaped into Naknek River in 2020, the largest escapement ever recorded for the river. Bristol Bay's 2019 run, with a return of more than 56 million fish, was the fourth largest since record keeping began in 1893. In the Naknek-Kvichak fishing district alone, 17 million salmon returned. Almost 3 million of those escaped up Naknek River, and as many as 600,000 salmon may have swum through Brooks River.* An unknown number, but at least several hundred to several thousand more, spawned downstream of the falls. All this came on the heels of 2018's astronomical run when 62 million salmon returned to Bristol Bay—the largest run on record.

The abundance of Holly and the other bears at the river is a direct product of the salmon that fought so hard to get here; fish that are now so near death or have already succumbed. Their story is far from over though. Salmon collectively transport billions of calories into Katmai each summer, feeding bears and dozens of other vertebrate species. Their decomposing bodies are devoured by countless insects and microbes. Their nutrients fertilize lakes, rivers, and forests. They sustain a multibillion-dollar fishing industry and tourism economy. Salmon live a never-ending story that sustains the survival of Katmai's ecosystem as we know it.

Brown bears on the Alaska Peninsula are some of the largest in the world, rivaled in size only by their close cousins on the Kodiak Archipelago. Adult males average 700 to 900 pounds in midsummer, weeks before they reach their maximum mass for the year. The size difference between these bears and those living as part of inland populations probably has some genetic component, but Alaska's bear populations, excluding Kodiak, do not experience absolute barriers to gene flow. Bears can only grow as large and fat as Holly when they have a lot to eat.

---

* The US Fish and Wildlife Service maintained a weir at the head of Brooks River from the 1940s to the early 1960s. Counts of salmon passing through the weir averaged about 20 percent of the overall Naknek escapement. This is the number I use to estimate the number of salmon entering Brooks River each year.

Isotope and mercury content analysis of hair from Kodiak bears revealed adult males eat more than 6,000 pounds of salmon, on average, per year; and 76 percent of the adult males derive almost two-thirds of their nourishment from salmon. Consuming such an extraordinary amount of fish cannot be done quickly. Katmai and Kodiak bears attain such great size and live at some of the species' highest densities not because they have access to salmon, but because salmon are ubiquitous across the landscape *and* are available for a great portion of summer and fall.

Consumers, whether deer seeking the most nutritious and tender leaves or bears on the hunt for salmon, move across landscapes to take advantage of optimal feeding opportunities. In the Wood River system, Daniel Schindler and colleagues from the University of Washington found that bears surf waves of incoming salmon. They move from stream to stream as the run pulses across a watershed. Schindler found bears concentrated their fishing efforts on cold lake tributaries in midsummer where salmon spawn earliest. Bears then shifted their efforts to lake beaches and large rivers where sockeye spawn later in the summer.

A similar dynamic occurs in the vicinity of Brooks River. By the end of July, as the sockeye's migration period ends but before Brooks River is cold enough to support spawning, bears disperse to concentrate their fishing efforts in the spring-fed tributaries of Lake Brooks and Naknek Lake where salmon spawn earliest. By late August at Brooks River, under waning daylight and colder air, salmon that had been staging at the inlet and outlet swim into the river to find and secure their spawning site. Dozens of bears follow, returning to the place where they feasted in early summer.

Bears may be the most conspicuous of salmon benefactors, yet dozens of other species rely on the energy that salmon bring to the landscape. Along coastal southeast Alaska, mink delay the timing of their breeding cycle so that they give birth and lactate when salmon carcasses become available. Salmon compose more than one-quarter of the summer diet of wolves in Katmai and adjacent Becharof National Wildlife Refuge. North of Katmai, in Lake Clark National Park and Preserve, salmon composed 89 percent of the summer diet of one individual wolf.

Bird species that feed on salmon extend from the obvious to the unexpected. Gulls, ravens, magpies, and bald eagles swarm over spawning streams to scavenge dead and dying fish. Mergansers feed extensively on salmon fry and smolt, and salmon can be their main source of food in some areas. Along parts of coastal British Columbia, calories from juvenile salmon provide young merganser broods with about 80 percent of their body mass at 10 days of age and 40 percent at 40 days. American dippers take salmon eggs just as eagerly as they swallow mayfly larvae. I once watched a mallard dabble flesh from a floating salmon carcass like she was rummaging through mud at the bottom of a pond. On a mid-July evening at the falls, I witnessed a white-crowned sparrow load its bill with flecks of salmon flesh to feed its chicks in a nest hidden within a tuft of grass.

Fish eagerly seek the energy provided by salmon flesh and eggs. Coastrange and slimy sculpin, tiny bottom-dwelling fishes that grow to no more than six inches long, gorge on salmon eggs. A large sculpin can consume over 50 eggs in a single meal. Larger predatory fish such as arctic char, Dolly Varden trout, and rainbow trout have a strong affinity for salmon eggs as well. During salmon-spawning season, their digestive tracts can be so packed with salmon eggs that their stomachs become visibly distended. The flux of salmon energy can provide most of the entire annual food budget for some populations of Dolly Varden. By consuming salmon eggs, flesh, and maggots that had scavenged dead salmon, Dolly Varden in the Iliamna River receive about 80 percent of their nutrients from salmon. At the Chignik basin on the central Alaska Peninsula, the extreme amount of energy provided by salmon eggs and flesh allows older and larger Dolly Varden to switch from an anadromous lifestyle to a completely freshwater residency.

The scale of the calories provided by salmon cannot be replaced by any other food source. Yet, calories are far from the only pathway through which salmon enrich ecosystems. When death overtakes a salmon, the fish journeys through a cycle larger than itself.

Katmai's freshwater habitats are low productivity environments. The growing season is short; lakes and streams are cold and nutrient limited. Little organic matter and free nutrients cycle through the system, and much of it inevitably flows downstream to the sea or sinks to the bottom of lakes. Sockeye smolts typically grow slowly in these environments and weigh less than an ounce after eating a modest diet of insects and near-microscopic plankton for one or two years.

In the sea, however, sockeye grow exponentially. Adults weigh 4 to 8 pounds, sometimes more, when they return to fresh water, representing a mass gain of more than 99 percent over their smolting size. When salmon return from the sea their bodies are conveyors of marine-derived nutrients. They become sacks of fertilizer for otherwise nutrient-starved freshwater and terrestrial ecosystems.

Understanding the flow of salmon nutrients through an ecosystem is no simple task, but since the tissues and bones of salmon are nearly all of marine origin, they carry a marine signature. Freshwater and terrestrial organisms that feed directly or indirectly on salmon incorporate this signature into their tissues.

Isotopes of nitrogen and carbon atoms are especially useful to trace salmon nutrients. Isotopes differ in atomic mass but not in chemical properties, so they can serve the same functions in an organism. On the periodic table, nitrogen has a molecular weight of 14 (or ^{14}N in shorthand), but some nitrogen atoms have an extra neutron, which increases the molecular weight to 15 (^{15}N). Likewise, carbon's molecular weight is 12 but it has heavier isotopes such as ^{13}C and ^{14}C. For both carbon and nitrogen, the proportion of heavier isotopes is greater in the ocean than on land or in fresh water. By looking for elevated levels of ^{15}N and ^{13}C (^{14}C is radioactive and decays at a steady rate so it is not useful in this regard), scientists can estimate the proportions of nitrogen and carbon coming from salmon and trace its pathways through freshwater and terrestrial ecosystems.

The extent of ocean-derived nutrients is widespread where salmon migrate and spawn. At a pink salmon spawning stream in southeast Alaska, macroinvertebrate densities were 8 to 25 times higher, and the amount of microbes covering submerged rocks was 15 times greater, than in parts of the creek where salmon could not reach. In western Washington's Snoqualmie River drainage, about 17 percent of the nitrogen in mayfly larva and more than 30 percent in juvenile coho salmon are of marine origin. When salmon carcasses were experimentally added to two small streams in southwestern Washington, overall densities of juvenile coho and steelhead increased, and the proportion of marine-derived nitrogen in their muscle grew by as much as 39 percent. The young fish not only ate insects enriched with salmon nutrients but also fed directly on the flesh of salmon carcasses.

Many studies have also documented increased plant growth in riparian areas where salmon spawn, but studies on the effects of salmon nutrients on vegetation are often confounded by soil characteristics and other factors that influence plant growth. To test the extent to which nutrients from salmon carcasses enhance tree growth, researchers collected and tossed dead salmon onto the north bank of Hansen Creek while leaving the creek's south side untreated. Over the course of 20 years, the researchers distributed more than 217,000 salmon—over 600,000 pounds of fish—doubling the carcass density on the north bank.

Prior to beginning the experiment, tree ring analysis indicated that trees on the south (and subsequently the experimentally depleted) bank grew faster than those on the north side, likely because south-facing slopes in boreal environments typically have warmer soils and longer growing seasons. After 20 years of carcass enrichment, spruce on the north bank experienced a growth spurt and grew nearly as fast as those on the south. Spruce needles on the north bank also contained significantly higher amounts of ^{15}N than on the south side. The south bank trees, however, continued to grow at about the same rate as before the experiment began. Perhaps the south bank trees were able to tap a reservoir of marine-derived nutrients in the soil, or maybe other factors influenced the consistency of their growth. Still, the results of this and other studies have left no doubt that salmon are good for plants.

Where scientists aren't available to throw dead salmon into the forest (that is, everywhere but Hansen Creek), bears play an especially important role in the distribution of salmon nutrients. The carcasses they carry out of the water are often partly consumed. The bears' leftovers facilitate access for scavengers, insects, and terrestrial decomposers. Bear scat and urine also function as nutrient vectors and provide plants and microbes with a ready source of food.

This dynamic is alive and well throughout coastal Alaska and much of British Columbia. Unfortunately, it has been broken in most of the western United States where brown bears have been extirpated from nearly all of their former range. Between 1880 and 1931, salmon contributed 33 to 90 percent of the metabolized carbon and nitrogen in the bones of bears living in the Columbia drainage. The tangential effects of their salmon-hunting exploits were likely widespread as well. Wherever the two species existed together, bears distributed the wealth of salmon beyond the immediacy of the riverbank.

Bristol Bay is one of the last places in North America where salmon runs equal or exceed those of the late 1800s or before, and where high concentrations of bears remain to reap the benefits. With salmon runs in the contiguous 48 states cleaved to a fraction of their historic highs, humans are the cause of and witness to the impoverishment of entire ecosystems.

On the north Atlantic coast, in what would become the United States, anadromous fish such as salmon, alewives, and shad were once a staple food of indigenous nations and early European colonists. Atlantic salmon occupied hundreds of rivers and streams from the Hudson to the Saint Croix until they fell victim to impassable dams, land-use changes, water pollution, and over-harvesting. The commercial US Atlantic salmon fisheries closed in 1948, and by the early 1980s, US wild Atlantic salmon could be found only in Maine. The 2,400 salmon that returned to Maine's Penobscot River in 1992 represented more than 70 percent of the returns along the entire East Coast of the United States that year. Despite some dam removal projects and other efforts to restore the population, annual returns in the United States are generally less than 1,000 individuals.

A similar tale played out on the West Coast of the United States. When Meriwether Lewis and William Clark explored the lower Columbia River, they found the riverbanks lined with people—and a regional subsistence and trade economy based on the river's salmon. In less than 150 years, it was gone. By 1999, wild salmon had disappeared from about 40 percent of their historic range in Oregon, Washington, Idaho, and California. About 30 salmon and steelhead populations on the West Coast are currently listed as federally threatened and endangered. Some of the others, such as Washington State's Baker River sockeye, remain wholly dependent on human intervention for their survival. Dams now completely block Baker River, so the fish must be captured and trucked around the dams to reach their spawning areas.

The dearth of salmon is more than an aesthetic or economic loss. It starves ecosystems of energy and nutrients. During the late 1990s, the biomass of returning salmon on the West Coast represented less than 10 percent of the historic highs in the 1890s and early 1900s. These numbers indicate that just 6 to 7 percent of the marine-derived nitrogen and phosphorous once delivered is now reaching the rivers of the Pacific Northwest.

When viewed in the context of modern salmon runs in the rest of the United States, the continued and consistent abundance of Bristol Bay's salmon seems even more remarkable. Mining companies have long ogled another resource in the Bristol Bay area though. We are now closer than ever before in Bristol Bay to setting in motion the same set of circumstances that killed salmon runs almost everywhere else.

The windswept tundra north of Iliamna Lake is an unlikely place to fight about. No roads penetrate the area. A few streams, headwaters really, begin their journey seaward. Bogs and kettle ponds speckle the low-lying areas. There's no park or permanently protected land, and it fails to garner the same scenic appreciation as the jagged peaks of the Lake Clark region to the east and Alaska's largest lake to the south. But at the apex of an inconspicuous divide between Nushagak River and waters flowing to Iliamna Lake is the site of Alaska's most contentious land-use battle in a half-century, one that will define the future of Bristol Bay and its salmon.

Pebble Mine is a proposed open-pit copper and gold mine that, if developed, would become one of the largest surface mines in the world. According to the US Army Corps of Engineers, the mine would remove 1.4 billion tons of material, and irreparably alter more than 13 square miles of currently undeveloped tundra and wetlands, including the permanent removal of 99 miles of streams. The open pit would gouge almost 2,000 feet into the earth and stretch over a mile-and-a-half wide—a hole so deep that the Washington Monument could be stacked on top of the Empire State Building and not reach the original land surface. Several earthen dams, including one more than 500 feet tall, would be built to hold waste rock and other tailings. Ore would be partially processed on-site, then loaded onto trucks and transported either by road or a combination of road and ice-breaking ferry to a newly constructed shipping terminal on Cook Inlet. A natural gas pipeline, laid on the floor of Cook Inlet then 60 to 80 miles overland, would supply fuel to power the mine site. Except for one variant in the Corps' final environmental impact statement for the proposed mine that would utilize 7 miles of existing road at the east end of Iliamna Lake, not a single piece of this infrastructure exists and nearly all of it would be located within two of Bristol Bay's most productive salmon-producing watersheds.

Open-pit mining causes permanent changes to soils, vegetation, surface water flows, and groundwater. It creates significant amounts of waste because most of the rock doesn't contain commercially valuable ore. Leftover tailings from ore processing are often toxic and remain so for decades or centuries. It's one of the most destructive and long-lasting land uses that humans have ever invented.

Pebble Limited Partnership, a subsidiary corporation of Northern Dynasty Minerals, a Canadian mining firm, says the mine can be built and operated without substantially altering salmon habitat. As a company fact sheet spins their point of view, "The area around Pebble constitutes less than 1% of the [Bristol Bay] watershed," and that "every drop of water will be carefully managed." The draft environmental impact statement for the mine from the US Army Corp of Engineers uses similar language. Regarding one salmon-bearing stream that will be destroyed, the Corp states, "In the context of the entire Bristol Bay drainage, with its 9,816 miles of currently documented anadromous waters, the loss of Tributary 1.19 represents an 0.08 percent reduction of documented anadromous stream habitat."

These statements downplay the importance of small streams in protecting a watershed's integrity and ignore the mine's long-term consequences. The loss of a single small tributary is not as insignificant as it may seem.

The otolith is a small oval bone housed in the inner ear of vertebrates. In salmon, otoliths grow proportionally with the length of the fish and produce growth rings akin to those in a tree trunk. When looking at a salmon's otolith, a skilled examiner can determine the fish's age and calculate its size at certain ages. Isotope analysis of otoliths takes this process a step further.

The Nushagak River watershed on the north side of Bristol Bay contains four distinct regions that differ in their bedrock geology and surface features, creating variations in the ratio of two strontium isotopes (^{87}Sr and ^{86}Sr). By analyzing that ratio in the otoliths from about 1,400 salmon returning to the drainage, Sean Brennan from the University of Washington and colleagues were able to determine which parts of drainage the fishes used as juveniles and which parts of the watershed contributed most to the overall productivity of the salmon population.

For Chinook and sockeye salmon, patches of high and low productivity shifted within the watershed across several years. Areas of high Chinook production in 2011 transitioned from the upper Nushagak River to the upper Multchatna River by 2014 and 2015. Sockeye experienced a similar shift. Greater production and growth of sockeye fry was concentrated in the Tikchik Lakes region in 2014. It then dispersed more evenly across the watershed in 2015, including atypical sockeye rearing habitats like the main stem of large rivers.

Since conditions for juvenile salmon growth within a river basin, or even a subsection of a river basin, are not consistent from year to year, then salmon runs and therefore fisheries and the ecosystem benefit from favorable conditions persisting somewhere in the basin. If the upper Mulchatna area, where much of the Pebble Mine footprint would be located, was unavailable as Chinook rearing habitat in 2014 and 2015, then significantly fewer juvenile Chinook may have survived long enough to run to sea. Similarly, just because spawning habitat for sockeye remains intact, it doesn't mean the population can be sustained if it doesn't have access to the right rearing habitats, whether that is a lake, river, or estuary. If we cut off or destroy one part of a watershed, the consequences may be proportionally greater than the mere loss of a few miles of flowing water. The entire landscape is involved in stabilizing biological production.

As proposed in 2019, and described in the mine's final environmental impact statement by the US Army Corps of Engineers, Pebble Mine would have a life span of at least two decades, after which plastic membranes and waste rock would be placed over some tailings while other tailings would be dumped into the open pit. An artificial lake would form in the crater as groundwater pours through the surrounding bedrock. The lake's surface would then need to be maintained below the surrounding water table *indefi-*

nitely to prevent groundwater contamination. We will *never* be able to walk away from it.

The most recent mine plan also taps a small portion of the estimated ore body. If the mine is established and the supporting infrastructure built, then the proposed mine would become a beachhead for a much larger and long-lasting mine as well as an extensive mining district encompassing the headwaters of the world's last great salmon run. Even the US Army Corp of Engineers acknowledges this as a "reasonably foreseeable" outcome.

On August 24, 2020, the Corps issued a press release stating that Pebble Mine "as currently proposed, cannot be permitted under section 404 of the Clean Water Act." The Corps required Pebble Limited Partnership to provide a new mitigation plan to offset the mine's impacts on streams and wetlands before it can receive a federal permit. In a letter to Pebble Limited Partnership, the Corps stated: "discharges at the mine site would cause unavoidable adverse impacts to aquatic resources and . . . those adverse impacts would result in significant degradation to those aquatic resources."

In early November 2020, Pebble Limited Partnership submitted a new mitigation plan. However, it failed to satisfy the Corps. On November 25, the Corps issued its record of decision on the proposed mine and denied a permit for it. The Corps wrote that the mitigation plan was noncompliant with Clean Water Act guidelines and insufficient in scope to overcome the damage the mine would do to the landscape, and that the mine was "contrary to the public interest."

While campaigning for the US presidency, Joe Biden stated that he opposed the mine. His election, along with the Corps' decision during the final weeks of Donald Trump's anti-conservation administration, serves as a death knell for this iteration of Pebble Mine. However, the ore remains on lands owned by the State of Alaska that are open to mining. Mine executives and investors will continue to ogle it. Even as the current Pebble Mine proposal is killed, a new version may rear its ugly head in the future. We came closer than ever before to sacrificing the last great salmon run, along with the regional economy and ecology that depend on it. Congress and the State of Alaska should work together to permanently protect all of Bristol Bay's headwaters from any development that is incompatible with the protection of salmon.

As salmon biologist Ray Hilborn noted in 2003, the stability of Bristol

Bay sockeye has been greatly influenced by different populations performing well at different times. "No one associated with the fishery in the 1950s and 1960s could have imagined that Egegik would produce over 20 million fish in one year, nor could they imagine that the Nushagak would produce more than the Kvichak.... It appears that the resilience of Bristol Bay sockeye is due in large part to the maintenance of all of the diverse life history strategies and geographic locations that comprise the stock....

"Defining the entire stock as healthy simply because a large component is doing well might lead to decline and extinction if the conditions that fostered the success of the healthy component disappear and the alternate strategy, which would have done well in the new environmental conditions, has been lost."

When Pebble Mine proponents argued that the mine would have had no population level impacts on salmon, they were guilty of the same fallacy committed thousands of times in the Pacific Northwest and New England—thinking their development would not matter to the whole. This is precisely how salmon runs disappear. We lose salmon not all at once, but with one impassible culvert, one dam, one patch of clear-cut forest, and one mine at a time.

The health and diversity of Bristol Bay's salmon run operates across a continuum of scales, from the microhabitats on the lee side of a submerged log to the vastness of Becharof, Iliamna, and Naknek lakes. Resiliency is built into these systems. For the Naknek watershed, resiliency is the countless yard-wide streams and the wild, unengineered rivers. It is the series of pristine lakes that support multiple populations of juvenile salmon and shelter incoming adults. It is clean and uncontaminated spawning beds of the upper Brooks River and the stretches of submerged beaches where a subset of fish find sufficient upwelling groundwater suitable for their own spawning events. It is the seemingly insignificant wetlands and the 0.08 percent of streams where salmon spawn and rear. Resiliency is the whole.

At the peak of the salmon run—when processing plants and salmon boats thrum with activity on the shores of Bristol Bay, when the water at Brooks Falls boils with salmon, when bears and gulls lounge with stomachs and gullets distended with fish—we witness an ecosystem whose potential is fully realized.

CHAPTER 13

DEATH

By late October, with the transition to winter well underway, the riverscape has appropriated an earth-toned palette. Birch and poplar trees stand bare, revealing their respective reddish and gray-colored twigs. Fallen deciduous leaves rest half frozen to the ground. Browned grass sags earthward, trampled by bears and matted by cold rain. A cap of fresh snow lines the mountaintops and tendrils of ice rim the nearby ponds. The sky is dark more often than light, making the scant hours between sunrise and sunset even more valuable for the few bears that have remained to scavenge the last of the year's salmon.

It was under this scene, not the optimism of spring, but the melancholy feeling of a near-winter day, that I witnessed one of the most poignant events of my career.

Late in the afternoon on October 21, 2015, while searching for content to post on Katmai National Park's social media pages, I found one of the park's webcams fixed on a mother bear and her two 9-month-old cubs. The family was resting in a pile near the river mouth. Problem solved, I thought. Everyone enjoys watching cubs. Without devoting much brainpower to it, I invited the park's online audience to watch. Moments later, regretting my haste, I understood this was no ordinary mother and cub scene. We had begun to watch a cub die a slow death.

During the two summers prior, 451 patrolled the river corridor rather unnoticed by the public. She didn't have any cubs or compete for space at the falls, so she rather easily blended into the background until she injured her right rear leg. The injury healed but her limp never went away, so when she returned in 2015 with three young cubs, she became immediately recognizable.

Despite her injury, 451 provided well for her offspring. They grew rapidly under her care, transitioning from small and timid animals at the beginning of summer to roly-poly fur balls, well provisioned with fat by the fall equinox. Sometime in early October, however, one of 451's cubs disappeared. Although its fate remains unknown, the event that took another cub makes me wonder about the fate of the first.

Not long before I tuned in to the webcam on October 21, a contingent of bearcam viewers watched one of 451's cubs struggling to keep pace with its mother and sibling. The family plodded on the dirt road that skirts the south bank of the river mouth. Reviewing the footage, I see one cub sit then lay on the road, her family a dozen yards ahead. The cub looks almost playful, her head torqued slightly to the side. She's pudgy enough for the season and her lumber-colored fur is dry and healthy looking. If this were all I saw, I would not discern anything out of the ordinary.

As soon as she stood, though, the cub began to struggle. She stumbled drunkenly to the side of the road. Regaining her composure momentarily, the cub walked wobbly footed to her mother and sibling before collapsing next to them. While she'll shift her position one more time in the next several hours, she will not stand again. Two days later, she stops breathing and dies with her mother and sibling at her side.

Even though thousands of bears live within the Katmai region, it's quite uncommon to find a dead bear or witness one die. Consequently, there is very little information on the specific causes of their mortality.

Biologists documented the natural deaths of 19 independent bears on Katmai's coast between 1989 and 1996. The cause of death was determined in about half of the cases, and nearly all of those suffered traumatic deaths. An avalanche killed one female, but nine others (including seven adult females, one adult male, and one subadult) were killed by other bears. The only nontraumatic death that was determined with certainty was caused by starvation due to muzzle and tongue injuries.

During the last 30 years at Brooks River, we know of about 25 bear deaths. When excluding cubs, though, park staff have recorded the death of only about eight independent bears. The cause of death could not be determined for three of those, while two likely died from an illness or disease. Trauma took the others.

For Katmai's younger bears, one of the biggest risks in their daily lives are larger bears. An incident in the late 1990s illustrates why young and small bears are so keen to avoid adult males, even if the overall probability of death by bear is low.

On a sunny July afternoon, rangers and a platform full of visitors witnessed BB attack and kill a subadult in the riffles downstream of Brooks Falls. Video of the attack is difficult to watch. It might be almost unwatchable if it had not been recorded on a low-resolution camera, as its heavy pixilation spares the viewer some of the goriest details. BB easily overpowers his subadult victim. He treats the other bear like he would a salmon and begins to feed on it before the subadult was dead. Images from the video remain firmly engrained in my memory, and I conjure them periodically to remind myself to give bears the respect they deserve.

Nontraumatic deaths are witnessed even less frequently. In October 2008, a large and battle-scarred adult male known as One-toe began to hemorrhage blood from his mouth as he walked through the lower river. He lowered his face into the water and never picked it up. The current wedged his body against the old floating bridge until park maintenance staff pried it free, allowing it to drift into the lake and disappear.

In July 2016, one of the river's largest and most dominant bears, Lurch, disappeared from the river. His absence wasn't uncommon or surprising; bears leave the river all the time, even during the peak of the salmon run. That August though, park staff discovered Lurch's well-decomposed body in a meadow not far from the falls. Little remained of the body except bones and fur. Lurch was identified by comparing photographs of his incisors and canine teeth with the pattern of those of the dead bear. The cause of death could not be determined.

Lurch was in his mid- to late teens when he disappeared, aged but not elderly for a bear, and he ranked among the river's most dominant animals. He was a frequent pirate and brawler that, like 856, used his size to intimidate other bears into yielding fish or space. During his last year of life, Lurch's most conspicuous feature was his lack of symmetry. He lost his left ear during a fight. The injury scarred over quickly but would forever remain a reminder of the physical conflict bears experience.

Whether it leads to immediate death, long-term disability, or temporary discomfort and pain, injury is a common part of a bear's existence. Wild bears suffer and persevere through more trauma than we realize, as revealed by the skeleton of a 20-year-old brown bear from Spain's Cantabrian Mountains.

From head to toe, this bear had experienced significant injury and illness. His teeth were a repository of dental issues. He had two missing teeth, broken canines, deep cavities, and other significant tooth decay. Fistulae connected the upper mouth and nasal cavity, and the enamel of all his molars were worn to expose the pulp underneath. He had suffered broken ribs and a broken right scapula. The bones of his paws had lesions consistent with infections. His seventh, eighth, and ninth vertebrae were fused, probably due to a systemic infection. He fractured his left fibula, right fibula, and right tibia. His right arm suffered a catastrophic injury in which the bones of the forearm, the radius and ulna, fractured or were somehow crushed. None of the fractures were fresh—they had all healed to the extent they could—but by the end of this bear's life his left arm was the only healthy limb he had. Finally, and this made me wince just reading about it, he broke his baculum. The scientists who examined the skeleton report: "This is a relatively frequent lesion produced in the heat of mating, and is of no consequence for bears." I wonder if the bear would agree.

Tundra, a young adult female that died in 2014, proves that very young bears also have the fortitude to survive through significant injury. As a yearling, Tundra sustained a bloody wound above her left eye that healed to leave a conspicuous scar. After separating from her mother, Tundra made

Otis practices his craft in the far pool of Brooks Falls. First identified in 2001, Otis has fished at Brooks River every year of his adult life. *Photo taken July 9, 2019.*

Grazer, one of Brooks River's most skilled anglers and defensive mothers, waits patiently for a salmon to leap within easy reach of her jaws. *Photo taken July 1, 2019.*

An experienced mother, 402 lounges with yearling cubs from her seventh known litter. Mother bears endure special challenges in order to raise their cubs. *Photo taken June 30, 2019. Photo © Jeanne Roy.*

Even old bears can learn new tricks: Lefty learned to fish the lip of the falls within days of arriving in July 2015. It remains his most preferred fishing spot and he rarely fishes other locations at Brooks Falls. *Photo taken July 6, 2019.*

After asserting his dominance, 856 turns his back and walks away from a rival male. Dominant bears like 856 have greater access to productive fishing spots at Brooks Falls and may secure more mating opportunities. *Photo taken July 1, 2019. Photo © Jeanne Roy.*

The subadult bear 910 tries an unconventional fishing technique. While bears have the instincts to catch salmon, fishing is a learned behavior. *Photo taken July 5, 2019.*

The view from the lip of Brooks Falls on a bear-free day. During years with a large sockeye salmon run, bears might fish at Brooks Falls every day between late June and mid-October. *Photo taken June 8, 2018.*

A subadult brown bear causes a bear jam at the south entrance of the old floating bridge. Bear jams caused so much ire among some commercial guides, park employees, and concession staff that the National Park Service replaced the bridge with a permanent elevated bridge in 2019. *Photo taken September 9, 2011.*

Brooks River begins at Lake Brooks (right) and flows for 1.5 miles
to Naknek Lake. It is one of the most historically and ecologically significant
areas of Katmai National Park. Brooks Falls is located about halfway
between the lakes. *Photo taken September 30, 2015.*

A National Park Service bear technician stands his ground and prepares to
dissuade a young brown bear from approaching Brooks Lodge. Rangers patrol
Brooks Camp in an attempt to prevent bears from utilizing the lodge and visitor
center area. *Photo taken September 14, 2018. National Park Service photo.*

Dozens of brown bears gather to fish at Brooks Falls during the peak of the early summer salmon migration. More than 100 bears have been identified using the river in a single year. *Photo taken July 7, 2009.*

At the peak of their early summer migration, thousands of sockeye salmon can fill the water immediately downstream of Brooks Falls. The Bristol Bay sockeye run is the last great salmon run on Earth. *Photo taken July 1, 2019.*

National Park Service wildlife biologists Sherri Anderson (left) and
Grant Hilderbrand (right) work to remove an illegally set wire snare from Divot.
While Katmai is one of the largest national parks in the United States, many of its
bears wander outside of the park boundaries where they may come into contact with
human-caused hazards. *Photo taken July 30, 2014. National Park Service photo.*

Park visitors enjoy the scene at Brooks Falls. Brooks River is the most popular
visitor destination in Katmai National Park, and perhaps the most iconic wildlife
viewing site in US national parks. *Photo taken July 14, 2019.*

Subadult bears enjoy a bout of playful sparring. While brown bears generally lead solitary lives, younger bears are often quite social, especially in habitats with abundant food such as salmon streams. *Photo taken July 14, 2019.*

Park visitors wait near Brooks Lodge for a bear jam to clear. Infrastructure and trails at Brooks Camp funnel people and bears into the same areas and create conflicts for space. *Photo taken September 11, 2018.*

Brooks River part of her home range, and she was often one of the few bears I would see along the river in May. She seemed to navigate the pitfalls of subadulthood well, and I expected to watch her mature into an adult and raise her own litters at the river.

Tundra's life was cut short, however. At the beginning of her seventh summer, rangers found Tundra in the forest, eviscerated and partly consumed. For public safety reasons (the body lay in an area frequently used by anglers, and bears can be very defensive while guarding a carcass), bear management staff decided to move her body away from where people would be prone to wander.

That was the end of the story, or so I thought, but park law enforcement ranger Dave Woodcock had the foresight to collect her skull and clean it so that we could use it for public education and interpretation. After state wildlife authorities documented that it was not from a poached animal, Dave brought it to me in the park headquarters. I was amazed by what I saw.

Tundra's bloodied forehead was more than a flesh wound. Her skull had been fractured or crushed above her left eye. The bone behind her orbital socket was misshapen, thin, spongy, and asymmetrical. Watching her as a living bear, I had no inkling the injury was so severe. She acted and behaved normally.

Neither Tundra nor the Cantabrian bear's injuries should be considered typical of all bears. It's only a sample of two, of course. Nevertheless, their bone biographies preserve stories of difficulty, pain, perseverance, and toughness. From the little we see and document, the end of a bear's life is seldom peaceful.

In contrast to Tundra, if a bear survives to adulthood, it has a good chance of surviving to the next year. More than 90 percent of adult females and 95 percent of adult males survive from year to year, and bears fortuned with good health and sufficient food can live over 30 years in the wild, although 20 is a more typical life span. The first year, specifically the first nine months, are the most uncertain and the most dangerous time in a bear's life.

When the cub first collapsed, 451 initially laid at her side. After a few minutes, mother feels an urge to fish or at least move to another location. She walks a short distance toward the river, but her ill cub does not follow. Four-five-one pauses, not as though she is groggy or sleepy, but with the sense of mind to understand she needs to return to her cub. Sunshine peeks through the overcast clouds. It's just after 4 p.m. and the low-lying sun casts long shadows over the land. The family remains in place overnight, sleeping in the trampled grass.

The next day, the cub is unresponsive as we watch 451 try to rouse her with a nudge from her muzzle and a gentle tap with her paw. With winter nearly upon them, any calories would increase their chance of surviving the upcoming fast, but 451 cannot bring herself to leave. Maternal instinct overrules her hunger. She remains at her ill cub's side for over two days, standing infrequently and venturing little farther than the river's edge.

The cub dies on the evening of October 23, mother and surviving sibling lying at her side. That night, the family sleeps in a pile near the deceased cub's body.

Due to the high-profile, unusual nature of the death, and the lack of scientific information about the mortality of cubs outside infanticide, the National Park Service (NPS) decided to collect and necropsy the cub. The next morning, NPS biological technicians Bob Peterson, Michael Saxton, and Leslie Skora arrive at Brooks Camp. Four-five-one had by then moved a scant 50 yards up the riverbank. A raven, quick to scavenge, lands next to the cub and begins to pull tufts of hair from the body.

Remaining wary of 451 and unsure how she might react, the rangers walk cautiously. Four-five-one is certainly aware of their presence but makes no effort to approach or defend. While Bob watches the mother, Michael and Leslie quickly examine the cub's body, photograph it, and then carry it back to the boat. From King Salmon, it's sent to Susan Knowles, wildlife pathologist at the US Geological Survey's National Wildlife Health Center, for necropsy.

Brooks River was only temporarily quiet. A few hours after the rangers returned to King Salmon, webcam viewers noticed a large brown bear-like object lying on the lakeshore. A bear lying on the beach was not out of the ordinary. Over the next two days, however, it didn't move. Although the cause of the cub's death was still undetermined, the possibility of another dead bear heightened concerns about a disease outbreak.

Bob, Leslie, and Michael returned to Brooks Camp on October 28.

They found the body of 868, a medium-sized adult male, lying on his side, undisturbed by bears or other scavengers. A gross necropsy (*gross* meaning basic, not disgusting, although it contained an element of the latter) revealed 868 was in good condition other than a probable broken nose, which rangers speculated may have been caused if he collapsed on his face. He had about 2 inches of subcutaneous fat on his stomach. Weighing an estimated 900 pounds, 868 was much too big to put in a box and ship away like the deceased spring cub, so only a few of his vital organs were removed. Unfortunately, natural decay of the organs limited analysis by the time they reached the lab of Alaska's state wildlife veterinarian, and so the cause of his death could not be conclusively determined.

In Wisconsin, Susan Knowles began to necropsy the dead cub. She found no sign of physical injury and few parasites. The cub tested negative for rabies and canine distemper but positive for infectious canine hepatitis, a worldwide contagious viral disease of canines, bears, and some felines.

Infectious canine hepatitis is caused by canine adenovirus (CAV-1). The virus spreads through ingestion of bodily fluids, and infected individuals can shed CAV-1 in their urine for about 6 months. It incubates in the upper respiratory tract then moves to infect the liver, kidneys, and bloodstream. Infected domestic dogs can experience anorexia, lethargy, vomiting, fever, diarrhea, seizures, paralysis, and death in severe cases.

Since bears hibernate for much of the year, a de facto quarantine and stay-at-home order, CAV-1 persists in Katmai through wolves, coyotes, foxes, and possibly lynx. With bears so curious about anything strong smelling, and willing to scavenge animal carcasses, a summertime outbreak could spread quickly through the population.

CAV-1 appears to be widespread on the Alaska Peninsula and Kodiak Archipelago and has been so for at least 40 years. Its prevalence among bears has increased in recent decades though. During the 1970s and 1980s, 9 to 16 percent of bears on the Alaska Peninsula harbored antibodies for the virus. Blood samples collected from bears between 2013 and 2016 revealed 26 percent of Katmai's bears had antibodies for it. Contact with the virus has grown even more substantially among Kodiak bears where antibody prevalence increased from 29 percent during the 1970s and 1980s to 93 percent during the mid-2010s.

Those with antibodies are survivors of the virus, and cubs could potentially become immunized against it if the antibodies are present in mother's
milk. Four-five-one may not have contracted the virus previously though,
or if she did her immunity for CAV-1 didn't transfer to her milk. Bear cubs
may also be particularly susceptible to canine adenovirus. Researchers did
not detect antibodies for the virus in bears under 2 years old in the Katmai
and Kodiak studies, raising the possibility that CAV-1 infections are highly
lethal for young bears. If so, perhaps outbreaks of the disease are a significant negative influence on cub survival rates in Katmai. Four-five-one's
cub was the first documented case of it at Brooks River though. If CAV-1's
lethality for bear cubs is truly high, I suspect we would have observed far
more cubs suffering from the disease. We need more information to draw
any strong conclusions.

Toughness is an innate characteristic of bears, even spring cubs. When
451's cub first collapsed and lay ill, I had seen enough bears persevere
through egregious wounds and fractures—injuries that would leave me
hospitalized for days or weeks—that in all honesty I thought she would
recover from whatever ailed her. I expected her to sit up, shake herself off,
and get on with other business in life. If she didn't recover, I certainly did
not expect the mother to remain at her side for so long, choosing instead
to focus on the survival of her healthy cub. As 451 held steadfast, I found
myself wondering what she felt about the whole thing.

Four-five-one's behavior could be explained through the frame of evolutionary function. She remained near her cub because she was vested in its
survival. Her motivation could have been to increase her own reproductive
success and ensure her genes were carried into another generation. I'm sure
this influenced at least some of her behavior. However, staying next to the
cub after it died made no sense. From an energetics and evolutionary perspective, concentrating on the survival of her other offspring would have
been a better move. Instead, she stayed. I couldn't help but wonder if she
was grieving.

As Jeffrey Masson and Susan McCarthy posit in their book, *When Elephants Weep: The Emotional Lives of Animals*, "That feelings may be complex and multifaceted or difficult to interpret does not mean they do not

exist." Masson and McCarthy later explain, "If humans are subject to evolution but have feelings that are inexplicable in survival terms, if they are prone to emotions that do not seem to confer any advantage, why should we suppose that animals act on genetic instinct alone?"

I cannot know what 451 felt while her cub lay dying at her side, but I won't deny she felt something.

After rangers left Brooks Camp, 451 returned to the spot where her cub died. Maybe she merely expressed a maternal instinct to seek her offspring. Yet unlike most mother bears separated from a cub, 451 was in no hurry to search. She spent a long time investigating the matted grass, sometimes sitting, sometimes standing, but nose often to the ground inhaling deeply where her cub's scent now mixed with that of the rangers. After several minutes, she slowly followed the cub's scent trail to where it was placed in the boat and taken away. She stood and stared toward the water.

PART THREE

HUMANITY

CHAPTER 14

BOUNDARIES

My handheld radio crackled, "Bear on the beach passing Generator Trail headed toward the river." Rangers broadcast hundreds of similar messages throughout the summer and they usually don't garner much attention. Being the bear-watching junkie that I am though, and with a moment free from immediate duties, I stepped out of the ranger station to take a look.

Through a gap between spruce trees, with midmorning sunlight reflecting off the lake, I spotted Divot and her lanky yearling. Having recently shed her old coat, Divot sported a midsummer shag of short dark brown fur and, oddly, a collar. From its loose and frayed end, a line of unknown composition arched stiffly upward to a ring of damp fur encircling the narrowest part of her neck.

After Divot reached the river and moved upstream of the bridge to fish, several other rangers and I began to confer on what the collar might be. My first thought was fishing line. Divot had a reputation for targeting salmon hooked by human anglers. I watched her play coy more than once on the banks of the lower river, acting like she wasn't paying attention to the person casting his line, only to charge into the water and chase a freshly hooked salmon. I had even photographed her with a fishing lure firmly entrenched in the fur of her left forearm. Whatever constricted her neck, however, was too substantial for fishing line.

When Divot returned to the river mouth, Michael Saxton photographed her on the shoreline, allowing us to conclusively identify the collar. It was a worst-case scenario. A trapping snare, set to capture wolves, girdled her neck. Made of woven steel wire, the snare would not loosen or decay. The wound it caused was destined for infection and would not have the opportunity to heal. The noose would tighten each time the frayed end snagged on anything. It threatened her life.

Humanity intruded upon her personal boundaries. We would have to cross them again if we were to save her.

I had last seen Divot at the river on July 13, two weeks before she returned with the snare. Her stay was brief, lasting a little more than a day before she disappeared with her two yearlings. Her destination, we would soon find, was much farther flung than expected.

On July 24, photographer Tina Crowe captured images of a bear and a single yearling fishing along Naknek River about 5 miles upstream of King Salmon, an area well outside the park's boundaries. The sighting would likely not have been particularly noteworthy except the otherwise healthy-looking mother had a wire snare around her neck.

After news of Divot's plight spread among Katmai's webcam community, Tina shared her photo in the bearcam chat. When I saw it, I recognized Divot immediately. She sat half submerged in water, clutching the sloppy remnants of a salmon between her front paws. Cinched tight around her neck was the snare. Only one of her twin yearlings accompanied her. The other had disappeared. Between July 13, when she departed Brooks Camp, and her return on July 28, Divot walked and swam at least 60 miles round trip, almost half of it in 5 days.

Traveling 60 miles in a few days is well within a bear's capabilities, but I was surprised by the extent of Divot's excursions. The salmon migration at Brooks River was near peak when Divot left and salmon were not yet widely accessible elsewhere. She was intimately familiar with the river, its food resources, and tolerant of crowds of people. So why would she leave?

A bear's home range encompasses the area it uses to forage, mate, and raise young. Males have a tendency to occupy larger home ranges than females in order to find mates and because their larger body sizes require more food. In habitats where nutritious food is widely dispersed, and mates are few, male brown bears may need over a thousand of square miles to make a living. Bears in relatively food-rich habitats, however, needn't wander so far.

In the interior of Lake Clark National Park and Preserve, a modeling study of brown bear home ranges determined that during the main period of salmon availability from mid-July to the end of August, males utilized about 23 square miles, while single females and females with cubs used 20 and 25 square miles, respectively. These home ranges are probably comparable to central Katmai at the same time of year, which suggests the bears of Brooks River aren't typically making forays to far-flung locations.

When necessary, though, Katmai's bears are more than capable of traveling long distances over short time spans. In June 1975, a trio of yearlings damaged a number of tents in the Brooks Camp campground. On June 20, rangers sedated, ear-tagged, and relocated a 12-year-old mother known as Moma and her triplets from Brooks Camp to Kukak Bay on Katmai's coast in the hope they would establish a new home range. The coast of the park seemed like an ideal site. It was remote, rarely visited by people, and contained a wealth of food. Kukak Bay was also 60 straight-line miles from Brooks Camp and separated from the interior of the park by the rugged crest of the Aleutian Range.

It didn't work. By July 14, the family (minus one of the three yearlings) had crossed the Aleutian Range and arrived at the Windy Creek Overlook on the northern edge of the Valley of Ten Thousand Smokes. The next day, the family was seen heading toward Brooks Camp, and by July 17 they had returned to the river.

Divot wasn't forced to travel to King Salmon like Moma had during her temporary exile to Kukak. Divot left through her own volition. Maybe Divot was motivated by a real or perceived habitat characteristic along Naknek River that could benefit her survival. Maybe she had utilized that area for years, unbeknownst to rangers and biologists. Maybe she still does.

Then again, perhaps Divot experienced nothing more than a bout of wanderlust and decided to take a chance to explore new territory.

The afternoon after Divot returned with the snare, the park's management team began to search for solutions. They could let Divot be, although this was the least preferable outcome. A person had caused her pain and threatened her survival, so we at least owed her the effort to try and help. However, feasible options were few. There were no live traps designed for bears at Brooks Camp. Even if one was available, another bear would likely take the bait before Divot. That left only one possible solution; we had to find and tranquilize her. In a national park as large and remote as Katmai, helping Divot would be no easy task, and we would need a lot of luck if we were to achieve our goal.

Grant Hilderbrand, the regional wildlife biologist for the National Park Service (NPS) in Alaska, was in Anchorage and, thankfully, available to clear his immediate schedule and travel to Brooks Camp to lead the effort. Yet, traveling to Brooks Camp, even from Anchorage, would require at least two flights, and scheduling restrictions would not allow Grant to get to Brooks Camp until late in the morning on July 29. Even so, this still represented a lightning-paced reaction and mobilization by a government agency in rural Alaska. I could only hope Divot remained at the river until then.

The next morning, Leslie Skora glanced out the window of her cabin on the shore of Lake Brooks. To her surprise, Divot was walking east along the road toward the river mouth. Knowing that if Divot entered the forest we'd likely lose track of her, Leslie, still in her pajama pants, slipped on a pair of shoes and followed.

Divot and her yearling walked to the river mouth then departed north along the beach where they had appeared the day before. Michael Saxton and Leslie (having since donned proper outdoor attire) shadowed Divot's progress along the shoreline, first on foot then by boat when it became increasingly difficult to keep pace. Divot remained on the lakeshore for 2 miles until she disappeared in the forest at the outlet of a small creek draining Dumpling's east face.

No more than a couple of yards wide, "Dumpling Creek" (it has no officially recognized name) originates from springs on the mountain's upper slopes. In late July, a small number of sockeye force their way through inches-deep water at the outlet to ascend the creek's lower reaches and spawn in pools almost as shallow as the depth of their bodies. Runs such as these are short in duration, sometimes complete within a week or two, but for bears that learn when and where they occur, they can provide especially easy fishing conditions, perhaps enough to keep Divot nearby, or so I hoped.

By the time Grant arrived at camp we had amassed a team from nearly every division in the park. Maintenance staff drove the boats and assisted in periodic probing searches in the forest, as did wildlife technicians and biologists. I tagged along to search and help document our efforts. The park pilot circled the forest hoping to catch a glimpse of the bears. Our search seemed more futile with every passing moment though, and when Divot failed to reappear by late afternoon, my hopes for success began to diminish.

Just as we began to discuss returning to camp, Divot and her yearling emerged from the trees and began to walk in our direction. We waited in silence, the boat floating only a few feet from shore as the family approached to our right. At the bow, Grant readied his modified 30-gauge shotgun but Divot's pace was quicker than we expected. She reached our position and walked past before Grant could fire. She disappeared into the trees.

I tried to remain optimistic as we traveled back to camp for the night, but I felt as though we had missed our one chance. It was an extraordinary effort to help a bear that found Katmai's wilderness not large enough.

For most of Katmai's history, conservationists sought to tweak its protected area in order to make it, from their perspective, more environmentally whole. When Robert Griggs lobbied for an expanded Katmai National Monument in 1931, he cited the area's usefulness as habitat for bears, salmon, waterfowl, and fish. President Franklin Delano Roosevelt enlarged the monument in 1942 to include all islands within 5 miles of Katmai's coastline to lessen the threat of poaching. In 1969, just hours before his presidency ended, Lyndon Johnson added about 94,500 acres to Katmai for "its protection of the ecological and other scientific values," subsuming the entirety of Naknek Lake within the monument. Although these were not the first proclamations to justify the creation or expansion of a park based on environmental considerations, they were a stark departure from the philosophy that created many of the first national parks.

During an era of rapid development, a shrinking frontier, and with populace that harbored more than a little bit of an inferiority complex toward Europe, many Americans in the mid- to late-1800s began to measure the nation's greatness not with thousand-year-old cathedrals and castles but with scenic splendor. The United States, the philosophy went, could establish its exceptionalism, in part, through its natural wonders. No other nation contained geysers like Yellowstone, forests of sequoia trees, or a canyon as grand as Grand Canyon. The sentiment carried well into the 20th century (Katmai was protected in part to afford "inspiration to patriotism") and continues to reverberate through our collective consciousness. National parks rank among our most vaunted landscapes.

Political expediency and economics, however, shaped the boundaries of the first parks as much as environmental ethics, perhaps more. The existence of many of the first national parks and monuments was frequently justified by their potential to attract tourists. Park boundaries were often cleaved in straight lines without regard for habitat connectivity, watershed protection, or the needs of migrating wildlife. Development outside of the boundaries for roads, homes, agriculture, and commerce increasingly severed pockets of protected areas. Today, we grapple with this legacy, while our influence over the parks and nature grows.

We've dramatically changed one of the continent's mightiest rivers in its mighty canyon for upstream water storage (the Colorado River in the Grand Canyon). We cull bison when their herds grow too large for their allocated habitat (as seen in Badlands, Theodore Roosevelt, and Wind Cave national parks) or when they attempt to migrate outside parks where they are not welcome (Yellowstone). Air quality frequently reaches unhealthy levels in our most majestic Appalachian parks (Great Smoky Mountains and Shenandoah). Invasive species and water diversion projects wreak havoc on unique ecosystems (Everglades). We alter wildfire regimes to protect infrastructure and communities (affecting most western parks) and are in the midst of forcing change on all parks by causing Earth's climate to warm.

In many respects, the scale of Katmai and adjacent protected lands are a triumph of conservation. Encompassing almost 3.7 million acres, Katmai is larger than Connecticut. The park's waters contain no dams, dikes, diversions, reservoirs, or flood-control structures, nor do any exist outside its boundaries. Along with the Becharof and Alaska Peninsula national wildlife refuges, the scope of federally protected lands extends across hundreds of miles and millions of acres of the Alaska Peninsula. With each boundary expansion, wildlife gained more protection and room simply to be wild. Katmai sustains not only one of the largest populations of bears on Earth but also one where the population is naturally regulated—it operates at the carrying capacity of the habitat and humans are not a significant cause of mortality. Nevertheless, Divot demonstrated that Katmai isn't big enough for all its bears.

Since the establishment of Yellowstone National Park in 1872, people have sought national parks to escape the storm of human development and modernity. We find refuge in their otherness. Parks are places to get back to "nature," where the land stands apart from humanity.

Yet, parklands were never unpeopled. The formation of parks followed on the heels of the United States' final wars on Native Americans. With the forced removal and genocide of indigenous peoples, as historian William Cronon explains in his essay "The Trouble with Wilderness; or Getting Back to the Wrong Nature," we created an "'uninhabited wilderness'—uninhabited as never before in the human history of the place." We've laid a boundary between national parks and the people who once found them home.

Russian fur hunters established their first lasting trading post on Kodiak Island in 1784. Scattered throughout the region were dozens of Native Alaskan villages and seasonally occupied camps. By this time or shortly after, the Russians also built a fur-hunting station and trading post at Katmai village.

Several decades passed before the Russians thoroughly penetrated interior regions of the northern Alaska Peninsula. In the early- to mid-1800s, the Russians didn't find people permanently inhabiting Brooks River. The nearest year-round settlement was Severnovsk (later called Savonoski) at the head of Iliuk Arm. Qit'rwik, the Alutiiq name for Brooks River, may have been a border area during a time of extended warfare between peoples living in southwest Alaska. After the wars ended, families from Savonoski occupied Qit'rwik seasonally to harvest fish and hunt game.

Russian and American colonization dramatically upset Native life-ways and cultures in the Katmai region. Russian fur traders conscripted Alutiiq and other indigenous men to hunt sea otters, and they often held women and children hostage to ensure the hunters met their obligations. In exchange for furs, a Russian *promyshlennik* provided a few trifling trade items, outright appropriated the furs, or gave the hunters tokens that could only be exchanged for goods at Russian-American Company stores. During times of famine, even small amounts of assistance from the colonizers constituted a lien upon the hunt.

The sea otter trade accelerated after Russia "sold" Alaska to the United States. Competing merchants drove up the price of pelts, leading to the wholesale slaughter of sea otters. As the otter population crashed to the brink of extinction, Native peoples who had become dependent on European and Russian trade goods were further impoverished. The salmon canning industry brought some economic relief to those living in the Katmai region around the turn of the 20th century. When the 1912 volcanic eruption struck, it set in motion a series of events that would further displace people from their traditional lifeways.

Griggs's explorations of the Valley of Ten Thousand Smokes revealed a devastated landscape buried in ash and pumice. Landslides and catastrophic floods further altered the land. The Katmai River valley remains a barren and fluvial maze of river channels and quicksand. Strong winds funnel blinding ash storms down the valley's throat. Ash so thoroughly buried the coastline and the Savonoski area that few people, if anyone, expected the landscape to recover quickly. As American Pete, a former resident of Savonoski, remarked to Griggs in 1918, "Never can go back to Savonoski to live again. Everything ash." Those who lived at Katmai village and Savonoski became volcanic refugees. They resettled at the newly minted Perryville 200 miles southwest or, like American Pete and his wife Pelagia Melganak, at New Savonoski along the lower reaches of Naknek River.

Unlike the Pacific coastline, which was downwind of the volcano, the Naknek Lake region was spared the eruption's worst effects. As life returned to normal, people from old Savonoski and fur trappers from Naknek began to use the Naknek Lake area again. Several families, including some who had lived at Savonoski prior to the eruption, were fishing and preparing salmon at the outlet of Brooks River when Mount McKinley National Park Superintendent Frank Been and NPS biologist Victor Cahalane visited in September 1940.

The establishment and expansion of Katmai National Monument, however, precluded people from returning on a permanent basis, and the monument proclamation prohibited many traditional subsistence activities. After Brooks Lodge opened for business in 1950, survivors of the 1912 Katmai eruption and their descendants continued to travel to the river to harvest salmon. Mary Jane Nielsen, who joined the harvest as a child, described how the experience changed as tourism grew in the area.

"While we were at Qit'rwik. . . . Grandma, Taata, and our parents would catch fish to split and dry. . . . The men built racks to dry the fish at the mouth of Brooks River on the south shore. Fish racks were still up in the 1950s when the National Park Service became more visible in the area. I have a visual image of the scene. I am not certain if the people standing across the river looking at us, at our tents, and at our fish racks were Northern Consolidated camp personnel or tourists. They may have been National Park Service employees. Thereafter, we traveled to Brooks River later in the season to catch and dry our redfish."

The Brooks Camp community remains small enough that there is little privacy. Everyone knows who you are and what you do. Rangers have even less anonymity than the bears. The Nielsen family's experience, however, was different. At best, the NPS viewed their presence as an annoyance or a sideshow. At worst, their salmon harvest was interpreted as an illegal act. In 1958, the NPS acknowledged the presence of this traditional use through the lens of what it might mean for tourism, not for the needs of people whose families had been fishing there for generations. "Though we are apt to think of their fishing camps more as nuisances and cluttered junk piles than as something of value, we must admit that it is part of the local color of the Monument, and eventually will be of visitor interest."

Congress legalized the traditional salmon harvest at Brooks River in 1996, but this is one of the few examples where people of indigenous heritage have regained any rights within a national park. When we consider how national parks are part of American identity, we must also consider the legacy of parks as a part of the colonialism imposed on indigenous nations by the United States. In contrast to their celebrated conservation success stories, park boundaries have very different and long-lasting consequences for people who once used these lands as home.

On the morning of July 30, with Grant scheduled to leave Brooks Camp that evening, Divot appeared near Dumpling Creek and then promptly reentered the forest. After another unsuccessful sortie to search the woods, we returned to the boats to wait offshore where we would not interfere with her movement if she appeared.

About 20 minutes after noon, two bears emerged from the trees several hundred yards east of the creek. My hopes rose as I peered through my binoculars and confirmed it was Divot and her yearling. We sat or stood in silence, the tinny sound of inches-high waves clanging against the boat's aluminum hull, as Divot approached and Grant readied his gun.

At Brooks Camp, few bears are more habituated to humans than Divot. On the beach in front of the visitor center I would have expected her to walk by a boatful of people without batting an eye. I felt apprehensive under the circumstances though. If she felt even slightly uncomfortable with our presence and turned into the trees, we'd miss another opportunity, and we couldn't count on another.

Divot continued her approach; 25, then 10 yards away. The moment she walked in front of the boat, Grant aimed and fired. The dart struck her right shoulder with an audible thwack, the impact triggering an internal charge that pushed a plunger forward to inject the tranquilizer.

Divot reacted almost as swiftly as the dart flew. Without a growl or roar, she turned her head back to snap at the projectile. Unable to reach it, however, and startled by the impact, she ran toward the creek on the gravel beach, her yearling following closely.

The tranquilizer, Telazol, was fast acting. Within 30 seconds, her pace slowed. Her rump sagged with the loss of motor control. Stumbling forward on her knees and elbows, her face lowered slowly to the gravel until she collapsed on her side. The yearling, confused by the events, watched from the edge of the grass as we exited the boat. For the next hour, it was never far as we hovered around its mother.

We waited several minutes to ensure Divot was indeed under the influence before approaching. Once at Divot's side, I stood out of the way to let Sherri Anderson, Katmai's then wildlife biologist, and Grant get to work. This was as near a perfect scenario as we could have wished for. Divot didn't run into the trees where finding her would be difficult and we couldn't be sure the drug had taken effect. Nor did she run into the water where she would drown if we couldn't keep her head above water. Grant explained that he wouldn't have tranquilized her in this location had her survival not been jeopardized by the snare, and he later remarked, "I thought for sure we'd be swimming." As I stood next to the 400-pound bear, I wondered about the struggle the snare forced her to endure.

Somewhere near King Salmon, Divot unknowingly pushed her head through the noose of a snare that should have been removed after the trapping season closed. The locking device cinched tighter as she moved forward until it pulled firmly against her fur and skin. She fought with all her strength to break free, but with a tensile strength greater than her body weight, the braided 1/8-inch-thick wire resisted and the noose pulled tighter. As she battled, the noose spun around her neck and cut into her flesh. The struggle lasted hours or days until the wire snapped at a kink that formed with Divot's twisting and pulling. By the time we reached Divot, the snare scored a girdling 1.5-inch-deep wound around her neck, exposing pink and raw flesh oozing pustules of blood and clear lymphatic fluid.

Sherri and Grant removed the snare using a pair of bolt cutters and treated her wound with an iodine solution to reduce the risk of infection. I took a moment to touch her shaggy and coarse fur, and then to examine her paws, the pads of which were textured just like a dog's—rough and pillowed for excellent traction and durability. Our last physical task was to pick her up and move her into the tree line where she would be more secure and less likely to roll into the lake as she slowly regained mobility over the next few hours.

With our effort successful, we returned to the boat elated that Divot was free of the snare. We kept a vigilant watch in case she got too close to the water or was approached by another bear before she regained full use of motor skills. Unable to walk initially, and likely experiencing a tremendous hangover, she crawled and dragged herself to the beach, panting from the effort and the heat of the day. Almost 2.5 hours after she was tranquilized,

Divot stood on shaky legs and stumbled with a stiff, uncoordinated gait to Dumpling Creek where she rested her belly in the cool rushing water.

Two days later, Divot and her yearling returned briefly to Brooks Camp before departing once again for parts unknown. The ring around her neck remained raw and prominent, but she now had a fighting chance to survive. By October, her thick fur hid most of the scarring. Only a thin parting of neck hair advertised her ordeal, which demonstrated that the boundaries between parks, culture, and the needs of wildlife do not completely overlap.

CHAPTER 15

IN A CROWD

The minute Jeanne and I stepped onto the platform at the river mouth, an old friend greeted us. Granted, the bear did not consider us friends, nor had we taught her to recognize us individually, but she was old. As 410 approached her fourth decade of life, each encounter with her was a special occasion.

Four-ten was one of the first bears I learned to recognize at Brooks River. With a round, dinner-plate-sized face, a prominent shoulder hump, and dark brown fur grizzled with lighter tips, 410 was an archetypal brown bear. Her thick, damp fur looked silky under the overcast light. With more than 25 years of worldly experience, she amassed a vast knowledge of the lower river and how to survive here. As we watched her snorkel in the river mouth, she moved in near silence, making noise only when she lifted her face from the water to exhale.

Apparently on the ebb of her multihour, hyperphagic eat-and-sleep cycle, she waddled out of the water to approach the platform where we stood. A set of stairs climbed to our position and 410 decided the best place to rest is underneath us. After crossing the gravel path to the platform, she pawed the grass in a belly hole 10 feet below the soles of my shoes and slowly lowered her body into it.

Not long after 410 settled into her nap, two of our National Park Service (NPS) coworkers approached the platform from the road. There was an end-of-the-season party for concession staff and friends at the lodge, and even though I doubted if anyone would mind if I attended, I've become far too introverted to enjoy drinking parties. Plus I'd rather watch bears.

We gestured to our coworkers to walk up to the back ramp instead of continuing straight to the gates of the old floating bridge. They followed our suggestion and hopscotched over 410 by utilizing the platform's walkway to access the stairs on the far side. Four-ten did not react to our conversations.

A few minutes later, two other park employees arrived, this time on bicycles. A small, inappropriately placed bike rack sat under the platform and that was their destination. By the time I saw my colleagues, it was too late to give them any warning. They rode within 30 feet of 410 before they saw her. "Wha'oh!" one of them exclaimed as he swerved to turn back. It was not the brightest move, riding a bicycle so fast in this area when the chance of encountering a bear at close range was so high, but one not uncommon at Brooks Camp. Four-ten continued to rest.

The opportunity to observe a wild bear so closely and safely is exceedingly rare and I have yet to tire of the experience. Yet, I am fully aware this specific experience would not have been possible without 410's tolerance of humanity.

She was undoubtedly cognizant of our presence as she exited the river to rest. We made no effort to hide or remain downwind and, regardless, two people standing quietly are well below her disturbance threshold. The events this evening added to 410's well-endowed credentials as perhaps the most human-habituated bear ever to use Brooks River. Her ability to adapt to the presence of people conferred many advantages, but what should we do if not all bears can accommodate our presence?

Habituation is a psychological term as applicable to wildlife studies as it is to a myriad of experiences in our daily lives. It is different from conditioning, which occurs when an organism increases the frequency or intensity of its response to a stimulus because of a reward or a punishment. In contrast, habituation offers neither reward nor punishment. It is the waning response to a neutral or nonthreatening stimulus. A new hand soap may seem strong-scented at first but over time we hardly notice its smell. Few of us regularly notice the scent of our own clothing, but the moment we don someone else's sweater their odor is immediately apparent. The deep thrumming of a locomotive wakes new residents in the middle of the night while the neighborhood's longtime townsfolk sleep soundly.

When a wild animal encounters humans, it must assess the situation carefully. Fleeing could save its life. On the other hand, running away or avoiding habitat when it isn't necessary can cost it energy and access to valuable resources. If there are no consequences (no rewards of food or play and no negative stimuli such as pain, injury, or energetic costs), then the animal can learn to ignore people. We remain a facet of the landscape that merits little attention. Habituation to humans, therefore, offers wildlife many advantages. When a "tame" squirrel in a city park habituates to people it can forage more efficiently, potentially access habitats with fewer predators, and avoid the energetic costs of running away unnecessarily.

Habituation can be used to promote a peaceful coexistence between humans and brown bears when people behave appropriately and bears have no motivation to break the code of conduct. The relationship is best exemplified at Alaska's McNeil River State Game Sanctuary, located north of Katmai. Beginning in 1973, access to the sanctuary required a permit, awarded through an application and lottery process. When Larry Aumiller, the sanctuary's manager for over 30 years, arrived in 1976 he began to manage McNeil to promote habituation of bears to people, a significant contrast from many national park areas like Katmai, which at the time, were being managed to discourage habituation. Each day, no more than 10 people plus a refuge guide walk to McNeil River Falls from an established camping area. The group always follows the same trails and is generally limited to the same viewing hours (10 a.m. to 8 p.m.). With the exception of the camping area and the group's personal boundaries, staff at McNeil try not to violate a bear's personal space. In the presence of bears, people are discouraged from making loud noises or moving in a manner that would confuse them. Bears, instead, choose their proximity to humans.

The management strategy at McNeil has been incredibly successful. Despite the close proximity of daily encounters—with bears occasionally approaching within a few feet of people on the ground-level viewing pad—

no one has been injured by bears at McNeil River under the current management system. Just as important, the number of bears using the sanctuary has remained high for the last several decades. Aumiller attributes this to the predictability of the situation. Bears know exactly when and where to expect people as well as how many are coming and how people are likely to behave. At Brooks Camp, however, habituation of bears occurred through a continual accident of circumstances rather than a planned strategy.

By all accounts, few bears used the river when Brooks Lodge first opened for business in 1950. Bears and any type of bear-management activities were absent from the reports of the first rangers stationed at Brooks Camp. Ranger Russell Todd, for example, never saw a bear on foot in the summer of 1954. The presence of people alone was apparently enough of a deterrent to displace bears from the river except at night. In 1957, biologists conducting salmon research at Brooks River for the US Fish and Wildlife Service reported bears "loudly evident" every night during September at the salmon-counting weir strung across the head of the river.

How many bears lived within the monument at that time remains an open question, but it was likely not many. The population may even have been at a nadir, the result of decades of heavy hunting pressure near the monument and, I suspect, the lingering effects of the 1912 eruption. After a two-summer biological investigation of the monument in 1953 and 1954, Victor Cahalane reported: "It is impossible to make even a rough estimate of the population of bears in Katmai National Monument." Yet he tried. According to his and other anecdotal sightings, including one from a pilot who claimed to have seen 60 bears along Savonoski River in early September 1954, Cahalane ventured that about 200 bears lived in the monument.

Steady levels of salmon and a reduction in hunting pressure outside the monument were probably the main factors that allowed the area's bear population to slowly increase, but at Brooks Camp people inadvertently helped accelerate the bears' use of the river. By the end of the 1960s, a small and growing contingent of bears had become accustomed to the easy access to unsecured food at nearby garbage dumps, the lodge's burn barrels, and unsecured supplies. By the mid-1970s, Brooks Camp had become well-known as a place to find at least a few bears, and several had begun to fish in the river during the day when people were active. Biologist Will Troyer found six to eight bears using the river corridor in July. Most bears, except those who were food conditioned, remained reclusive though. Through the 1980s, bear sightings and numbers continued to grow, and when 410 was born in 1989 the number of bears using the river reached 26 in July and 31 in the fall, while human visitation climbed to about 10,000. The stage was set for 410 to become one of the most habituated bears ever at Brooks Camp.

A substantial number of Brooks River's bears display a high level of tolerance for people, but probably none in the park's history have attained the level of habituation of 410. In 2007, my first summer at Brooks Camp, 410 had long attained a status all her own. Everywhere except the lodge porch was her domain.

Her first year of life wasn't without its risks. On a late July morning, Chowmane—as 410 was known before she acquired her ID number[*]—accompanied her mother, Goatee, to the falls. While waiting at the base of a spruce tree as her mother fished, a young adult male rushed Chowmane and her sibling. Four-ten escaped up a tree. Her sibling did not and was killed.

For three summers, Goatee brought 410 to the river. Goatee was habituated to bears and people, and she exposed her cub to both. They braved the falls in July, but they also made frequent use of the lower river where people are most active. They investigated human-made objects and structures, often while visiting the campground and lodge. Four-ten seemed fascinated with glass. She pawed plexiglass sign covers and stretched up to get her muzzle to windows. The repeated exposure to people reinforced 410's tolerance of humans, even as rangers occasionally hazed the family with firecracker rounds blasted from a shotgun. After Goatee emancipated Chowmane in 1992, 410 easily transitioned from habituated cub to very habituated subadult.

By the end of her life, one that extended almost 30 years (410 was last seen in 2018), she displayed an extreme tolerance for people, our motor vehi-

---

[*] Four-ten had at least two different nicknames in the 1990s (Chowmane and Cubless) plus at least one more after that (Four-ton). By the time I arrived at the river in 2007, however, no one called her anything but Four-ten.

cles, and noise. Visitors and staff consistently pushed her personal bound-aries and reinforced her habituation when they expressed an unwillingness to wait for her to move. Maintenance staff would operate heavy equipment within 15 yards of her. The lodge tour bus, taking visitors to the Valley of Ten Thousand Smokes, sometimes came closer. She slept on the beach in front of the lodge at midday, next to our cabins, and along the footpath at the base of the lodge, hardly turning an ear to planes or small vehicles.

With her level of habituation, the whole river was available to 410, and not only because she tolerated people. She had a reputation among bears too. At the falls, bears recognized her nonthreatening, if not gentle, dis-position. In her twilight years, not once can I remember her aggressively displacing another bear. Instead, she found room to fish in the far pool as best she could, while in September she found ample fishing opportunities at the lower river. Even dominant males like 747 and 856 allowed her to fish nearby.

Four-ten's habituation caused many management challenges. In the fall, when she exited the water near the platform or bridge, I knew she would almost certainly nap near the trail or along the road, stalling visitor access for an hour or more. Keeping people from approaching her, while ensur-ing their experience remained enjoyable, was not often an easy task for my fellow rangers or me. (Herding people is very much like herding prover-bial cats.) Yet, I loved watching 410. Her ability to adapt to the presence of people made her a remarkable bear to observe. For some people, however, 410's tolerance for humanity somehow made her less wild and less worthy of our attention.

Unless we arrive at a park in complete ignorance of its features, we visit with some preconceived perception of what that park should be. Photos, books, and nature documentaries artfully display the nation's most iconic landscapes, generally with a lack of people in the frame, and they condi-tion our mind to expect certain experiences. Parks often meet or exceed the expectation. I had seen more photos of the General Sherman Tree, the largest tree in the world, than I can remember. I read about and studied its characteristics; trying to envision its 110-foot circumference; how one of its branches before falling off in 2006 was larger than most trees east of the

Mississippi; and how it is the fastest-growing tree in the world, accumulating more cubic feet of wood annually than any other tree despite its 2,000 years of life. When I finally visited Sequoia National Park and stood in its shadow, I was no less awestruck by the tree's otherworldly scale.

Visiting the General Sherman Tree was a curated experience, however. I camped in a developed campground the previous night. I drove on a paved road to get there and parked less than a mile from the tree. A wide, well-trodden trail led me through the forest to its base where I was met by a log-rail fence placed to discourage visitors from creeping to its trunk.

These observations shouldn't be construed as complaints. The infrastructure allows tens of thousands of people per year to visit the tree while attempting to protect its health and continued longevity. Providing for both enjoyment and protection is a dichotomy in national parks. The US national park system is guided by the Organic Act of 1916 where the fundamental purpose of the parks is "to conserve the scenery and the natural and historic objects and the wild life therein and to provide for the enjoyment of the same in such manner and by such means as will leave them unimpaired for the enjoyment of future generations." How the NPS achieves this goal, commonly referred to its mission statement, has been a source of debate for over 100 years.

The Organic Act established the National Park Service but was silent on issues of ecological preservation as we understand the term today. "Enjoyment" seemed to require reasonable access such as roads and trails as well as amenities like campgrounds, lodging, and shops selling key chains, stickers, and other fine trinkets. "Unimpaired," therefore, could not have been meant in its strictest sense. Otherwise, parks would largely, if not completely, have become people-free areas and infrastructure would not have been developed. And although "scenery" was never formally defined, it was a term clearly understood by those who participated in the congressional hearings leading up to the passage of the act. According to historian Robin Winks, it was intended to include the aggregate landscape, especially its natural beauty.

Winks concluded that through the use of rhetoric—stating the most important argument first—Congress intended that the conservation of "scenery" take precedence over enjoyment. Therefore, the NPS mission is not a contradictory mandate that requires we balance protection and preservation equally with enjoyment.

Regardless of whether the rhetorical arguments ring true for the NPS mission, Congress strengthened the conservation mandate of parks through two acts in the 1970s. The 1970 National Park System General Authorities Act stated parks "derive increased national dignity and recognition of their superb environmental quality through their inclusion . . . in one national park system preserved and managed for the benefit and inspiration of all the people." Winks argues that this holds national parks to an increased standard of protection, one based on a superb environmental quality. Degradation in the quality of one park becomes a threat to the integrity of the whole national park system. In 1978, through an act that expanded Redwood National Park, Congress declared all national parks were to be protected "in light of the high public value and integrity" as well as in ways to avoid "derogation of the values and purposes" for which the parks, collectively and individually, were created. Winks reiterates, "Virtually all commentators at the time and since have concluded that the 1978 provision added to the Park Service's mandate to protect ecological values."

These acts may have muddied the waters in a different way though. Winks argues that the 1970 and 1978 laws apply to action, not inaction. Was the NPS required to mitigate deleterious impacts to parks or merely prevent future intrusions? The NPS has moved to do both by, for example, reintroducing extirpated species, removing or relocating facilities, and controlling invasive species.

Defining "scenery" for our parks is still subject to cultural norms, especially regarding the behavior of wildlife. Most NPS managers have historically viewed habituation as undesirable—wildlife ought to show an avoidance response, because, as the reasoning goes, that is the most natural and wildest form. On the other hand, boldness and habituation are regarded as unnatural and dangerous. Wildlife is also managed through the lens of populations, not individuals that compose a population. But when individual animals possess the capacity to habituate, to live alongside humans without conflict, is that any less natural than one that flees? For many individual animals, it is the only way they know how to live, and as parks become increasingly crowded with human visitors, wildlife will be forced to increasingly share space with us. Bears do not habituate to people for our benefit. They habituate to people in spite of us.

Habituation allows bears access to natural foods and other resources that exist near centers of human activity. At Yellowstone, bears that habituate to roadsides exploit habitat that would otherwise be off limits to the grizzly population at large. Habituation can also allow certain bears to avoid confrontation and conflict with bears that might be threatening or dangerous. Bear viewers, for example, can displace large males from feeding areas, providing more foraging opportunities to habituated subadults and females with cubs.

Many lines of evidence also indicate habituation helps keep people and bears safe. McNeil's record speaks for itself. At Glacier National Park, habituation of grizzly bears to hikers can lessen the rate of charges and, consequently, human injuries. At Yellowstone, grizzlies feeding on natural foods at roadsides have not injured people despite the park's famously chaotic bear jams. And at Brooks River only three people have been injured by bears since the lodge opened in 1950.

Although there are brown bears everywhere that possess at least some capacity to become habituated, those living in coastal Alaska seem more inclined to it than other populations. The bears of Katmai and Kodiak live at densities an order of magnitude larger than grizzlies in Denali or the Northern Rockies. Bears interact frequently within these high-density populations and naturally habituate to each other to access food resources. Bears at Brooks River also become more habituated toward each other seasonally. The rate of aggressive encounters and active displacement by bears at Brooks Falls is greatest in late June and July, which is when bears are hungry and have not interacted closely since the previous year. Their aggressive responses to each other wane over days and weeks of repeated encounters. As a result, more fishing spots become available at the falls during the last two weeks of July than the first two weeks. Bear biologists Tom Smith and Stephen Herrero argue that this bear-to-bear habituation is primarily responsible for the tolerant demeanor bears exhibit toward each other and "sets the stage for humans to commingle at close range without great risk."

Yet, the capacity to habituate is not universal. It varies widely among individual bears. While 410's habituation worked to her advantage, we must consider the consequences of our presence for bears that cannot adapt.

My first summer at Katmai, I watched a shy young adult male slink to the far pool at the falls but venture no farther. As salmon swam through the shallows, he pounced on them with skill and accuracy, but he always fished in the same manner, standing perpendicular to the current with his butt pressed against the rock wall. When other bears approached, he almost never made any attempt to defend his fishing spot or stand his ground. He practiced abundant caution, routinely yielding space, sometimes at a running pace, to avoid most other bears. He reacted even more warily toward people, eyeing the platform with suspicion. He approached the lip only rarely and usually only at night in the absence of people. The lower river, where human activity is most pronounced, was completely off limits to him. From the falls platform one evening, I watched him shuffle into the riffles when no people stood on the adjacent downstream platform. A pair of bear watchers arrived within a few moments and interrupted his sanctuary. In a spray of water, the aptly nicknamed Scare D Bear fled across the river and into the forest.

By 2019, Scare D had grown significantly and ranked among the largest bears at the falls, but his comfort level near people had changed little from the time when I first observed him. Even as he experienced the prime of his life, he rarely visited productive fishing spots like the lip or jacuzzi, not because he lacked the knowledge or skill to fish those places, but because those fishing spots are too close to the wildlife-viewing platform and the humans who stand on it. The areas with people are occupied territory, places so thoroughly permeated by humanity as to render them off limits to nonhabituated bears.

The impacts of people on the bears' use of the river was described in detail by Tammy Olson during her graduate thesis studies in the late 1980s and early 1990s, a time when visitation at Brooks River skyrocketed to then unprecedented levels. She systematically observed bears for more than 1,600 hours over three summers from the platform at the falls, a tree stand halfway between the bridge and the falls, and a stand set on scaffolds near the river mouth. These three locations allowed her to observe all of the river from the falls downstream to Naknek Lake and track how individual bears utilized the different spaces. To track the bears across seasons and years, Tammy photographed each bear and recorded detailed notes on their physical characteristics and behaviors. Bears were then assigned identification numbers and further classified by their tolerance for people. Bears that were consistently tolerant of people less than 50 meters away were deemed habituated. The others were classified as unclassified or not consistently tolerant. Tammy's work became the foundation of the Brooks River bear monitoring program that the park still utilizes today, and her observations revealed stark contrasts in the ways bears used the river.

From 1988 to 1990, nonhabituated bears accounted for 62 to 77 percent of the individual bears observed at the river, but they spent less time on the river and arrived later in the season than their habituated counterparts. The availability of fish didn't seem to influence their foraging patterns either. Nonhabituated bears used the zones adjacent to Brooks Lodge and the bridge significantly less than habituated bears, even during late summer when the lower river filled with dead and dying salmon. The disparity was particularly apparent with family groups. The area downstream of the bridge was used almost exclusively by habituated mothers and their cubs. Nonhabituated families accounted for less than 2 percent of the total "family group minutes" at the lower river, even though the numbers of habituated and nonhabituated families were about equal. Bears at Brooks River were also mostly crepuscular, which contrasted with the pattern of use at Margot Creek, a stream about a dozen miles from Brooks River and with no human visitation in the early 1990s. There, Olson found bears distributed their activities uniformly throughout the day.

An extension of the lodge's open season offered Olson an opportunity to assess the effects of increased human use at the river during a time frame when bears had experienced relatively few people. Prior to 1992, Brooks Lodge closed for the season on September 10, but in 1992 the season was extended to September 18, which is where it currently remains. After the lodge closes, winterization work by the NPS and concession employees extends the period of human activity an additional two to four weeks.

The effects of the extended lodge season were readily apparent. Non-habituated adults significantly delayed their use of the river in 1992, and arrived on average 17 days later than 1988 through 1990. In contrast, arrival dates did not differ for both habituated adults and subadults.

Tammy Olson's conclusions are now part of a large and growing body of research documenting the impacts of people on brown bears. At Pack Creek on Admiralty Island, highly habituated bears tended to use the creek area during midday periods of high visitor use more than other bears. When the Pelican Valley of Yellowstone National Park is open to visitors, hikers significantly reduce bear activity in meadows more than a third of a mile from forest cover. At Chilkoot River near Haines, Alaska, people were involved in about half of the instances when bears left the river. At Kulik River, a very popular sport-fishing location in northern Katmai, bears alter their use of the river to accommodate human activity by seeking times and places where human use is lowest. In northeast Katmai, adult males in the Douglas River area reduced their use of salt marshes by 15 percent when groups of bear watchers utilized the same habitat. On the salt marshes, bears also extended the time spent in vigilance behaviors when people were present, but these behaviors also declined when people were more than 100 meters away.

Bears can forage on berries and sedge at any time of day or night, but when feeding opportunities are time constrained then the impacts of benignly acting people can become significant. By analyzing three summers' of time-lapse photos from Geographic Harbor, a popular bear-viewing area at the head of an intricately carved fjord on Katmai's coast, NPS biologist Carissa Turner found bears active at all times of the day, yet there were discernable peaks. The first peak in bear activity occurred in the morning (from 6 a.m. to 12 p.m.) and the second occurred in the evening (from 6 to 10 p.m.). Meanwhile, human visitation was highest during midday hours.

At the outlets of many small coastal streams, salmon are typically only available to bears during the early stages of the incoming tide when the overall water level remains low. At stages closer to high tide, the water level becomes too deep for bears to forage efficiently. When the presence of people coincides with optimal bear fishing times, as the midday depression in bear activity at Geographic Harbor suggests, nonhabituated bears may be displaced from an already limited foraging opportunity.

Not all biologists perceived these impacts as negative. At Glendale Cove in British Columbia, the presence of people displaced large males and allowed subordinate bears, including females with cubs, more time to fish. When people were absent large males were more active and females with cubs spent less time fishing and more time remaining vigilant. This led the study's lead author, Owen Nevin, to conclude, "By displacing large males, viewing activities created a temporal refuge, enhancing feeding opportunities for subordinate age/sex classes. Here, we have shown that appropriately managed wildlife viewing may have real, direct benefits for the animals viewed."

However, are those the benefits we want, especially in the context of US national parks? (In fairness, Nevin's study location is not part of a national park but is located on First Nations territory.) If national parks were mandated by legislation to grow a bear population, then increasing foraging opportunities for mother bears and their cubs could be an important way to increase reproductive success. National parks aren't wildlife farms though, nor are they only for bears that possess a tolerance for humans. Importantly, in the case of Brooks River, nonhabituated mother bears experience a tremendous disadvantage. The presence of many adult males can displace them from the falls, while the presence of people displaces them from productive fishing areas of the lower river, leaving these human-intolerant mothers with precious little room to make a living.

Since Olson's original studies the number of bears at the river has ranged from a high of 114 bears in 2010 to a low of 40 bears in 2014, but the pattern of bear use has remained consistent. Some nonhabituated bears find space near the falls, but the lower river continues to be the almost-exclusive realm of humans and human-habituated bears. In 2019, more than 14,000 people visited Brooks Camp, but "visitor use days," the total tally of days visitors spend at the park, reached about 16,000. Brooks Camp received 9,000 visitor use days in July alone. Available habitat for bears is further restricted as more people than ever venture into the river to fish or photograph. Outside of a few specific individuals, almost no adult males utilize the lower river area during midday hours, even in September when the fishing is easy and productive.

There's one anomaly among this pattern though—Brooks Falls. At the falls, we have the opportunity to watch the largest and most dominant bears as well as those showing little tolerance for people. Four-ten found room at the falls because of her tolerance for other bears and her lack of concern for people. Scare D Bear finds less space at the falls, but still some, because regulations restrict people to the wildlife-viewing platforms between June 15 and August 15. In addition, those platforms close from 10 p.m. to 7 a.m. This allows nonhabituated bears more unobstructed fishing opportunities. As Tammy Olson and her late husband Ron Squibb wrote in their 1993 book, *Brown Bears of Brooks River,* "Predictable human behavior seems very important to non-habituated adults. At Brooks Falls, people stay off the river and remain on the viewing platform to the south of the falls. Access is mostly by one trail and people are rarely there at dusk and dawn. These simple and predictable human patterns seem acceptable to bears that avoid other parts of the river where human use is unrestricted."

Some people argue we needn't change our behavior to accommodate the needs of bears in Katmai, because there's relatively little risk to human safety. Bo Bennett, a former fishing guide for Katmailand, the concession that operated Brooks Lodge from the early 1980s to 2016, and the author of *Rods and Wings: A History of the Fishing Lodge Business in Bristol Bay, Alaska,* sums up the attitude when he writes, "Because I am a fisherman and have spent many years fishing the bear-infested streams of Alaska and northern Canada, I don't think that fishermen are perceived to be much of a threat by bears."

There is an underlying truth to Bennett's statement. When you are fishing and the bears you see behave like 410, it's easy to conclude that bears don't care about our presence or see us as a threat. But not all bears are 410. While habituation allows certain bears to tolerate people, for other bears even a lifetime of exposure to humans isn't enough. Nonhabituated bears aren't going to jump out of the forest and charge us as we fish or if we wade the river looking for the perfect photo or if we have a loud conversation on the platforms. They'll either leave or avoid the area. The presence of people creates a landscape of fear among bears that are intolerant of humanity. When instinct compels caution, bears may not be able to distinguish between someone who intends harm and those with more benign motivations such as photography or fishing. Animals rarely have perfect information. As a result, they generally err toward overestimating risk rather than underestimating risk. Humans have represented a real threat to bears for thousands of years. It's difficult to shed that evolutionary baggage.

More than 15 years after Scare D Bear first made his way to the falls as a timid subadult, he still will not approach the lower river when people are present, and if he makes his way to the lip, his deliberate movements suggest an extreme wariness of innocent onlookers like myself. One could argue that Katmai is a big place and Scare D Bear can just go somewhere else if he doesn't like people. With Katmai's bear population existing at or near the habitat's carrying capacity though, another place may not be available. Brooks River's early summer and early fall feeding periods also represent the first and among the last fishing opportunities of the year. A bear displaced from Brooks in September has no local alternatives.

None of this is to suggest we shouldn't visit Brooks River or other areas with wildlife, only that we need to consider how to visit most ethically. Brooks River is currently managed with few restrictions on where people can go and no restrictions on the number of people who can visit during the day. On the busiest days, hundreds of people fill the platforms while dozens more walk in the river. Currently, room for the human-shy bear is exceedingly rare and, as a result, Brooks River has become the realm of the human-habituated.

If, like Robin Winks concludes, parks are to be held to a higher standard of protection, if they are to be places where natural processes dominate, then we must self-sacrifice part of our experience to protect wildlife and the experience of people who come afterward. Not one person needs to stand in Brooks River to make a living. However, every single bear does.

To accommodate a full spectrum of bears, we must fundamentally rethink how we use and enjoy the river. During seasons when bears need to use Brooks River to fish, I no longer walk the river or stray from established trails unless absolutely necessary. I can't, certainly not while knowing that my presence physically displaces bears from the habitat. Watching from the platforms and sites adjacent to buildings is more than a satisfactory compromise.

While I treasure my experiences watching 410, Brooks River shouldn't be a place for only the most human-habituated of bears. Nor do I want every bear to run from the sight, sound, or scent of a person. Sharing habitat with wildlife ought to include opportunities for all of a population's individuals to find space. Some habituation is necessary for bears to coexist with people. Four-ten found a way. We should do the same for bears that are unable or unwilling to follow her example.

CHAPTER 16

BEAR IN CAMP

While 273 ventured to the falls as a young subadult, the lower river and camp area were her most frequently used domains. When I first came to know her, it wasn't 273's fishing skills that garnered my attention. Rather, she would have blended into the crowd of about 30 subadults identified at the river in 2010[*] if she hadn't expressed a keen interest in people and our objects.

Two-seven-three was prone to follow people, either out of curiosity or to test the limits of her dominance. The bridge gates were a common source of amusement for her, and they became heavily scarred from her claws and teeth. She proved difficult to haze when she ventured close to the lodge and park housing area, a territory rangers try to manage as a bear-free zone.

Her behavior changed as she matured into a borderline adult and she seemed to grow out of her curiosity toward people and our objects. For a couple of years, she visited the camp area less frequently and wasn't implicated in any instances of property damage. Once she became a mother in 2015, however, her old habits soon resurfaced.

---

[*] Two-seven-three first appears in the NPS bear-monitoring database in 2011. However, she was likely present at the river before then, only identified as a different bear, 198.

Early that August, I spent six days exploring the Valley of Ten Thousand Smokes, Katmai Pass, and parts of the Katmai River valley. I forgot about Brooks Camp, living in the moment as I trekked across the trail-less landscape, watched caribou, play-bowed with a curious fox, and forded numbingly cold glacial creeks. When I returned to Brooks Camp, with my vocal cords not yet woken from their torpor, I found fellow rangers in a state of frustration. Two-seven-three and her cub had decided to play with almost any human-made object they could find.

In my field notes from August 11, I scribbled a litany of charges: "273 has damaged several buildings around camp. She tore the screen door on the superintendent's cabin, tore the tarpaper off the wader shack and took boots and PFDs out, and damaged a tent frame. 273 also damaged the bridge. Few staff [are] here to deal with it. Tensions and stress level[s] are high."

Rangers at Brooks Camp work on the front lines of a decades-long struggle. Although peaceful coexistence is the goal, Brooks Camp is the center of conflict between the park's two most dominant mammal species.

Although preserving the spectacle and promoting tourism-potential served as the impetus to create the first national parks, the newly protected areas immediately became refuges for wildlife species that were becoming rare across the contiguous 48 states. By the 1880s, Yellowstone harbored the last wild herd of bison in the United States, a mere two-dozen individuals from the tens of millions that once roamed the continent. Even then, rangers had to take heroic efforts to save this herd from poachers hell-bent on exterminating the animals.

Wildlife wasn't protected uniformly, however. Species were often judged by their aesthetics and perceived usefulness. Well into the early 20th century, Yellowstone rangers shot and poisoned predators to favor animals viewed more amicably such as elk and deer, a decision that reflected the cultural values of the people charged with managing parks as well as the public at large.

As the science of ecology and yearning for a wilderness ideal grew, Americans started to reconsider wildlife management and the role national parks should play in it. In 1963, an advisory board for the Department of Interior issued *Wildlife Management in the National Parks* (or the Leopold

Report, after the board's chair, A. Starker Leopold). The Leopold Report catalyzed a time of soul-searching for the National Park Service. Surging visitation and increased development had altered the face of many national park areas, while heightened awareness for environmental issues grew within the public. The report acknowledged that few parks were large enough to be self-regulating ecosystems and asked, "How far should the National Park Service go in utilizing the tools of management to maintain wildlife populations?" Although admittedly conceptual, the report recommended the NPS manage parklands as "vignettes of primitive America." Parks ought to resemble the prevailing conditions experienced by the first Europeans on the continent, a philosophical shift that looked to the past to define the present and future.

It was under this context that bear management evolved at Brooks River. With so few bears using the river in the 1950s, at first there was little to no need for wildlife management of any kind. As the bear population grew, however, conflict between bears and people became an inevitable facet of the Brooks Camp experience.

Just a few years into the lodge's history, conflict with bears began to slowly rise, mostly because people were tempting them. In July 1953, bears "invaded" Victor Cahalane's campsite about 1 mile north of Brooks River, chewing into canned goods stacked on the ground. The next summer, he left food outside for several nights "in an 'experiment' to determine if brown bears were sufficiently bold to enter the camp while it was manned." At least one was. A medium-sized bear took the food and carried it off.

Garbage proved to be equally attractive to the local bears. For Brooks Lodge and the few NPS personnel at the time, trash was most easily and economically disposed in the park. Initially, bottles and cans were sunk in the lake or buried in the forest. In the early 1960s, an open dump was established on the shore of Naknek Lake, which soon attracted several bears. With bears scarce around camp for a brief time, the lodge manager guided guests to the dump to see them, creating perhaps the first guided bear-viewing opportunity in the monument.

Lodge employees began to feel unsafe transporting garbage to the lakeside dump after a small coterie of bears learned the trash barge's schedule, so the dump was moved 2 miles southeast of camp on the Valley of Ten Thousand Smokes Road. To keep bears away, a bulldozer covered the garbage once per week and the NPS installed an electric fence around the landfill. Electric fences work well with curious bears but are not a significant deterrent for strongly motivated individuals. As a result, these measures failed to keep bears away.

The dump was also relatively inaccessible, because no bridge extended across the river. Trash had to be ferried across the water, then trucked to the dump. To lighten the load, the NPS installed burn barrels at Brooks Camp in 1966. Trash, and the smell of burning trash, soon attracted bears to the lodge area, and this may have contributed to the first and most serious bear attack in Brooks Camp's history.

Located a five-minute walk north of the lodge, the Brooks Camp campground is tucked in a grove of balsam poplar along the shore of Naknek Lake. The campground is currently surrounded by an electric fence, and rangers instruct campers to prepare food only at the campground's cooking shelters. At all other times, food must be stored within the food cache along with any cooking utensils, dishes, pots, and pans. Although a Lincoln Log–style food cache, elevated on stilts, sat in the campground when John Huckabee crawled into his sleeping bag and dozed off on the evening of July 21, 1966, there was no electric fence, nor was proper food storage and camp cleanliness an emphasized part of the Brooks Camp experience.

Before going to sleep, Huckabee panfried and ate a lake trout he had caught earlier in the day. His meal was too big to finish in one sitting so he stored the leftover fish on a rock and his unwashed frying pan next to the fire. The evening was clear, and with no sign of rain, Huckabee chose to forego his tent to sleep under the stars. That night, he woke to the sound of a bear rummaging through his campsite.

"I looked at it for a moment, and it did not appear to see me. I decided it was too close to run, so I elected to lay low. After a few minutes, it walked over towards where I lay. I remember the audible soft thud of its footsteps. I was on my abdomen, and the bear began to sniff my sleeping bag."

A bear needs only take a small mental step to go from eating garbage to seeking out people and our possessions for other sources of food. We don't know whether the bear that stood over Huckabee had fed on garbage at

Brooks Camp, but its boldness suggests it had. Huckabee lay still, unsure of what to do.

"It rather delicately hooked under my hip with [its] fore claws and rolled me over. I decided that a bite on the backside was better than a bite in the abdomen, so I rolled back over." That's when the bear bit Huckabee in the buttocks and thigh. It began to drag him away.

"I yelled as loud as I could, and my impression was that the animal was startled. I do not recall—never did—any details while I was in the thing's teeth. It dropped me about 3 to 4 meters away."

Another camper heard the yell and scared the bear away by making noise. Huckabee needed surgery to repair his wounds and remained in the Anchorage hospital for five weeks before he was released.

The attack was a wake-up call for everyone, but the relationship between the NPS and concessioner became increasingly antagonistic regarding bear management. The NPS told the concessioner to keep all food indoors until it could be hauled to the dump. The concessioner, though, according to National Park Service historian Frank Norris, "paid scant attention to the plan and took the attitude that it was the Park Service's responsibility to keep the bears away from the buildings, if necessary by relocating them." In 1969, surely with the Huckabee attack fresh in many staff's minds, the concessioner continued to leave garbage in a can outside the lodge overnight, while the fish cleaning shed, a screened-in frame structure, was cleaned about twice a week. Between cleanings, fish entrails sat in a wooden bucket on the floor. When it came to food and garbage "the concessionaire appeared to have the upper hand and was doing a great deal of whatever he desired," wrote University of Alaska Fairbanks professor Frederick Dean in his 1969 review of Brooks Camp bear management.

As the garbage issue persisted, the NPS implemented reactionary tactics to prevent bears from becoming too comfortable around camp. Capture and relocation were used, but the practice proved to be largely ineffectual; most transplanted bears returned within days or weeks. Heavy-handed hazing techniques were more successful, at least with some bears. In particular, rangers began to "pepper" bears that approached burn barrels or lingered too close to buildings with shotgun shells filled with rock salt.

The 1970s marked a shift in bear management success at Brooks Camp.

While issues persisted, the NPS expanded its effort to educate visitors on proper etiquette in bear country and the burn barrels were finally eliminated. A trash compactor was installed and garbage was hauled by barge to the west end of Naknek Lake and then trucked to the Naknek dump.

The culture regarding food storage was slow to change though. Garbage was one thing. Preventing bears from getting people's fish and lunches was another. Park regulations and policy hadn't kept pace with the increasing frequency of encounters between bears and people. The still-relaxed attitude regarding food was about to take another casualty.

Sister was almost 4 years old when Will Troyer fitted her with a radio collar and ear tags in 1978. While hibernating on Mount Katolinat that winter, she gave birth to cubs. She was quite young for a first-time mother in Katmai. Evidently habituated to people, Sister was frequently seen at Brooks River during the next few summers. Her habituation would soon provide her with too-tempting opportunities to acquire easy meals.

On July 5, 1982, Sister and her two spring cubs from her second litter found an unattended backpack in the oxbow area upstream from the lodge. The backpack contained cookies, orange juice, used coffee cups, a thermos filled with coffee, a camera, and a .32 caliber pistol. The next day, she tore into an angler's unattended backpack that contained two salmon. Later that day, the family damaged an airplane float near the lodge that also contained salmon. On the morning of July 23, Sister climbed the elevated food cache at the campground and pulled down five backpacks from the storage area, and in mid-August, she took two backpacks from an unattended canoe.

The next year, Sister and her yearlings began where they had left off, and temptation remained everywhere. Around 11 a.m. on June 12, 1983, the bear family followed two anglers in the upper river. Around noon, they approached within 10 feet of an occupied tent in the campground. At 12:30 p.m., they found an unattended day pack on the riverbank while its owners sat on a rock in the river. The day pack contained no food, but the bears picked up a camera, nosed the pack, and looked at the two people for a few minutes before moving off downstream.

At about 1:00 p.m., the two anglers who had met the bears in the morning stopped to have a picnic lunch beneath the platform at Brooks Falls. When Sister and her yearlings found them, the anglers abandoned their food and moved away. The bears ate the rest of the picnic. Rewarded once again for the effort, the family approached another pair of anglers, who narrowly escaped by climbing a steep bank where a downed tree temporarily impeded Sister's progress.

The next day, Sister damaged two tents and other equipment in the campground. Even though none of those items contained food, park staff believed the family's behavior had progressed to a point in which they unacceptably threatened human safety. Superintendent David Morris gave the order to kill Sister.

Rangers set a trap, baited it with garbage, and waited for the family's arrival. By midafternoon, Sister had picked up the scent. When she arrived in the small, gravel-covered leach field near the NPS housing, rangers shot her and then hazed the yearlings away.

Sister wasn't the first bear killed by rangers at Brooks Camp but she was the last. For decades, Brooks Camp grappled with food and garbage management issues. The management response was often piecemeal, and the necessary cultural buy-in from visitors and staff was slow to evolve. Sister's death was entirely preventable and it sparked the rule changes that serve as the foundation of bear management at Brooks Camp today.

Adjusting to life at Brooks Camp can come as a shock. Upon arrival you're whisked into the visitor center for a mandatory "bear orientation" where a ranger instructs you to follow a peculiar set of guidelines.

You can't set anything down and walk away from it. And, really, this includes all your possessions. Your backpack stays on you or within arm's reach at all times. You don't leave shoes or anything else on your cabin porch. With large and potentially dangerous animals using people trails and passing through the lodge area, moving from place to place requires greater than usual attention to your surroundings. You walk in groups and talk to each other so you don't surprise bears. You stay 50 yards away from bears except when you're on the platforms.

Food and drink require especially careful consideration. They can only be prepared and consumed in designated picnic areas or inside of buildings. Outside these places, you cannot possess food, not even chewing gum or flavored drinks, except for the sole purpose of transporting it to a building or picnic area. Plain drinking water is fine, but eating a candy bar or anything else when not inside a building or at a picnic area equates to breaking the most sacred Brooks Camp taboo.

Do you plan to go fishing? All fishing must cease and all lures must be removed from the water when a bear is within 50 yards. All areas upstream of the bridge are catch-and-release only. Downstream of the bridge, anglers can only keep one fish per day. If you do keep a salmon, don't expect to enjoy it as part of your evening meal. It must be placed in a plastic bag and taken immediately to the Fish Freezing building to be stored until you depart. No public fish cleaning facilities are available. If you want to clean your fish, you have to travel outside the Brooks Camp Developed Area—the bureaucratic designation for the bear management area encompassing all land and water within 1.5 miles of Brooks Falls.

Got it? Good.

The rules are inconvenient but they work. Between 2003 and 2006, park wildlife biologist Tammy Olson and her staff documented only three incidents when a bear took a fish from an angler. Additional "fish stealing" events continue to happen, including several that I have witnessed, but they almost always occur when an angler is careless and continues to fish when a bear is too close. Other food-related incidents are even more rare.

Since the early 1980s, the culture around bear management has shifted from one blaming bears for "bear problems" to blaming people for "bear problems." However, that doesn't mean Brooks Camp's rules are universally accepted as necessary, especially regarding the infamous 50-yard rule.

There is no simple formula to determine how close people should approach bears. "However, a good barometer," as bear biologist Stephen Herrero explains, "is to not cause the bear to overtly react in any way." Without the ability to ensure that everyone who visits parks has a thorough understanding of bear behavior and the motivation to remain safely separated from the wildlife, some national park areas have defined an appropriate distance through regulation. At Denali National Park you cannot approach or engage in photography within 300 yards of a bear. Glacier National Park prohibits approaching, viewing, or engaging in any activity within 100 yards of bears or wolves. Yellowstone's wildlife distance regulation is probably most specific. It prohibits willfully approaching, remaining, viewing, or engaging in any activity within 100 yards of bears and wolves, "except when completely inside a legally positioned motor vehicle; within any distance that displaces or interferes with the free unimpeded movement of any wildlife; within any distance that creates or contributes to a potentially hazardous condition or situation; [and] failing to remove oneself to prescribed distances during inadvertent, accidental or surprise encounters with wildlife."

Katmai's wildlife distance regulation reflects the specific nature of bear encounters within the park. "Approaching a bear or any large mammal within 50 yards is prohibited. Continuing to occupy a position within 50 yards of a bear that is using a concentrated food source, including, but not limited to, animal carcasses, spawning salmon, and other feeding areas is prohibited." Exceptions include instances when people are "engaged in a legal hunt, on a designated bear viewing structure, in compliance with a written protocol approved by the Superintendent, or who are otherwise directed by a park employee."

Fifty yards seems about as arbitrary a distance as any other, but it was chosen, like those of other parks, as the minimal distance at which a bear is unlikely to react defensively. In the first systematic descriptions of brown bear social behavior, wildlife biologist Allan Egbert found most encounters between bears on sedge meadows at McNeil River were settled at distances of 50 meters or more, usually by one bear simply moving away. At Brooks River, bears that are separated by more than 50 yards almost always resolve their differences peaceably, typically with one bear departing voluntarily or letting the other pass at an appropriate distance. In contrast, grizzlies in Denali, Glacier, and Yellowstone usually have much larger personal space bubbles.

Violating a bear's personal space is risky business, and wildlife distance regulations are often framed around the need to protect human safety. Yet, the regulations are used to protect bears just as much as people. The closer we are to bears, especially outside of closely managed situations, the more likely we are to violate its space, cause it stress, and cause it to move away or react defensively.

A prior iteration of Katmai's wildlife distance regulation found in the park's archives was straightforward. In 1984 it stated, "No person may approach or remain within 50 yards of a bear except while on the bear-viewing platform at Brooks Falls." The current regulation makes a point of calling out a specific circumstance: You cannot remain within 50 yards of a bear using a concentrated food source. Although the presence of salmon clearly meets the intended definition of a concentrated food source, guides and longtime visitors who seek opportunities for close encounters conveniently ignore the provision, and lax enforcement tacitly allows it.

During one of my most recent trips to Brooks River, I watched a photographer position himself in an area of the river that is often used by bears. Shortly thereafter, a young subadult emerged from the trees and began to fish. The photographer had the opportunity to move away and do so safely to give the bear space, but he didn't. Instead, he kneeled and then lay on his stomach to improve his camera angle with the bear only 25 yards away.

Other than lying down, this strategy is incredibly common in Katmai. It gets people close to habituated bears but violates the spirit of the regulation, and it displaces nonhabituated bears from feeding areas. The rule's spirit, like those at other parks, isn't to prohibit people from standing their ground when they feel threatened by a bear (often a safe choice during a surprise encounter); it's to discourage people from unnecessarily risking their safety and disturbing wildlife. Purposefully placing yourself in a position where a bear is likely to travel, such as standing in the river, and remaining there even after you see the bear coming from a safe distance, is intended for thrill or photography, not for human safety or the welfare of bears.

Outright harassment of bears is thankfully uncommon in the park. Most visitors try to behave responsibly, but with relatively few rangers and little restrictions on where people can go, only a modest amount of unethical or dangerous behavior is necessary to have a disproportionately negative effect on bears. Many more bears might care about our proximity than we realize.

By using surgically implanted heart rate monitors on GPS-collared wild black bears, Mark Ditmer from the University of Minnesota and colleagues discovered that bears responded physiologically but not physically when they were approached by aerial drones. In all 17 drone flights, bears experienced elevated heart rates. The heart rate of a female with cubs increased 123 beats per minute above the predicted normal rate and didn't recover for 10 minutes after the drone left. However, despite their internal reactions, bears did not flee or increase their movements. A follow-up study on captive black bears found that they were able to habituate to drone flights over time, so their wild counterparts probably possess the same capacity. The habituation might also be context specific. A hovering drone is not an unpredictable human.

Bears live in a world of threat and bluff. They do not readily show their vulnerability or submission. Around people, they are more likely to project a calm demeanor even as warning lights flash in their brains and heart rates soar. As Katmai's Bear-Human Conflict Management Plan explains, "[Bears] must be pushed even to exhibit less dramatic, but fairly observable indicators of stress such as yawning or excessive salivating. Typically, when people approach too close, or try to displace bears by shouting, the bear will continue its behavior, but slightly alter its course, so that it does not appear submissive as it withdraws from the area. . . . This tendency for the bear to appear to feign disregard makes it easy for people harassing bears to argue, and even to convince themselves, that they did not change the bear's ongoing behavior."

Complicating wildlife distance issues is the rapidity in which people get used to bears. Habituation is a two-way street.

The trail to Brooks Falls is mild; its greatest physical barrier usually nothing more than a shallow pothole. The first time I walked it alone, however, I was filled with heightened anxiety. Every other spruce tree seemed to be cleaved by claws and teeth. Yard-wide animal trails with footprints as wide as dinner plates crisscrossed the forest floor. So focused on scanning for bears, I failed to hear the high-pitched whistling songs of the varied thrush or the hurried trill of yellow-rumped warblers.

A few days later, I hiked alone to the summit of Dumpling. I had seen bear sign along the way to the tundra-covered summit knob, mostly in the form of grass-filled scat, but it was not particularly fresh. Bears didn't appear to use this habitat nearly as much as the river corridor, and with greater lines of sight I felt more comfortable wandering alone. While this too was a novel experience, bears would not go unseen.

I walked over broken rocks covered in rock tripe, a lichen species resembling charcoaled potato chips, to the north edge of the summit knob and peered down a small cirque toward Naknek Lake. On a ridgeline leading to my vicinity, I caught sight of a bear silhouetted against the overcast sky. Alone and having not been issued bear spray, I carried no deterrents except my very much untested wits.

I followed the advice I had read or been given, at least what I could remember of it. I made noise and began moving away. I don't know whether the bear was curious, defensive, or indifferent, but it must've heard me. I shouted for five minutes as I hiked downslope.

I became more comfortable around bears during the next few weeks (thankfully, because a ranger who doesn't know what he is doing or is too nervous to set a good example is not an effective ranger), and I soon found myself enjoying the slow walk to the falls or up Dumpling. I looked for signs of bears with a feeling of companionship, as I still do. Knowing they inhabit the same places as me makes the landscape seem less lonesome.

My change in attitude, a personal habituation toward bears, is common at Brooks River. While the process took more than a month for me, it can occur surprisingly fast for other people. Human-to-bear habituation proceeds in the same manner as bear-to-human habituation. Namely, frequent and innocuous encounters lead to less overt reactions.

Shortly after arriving, you see a big scary-looking bear while walking from the lodge to the falls. Yet, it doesn't charge or attack. The experience is nerve-wracking, but you are fine. On the way back from the falls, you encounter a mother with cubs. She seems to mind her own business as well and disappears into the forest without incident. You are still fine. Wash. Rinse. Repeat. Eventually you become comfortable, perhaps even complacent, with the experience and so you are more willing to push boundaries that you wouldn't have pushed during your first bear encounters.

I've met and spoken to many visitors and employees who felt genuine concern for their safety after arriving, only to become quite relaxed in the company of bears. Repeat visitors rarely express concern about the close proximity to bears (it is often one of the reasons they return).

Bear-habituated humans present a strange dichotomy for rangers. On one hand, their relative calmness enhances their experience and sometimes that of others who might be nearby. No one particularly enjoys standing near someone commenting incessantly about their fear of bears or their willingness to kill one (the latter a bluster that often masks fear). However, with habituation a person's initial wariness can give way to a careless casualness. Habituated humans may approach bears unnecessarily, engage in risky behaviors near bears, and ignore a bear's warning signs. It's not danger through ignorance. It's danger in spite of knowing better.

The dilemma of habituated humans has been on the NPS's radar for decades. In 1989, Katmai Superintendent Ray Bane explained that within a short time, "people who arrived in terror of being attacked are confidently approaching bears or disdainfully dismissing them as nuisances." Almost 10 years later, bear biologists Christopher Servheen and John Schoen, when describing human-to-bear habituation at Brooks Camp, wrote that habituated bears "are often described as 'cute' by people and these people tend to lose their common sense by getting too close."

A most extreme version of the habituated human manifested in Timothy Treadwell, the brown bear advocate who, along with Amie Huguenard, was mauled and killed by bears at Kaflia Bay on Katmai's coast in 2003. Treadwell underwent his own process of habituation that, according to his book, *Among Grizzlies: Living with Wild Bears in Alaska*, happened after only a few close encounters.

I don't wish to rehash his story. It's been covered thoroughly in film and in print. I only bring him into the conversation because Treadwell's behavior was not as unique as the media portrayed it to be. Uncommon? Certainly, but he was not the last person who sought the close company of Katmai's bears or placed themselves in compromising positions near them. Some guides openly brag about it, referring to themselves as "bear whisperers." Others show their bravado by behaving questionably around bears and posting photos of it online. Spend any significant time at Brooks River during the bear-watching seasons and you'll see staff, private guides, and visitors frequently violating a bear's personal space, either out of disregard for the bear's needs or a mistaken attitude that the bear doesn't care.

Treadwell's death was tragic, but he was right to promote the idea that we should respect bears, not fear them. He failed to adhere to his own mantra, unfortunately, when he didn't respect their space. Any overly habituated human risks the same.

In a morning meeting, we discuss options to deal with 273. We agree she must be hazed more thoroughly, but we do not agree on the methods. Some argue that her behavior justifies the use of nonlethal projectiles— rubber bullets, beanbag rounds, and such. The problem with those, as I saw it, was the potential for things to go wrong too quickly. Rubber bullets and beanbag rounds require lethal backup; shotguns loaded with lead slugs in case the nonlethal rounds trigger an aggressive response. It seemed unnecessary to risk killing 273 for tearing some tarpaper off an old cabin, so I argued against it. I thought we needed a more consistent and united response—more people keeping watch and more people using low-level hazing techniques anytime 273 approached the buildings. She could be taught to stay away.

Because bears are smart and risk averse, if we make the things we don't want them to do difficult and the things we want them to do easy, then bears will typically choose the latter. This is the philosophy behind aversive conditioning, a process that pairs a negative stimulus such as pain or loud noise with an undesirable behavior. Like the reverse of Pavlov's dog, instead of involuntarily drooling at the sound of a metronome, bears can be taught to avoid certain places and behaviors if they learn to associate the experience with something uncomfortable.

At Brooks Camp, hazing is used to apply aversive conditioning and teach bears a code of conduct. The task most often falls to rangers known as "bear technicians" who patrol the lodge and visitor center areas to protect buildings from bears and reduce the frequency of bears moving through that area. Since bears can habituate to hazing, Katmai's bear techs have found it most prudent to haze using low-level techniques such as yelling, foot-stomping, and standing their ground before resorting to loud noise makers, pepper spray, and finally deterrent rounds. Although yelling and clapping may be considered low-level hazing, they require an advanced knowledge of bear behavior, and more than a little confidence, to perform correctly. And, absurd as it may sound, bear techs often haze while working solo and usually with nothing more than their experience and a holstered can of bear pepper spray for protection, underscoring the generally mild-mannered nature of Brooks Camp's bears. While I never enjoyed hazing—I was usually pulled reluctantly into such affairs—I've worked with several people who found it an adventurous and worthwhile vocation.

We couldn't haze 273 just anywhere. She had to be caught in the act of doing something we'd rather not allow her to do. Otherwise, she would only learn that people dressed in green and gray uniforms are obnoxious. Or worse, our hazing would be too effective and discourage her from accessing the river where she needed to feed. So we waited for her to arrive at camp.

She and her cub show up late that morning. After fishing near the bridge, she exits the water and walks toward camp. Five rangers, including myself and some armed with shotguns, stand at the base of the hillock below the lodge gift shop. To our right, I see the shack where, just a day or two before, 273 clawed off the tarpaper siding then removed and chewed on life jackets and rubber boots.

By staging ourselves in her potential path, we posed a visual, olfactory, and dominance barrier. We couldn't compete with 273 physically, and she required additional respect because she was a current mother. Our intent, therefore, was to draw a line in the sand and bluff her into thinking we were more dominant.

Keeping the lodge and visitor center area clear of bears has been a mul-tidecadal, yet unachievable, goal for the NPS. The facilities occupy natural travel corridors that bears use when moving between the river and the lake. Bear techs must devote near-constant attention to this area to catch a fraction of the successful or attempted ursine trespasses. Since there aren't enough bear techs to patrol the boundaries of camp 24 hours a day, nor would it be safe to do at night, the true frequency of bears trespassing in camp is not known, but it happens hundreds of times per year.

The NPS accepts the hazing of bears for the protection of property as one of the costs of occupying Brooks Camp. Since 1998, though, Katmai's bear management plan has included the option to haze for the convenience of park operations. Bear techs are commonly asked to implement this pol-icy. They are required to haze bears from the 100-yard section of beach between the visitor center and lodge solely so that concessioner floatplanes can park there. (The Naknek Lake beach north of the river is half a mile long.) And, although a newly constructed elevated bridge has reduced the frequency of Brooks Camp's infamous bear jams, they still occur. When a bear decides to rest along a roadway or trail, preventing tourists or workers from reaching their destination, bear techs will sometimes haze bears to move them out of the way so traffic can flow again.

Seeing my coworkers and friends placed in these positions, and sometimes participating in it as well, I've often wondered how much risk is appropriate in order to provide convenience. If the concessioner and park workforce accepted these delays as a cost of doing business, then it's likely that bear techs would not be tasked with hazing for convenience. A small, yet not insignificant number of park and concession staff view most any bear-caused delay as unacceptable. Commercial interests hold considerable political sway over the park too. Congresspersons and senators are not shy about expressing the concern that a government bureaucracy has wronged their constituents. At Brooks Camp, being wronged is frequently defined as the inconvenience and delay caused by a bear jam.

Hazing can be largely ineffectual with extremely habituated bears. Four-ten became so used to our bluffs that she almost always ignored it. Escalating the level of hazing to deterrent rounds might've worked, but bears can habituate to these techniques or simply learn to avoid the people who threaten them with it. Then there's the element of safety regarding firearm use in a place where it is difficult to know where all people are located. As a result, bear techs rarely consider the use of deterrent rounds.

From the perspective of human and bear safety, the modern bear management program has been very successful. Since the Huckabee attack in 1966, only two people have been injured by bears at Brooks Camp, and thankfully both incidents resulted in minor injuries. After Sister's death in 1983 no bears have been killed by people. Visitor education and relatively strict regulations have played an important role in the effort, but we also need to acknowledge the temperament of the bear population in reducing bear and human conflict. Between 2003 and 2006, bear management staff recorded more than 1,700 bear and human interactions, but only 49 bears directly or aggressively approached people, and 45 percent of those involved anglers, who not coincidentally occupy the same places where bears need to fish.

Over the same time span, park staff documented more than 1,000 instances of bears trespassing or attempting to trespass in Brooks Camp. NPS personnel hazed bears in over 600 of those instances. Most of the rest of the trespasses were learned about after the fact. There were 49 documented accounts of NPS personnel hazing bears to open trails and roads, or so that people could access parked aircraft.

Although recent history suggests the experience and work environment at Brooks Camp will remain relatively safe, I worry. No injuries to people or bears are acceptable, yet each summer we play with fire near a pile of oily rags.

The five of us present a united front as 273 and her cub approach the lodge. She reaches the trail junction not 25 yards from our position and faces a choice. Turn right and go to the beach where she can walk but may not be allowed to rest. Turn left and perhaps find a secure location to hide in the forest or the marsh. Or, challenge our presence on the hill.

I cannot know for sure if our presence helps her make the decision, but she chooses option two before we need to consider raising our voices, scuffing our feet on the gravel, or sounding an air horn. I catch glimpses of her shoulder hump projecting above the grass as she enters a willow and alder thicket behind infrastructure that is representative of Brooks Camp's ongoing and impossible struggle to prevent bears from damaging human property. Two-seven-three avoids the sagging electric fence protecting a sump pit for the sewage system. Next to the fence, at the former site of a screen-covered fish cleaning shed, she walks behind the Fish Freezing building, its log frame scarred with claw and bite marks.

We watch the grass rustle as the family beds down for a nap a scant 30 yards from the lodge gift shop. Once again, rangers are forced into an awkward compromise. One or two of us keep watch while business as usual goes on. Tourists enter and exit the gift shop and adjacent lodge office. To reach the river, they follow the trail whence 273 came, all the while a mother bear and her cub sleep less than a stone's throw away.

CHAPTER 17

CLIMATE

I could hardly believe the weather. On July 4, 2019, the weather station at the visitor center, located 30 feet in the air, records a high temperature of 87°F. Closer to ground level, the thermometer at the lodge climbs to 90°F, while the airport at King Salmon reaches 89°F, an all-time record high for the community. While watching bears at the falls that evening, I stand nearly stationary for three hours and can't stop sweating. Today is the hottest day I ever experienced at Brooks River.

Under sunny skies, the heat persists over the next week and sunburned tourists begin to circulate in large numbers. The bears cope by seeking cooler conditions in deep shade or by resting in the river. Their meals become more infrequent as a dramatic spike in water temperature begins to affect the salmon. On July 6, the run begins to slow, and on July 7 it stops. Through July 10, I see very few salmon move upstream or stage in the lower river. The run has evaporated at the time of year when it normally peaks.

The heat wave's effects are widespread across Alaska, a landmass more than twice as large as Texas. Chum and king salmon in the Yukon and Kuskokwim rivers turn belly up and die as water temperatures exceed their thermal tolerance. Large numbers of pink salmon die in tributaries of Norton Sound. Anchorage records the first 90°F temperature in the city's history.

Large wildfires spread throughout the state's south-central and interior regions, plunging air quality in nearby communities to levels among the lowest on Earth.

July 2019 was an incredible month for the state and the world. Its first week was Alaska's warmest week ever recorded. The month was the warmest month ever for the state. Worldwide, July 2019 was the hottest month in recorded history during the second hottest year in recorded history. The average global air temperature approached 2°F warmer than the 20th-century average.

The greenhouse effect is a natural phenomenon through which heat-trapping gases in the atmosphere insulate the planet from the vacuum of space. Sunlight warms Earth's surface. The infrared energy radiating back into the atmosphere is partly absorbed by greenhouse gases like water vapor, carbon dioxide, and methane. By burning fossil fuels such as coal and oil as well as through land use changes like deforestation, we've released excess carbon dioxide into the atmosphere and effectively increased the atmosphere's insulating properties, forcing the climate to warm.

With carbon dioxide emissions continuing to rise, Alaska's anomalously hot and dry summer of 2019 portends the near future. No place on the planet will be spared the consequences of human-driven climate change. Its fingers have already begun to reshape Katmai, and the park will emerge a different place in its wake.

Robert Griggs and his National Geographic Society expeditions visited Katmai when the landscape remained wounded from the 1912 eruption. Reaching the Valley of Ten Thousand Smokes from Shelikof Strait was an arduous endeavor, so after realizing the relative ease in which the Valley could be reached from the west, some of the last National Geographic Society expeditions to the area utilized Naknek Lake as their preferred travel corridor. In the lakes region, they hunted bears, chased waterfowl, and became infatuated with the scenery.

Lowland areas near the lakes also offered another contrast from the ash-covered Pacific coastline. It remained blanketed with plant life. Travel through Katmai's forest and thicket was often difficult, but the effort of bushwhacking eased for crews when they reached higher elevations or explored the Bristol Bay lowlands to the west. Granitic ridges bordering Lake Grosvenor were mostly bare. Trees were absent from elevations above 800 feet on Dumpling. Farther west, Jasper Sayre, one of the botanical assistants dispatched to the Valley by Griggs in 1918, photographed little more than sapling birch and spruce growing on the tundra near the future site of King Salmon.

During the 100 years since, the growth of woody vegetation has expanded markedly across the area. Alder and willow thickets have exploded in abundance along the coastline. The tree line has steadily crept upslope. In the lowlands west of the park, more trees than ever before grow where tundra had historically predominated, and vegetation is greening earlier in the spring.

Along the Pacific coastline, as much as 3 feet of ash buried the original soil surface, and acid rain devastated what stood above. Many of the vegetative changes we see there today are attributable to normal recovery from the eruption's effects. Upwind of the eruptive center, however, ashfall was considerably less. Thirty miles from Novarupta, about 6 inches of ash coated Brooks River. In King Salmon, 60 miles away, 1 to 2 inches covered the ground, and little more than a trace blanketed Naknek on the shore of Bristol Bay. Ashfall and other volcanic effects, therefore, were unlikely to have been a reason for the lack of vegetation photographed by Sayre and Griggs along the lakes and farther west. Then, as it remains today, climate exerted a stronger, long-term influence.

The Katmai region harbors the southern extension of a longitudinal tree line that stretches north through western Alaska to the Noatak and Kobuk regions above the Arctic Circle. East of the divide lies a vast boreal forest. To the west, tundra and scattered shrublands spread to the Bering Sea coast. Weather, wildfire, soil conditions, and the length of the growing season drive the vegetative differences between the two environments. Summer soil temperatures, for example, have been historically too chilly to support the growth of spruce trees in the lowland areas near Bristol Bay.

As Alaska's climate warms, higher summer temperatures and a longer growing season may at first seem to be a good thing for trees, but tree growth is influenced by a myriad of interwoven factors that paint a much more complicated picture. Since the 1970s, the growth of white spruce has slowed in Interior Alaska as summer temperatures creep above the ideal temperature range for the species. The temperature increase causes drought stress in the trees either through reduced soil moisture or excessive evaporation from the needles. More frequent fires are also suppressing regeneration of spruce. Interior Alaska now has less acreage of older spruce forest and more postfire, early-successional vegetation such as willow and aspen than it did prior to 1990. The combined changes may become severe enough to cause a wide swath of Alaska, from the interior south to the Kenai Peninsula, to exchange much of its boreal forest for habitats like grasslands that are better adapted to frequent fire and drought.

Western Alaska's forests are on a different climate-driven trajectory. White spruce is a relatively recent addition to the King Salmon area, having established its presence sometime around the beginning of the 1800s. The warmer climatic conditions over the last few decades have raised soil and summer temperatures to within a more ideal range for white spruce in this area. These changes represent the beginning of many biome shifts that will transform Alaska's ecosystems.

As the forest in and around Katmai expands into previously unoccupied territory, its trees also experience forces that work to halt their growth. In 2007, the canopy of spruce along the Brooks Falls Trail reached 40 feet high. Their needles intercepted so much sunlight that only shade-tolerant plants survived in the understory. Along the trail to the falls, I enjoyed the company of ephemeral wildflowers and the spongy mosses that grew between the trees. The spruce, however, were under attack.

Aided by warm spring and summer temperatures, crops of bark beetles invaded the trees. Despite their 1/4-inch-long size, spruce bark beetles have a tremendous ability to alter forest habitats. Adults burrow into a tree's inner bark to mate and lay eggs. After hatching, larvae eat their way around the trees, feeding on the thin living layer of tissue between the tree's outer bark and the heartwood underneath. When larvae numbers reach a critical mass their galleries girdle the tree, preventing it from passing water and nutrients up and down its trunk. Severe beetle outbreaks can quickly kill large numbers of spruce.

The recent outbreak was driven by a series of warm springtime conditions, which allowed overwintering adult beetles to disperse and enter trees while the soil remained frozen, compromising the spruces' ability to transport sap and defend itself from the attack. The beetles gained an overwhelming advantage over their hosts as the outbreak expanded from one to two to three summers. The trees became scorched, almost kiln-dried, by the attack. Their dark green needles faded to a brittle, rusty-brown as the life drained from their tissues. Today, they stand as bare skeletons or lie in tangled heaps on the forest floor.

Spruce bark beetles are native to Katmai and just about everywhere spruce grow. This wasn't the first outbreak to occur in the area. Tree-ring analysis indicates the forest had sustained several other beetle outbreaks in the past 200 years, but this one was particularly intense, wiping out almost every mature spruce within miles of the river.

In the aftermath, light flooded to the forest floor. Long dormant and sun-starved plants flourished. Thickets of willow, birch, and bluejoint grass currently grow where I kneeled to observe various *Pyrolas* and bunchberry dogwood. Berry plants such as currants, highbush cranberry, and elderberry have also used the opportunity to thrive where few had grown before. During warm summers—conditions that will very likely become the norm in coming decades—berries are ripening earlier too, potentially altering the foraging choices of bears.

I considered my berry-picking excursions on Dumpling as somewhat of an annual ritual. Each August, I followed the seldom-maintained trail from the campground through the head-high cow parsnip and bluejoint grass to reach the alder thickets, meadows, and finally mountaintop tundra.

Cladonia, the reindeer lichen, its branches reminiscent of sun-bleached caribou antlers, filled gaps between stems of evergreen plants such as black crowberry and alpine azalea. Autumn arrives early on the mountaintop and the foliage of arctic willow and Kamchatka rhododendron beamed their respective vivid yellow and crimson. While I enjoyed these sights, my search was focused on tiny glaucous-blue orbs, the blueberries of *Vaccinium uliginosum*.

A fine line exists between gathering blueberries when they are perfectly ripe and too soft, so I sometimes checked my picking areas two or three times before committing to the harvest. With *V. uliginosum* growing as a ground-creeping shrub, harvest is a hands-and-knees effort and I often needed a couple of hours to collect a gallon of berries. (Yeah, I like blueberries.) Even so, the trip usually cost me little more than a spare morning or afternoon, and I could rely on my cabin's well-stocked pantry to meet my caloric needs if I returned empty-handed. But bears that miss out on this meal face a different set of consequences.

Berries and salmon represent the only regularly abundant, highly digestible, and energy-rich foods for bears in the Brooks River area. Historically, the availability of these foods has been temporally staggered. Salmon become widely available in early to mid-August. As the runs dwindle and play out, berries come into season and many bears switch from fishing to berry harvesting. The warming climate, though, could cause these previously asynchronous foods to overlap in availability.

On a section of Kodiak Island, biologist William Deacy and colleagues found the timing of elderberry ripeness varied considerably. Since 1949, it ranged between July 14 and September 28, but the berries typically ripened in mid-August. Salmon spawning activity was relatively consistent and far more constrained in its timing, ranging between July 19 and August 2. During recent years with anomalously high spring air temperatures, elderberries ripened several weeks earlier than average and coincided with midsummer salmon runs. Bears were suddenly faced with a choice between foods and many, surprisingly, switched from eating salmon to elderberries.

The change seems counterintuitive given that salmon provide a much denser bundle of energy than berries. But recall a diet balanced in protein, sugar, and fat allows bears to gain body mass more quickly than any of those foods alone. Deacy argues that the bears' search for the optimal macronutrient ratio will lead some bears to abandon salmon fishing in exchange for berry harvesting, potentially disrupting the trophic cascade in which bears disperse salmon nutrients across terrestrial habitats. The synchronization of two key foods also reduces the duration of total food availability. Instead of having the opportunity to forage on salmon for two to three weeks and then on berries for a few more, both can arrive at the same time. Whether overall food availability or the duration of availability matters more to bears remains an open question as do the ecosystem-wide consequences of fewer bears feeding on salmon.

From a population perspective, Katmai's brown bears are well positioned to weather climate warming and shifts in food availability due to their omnivory. Salmon, however, may not be able to dodge the sword of climate change so easily.

On July 8, well within the midst of the heat wave, I task myself with cleaning the underwater webcam after a crud of algae blooms on its lens. Since the webcam is located too far below the deck of the bridge for me to reach, I'll need to get wet to access it. I take off my shoes, leave them safely stashed on the elevated bridge, and wade up to my armpits in the river.

Typical summer weather at Brooks River is cool and damp. Sunny or partly cloudy days are recorded only one day in five. In the mid-20th century, the area averaged only five days in July when the air temperature exceeded 70°F, and the average monthly temperatures for June, July, and August were 50°, 54°, and 54°F, respectively.

During a normally overcast day, with a breeze off the lake and air temperatures in the 50s or 60s, my tolerance for a fully immersive cold water experience would be limited to a few minutes before signs of hypothermia would begin to take hold. I'd feel some effects, like numbing feet and hands, almost immediately. Depending on the depth and duration of the task, I may not enter the water without a dry suit and a layer of fleece pants underneath.

When I enter the river after it has cooked for almost a week under sunny skies and daytime air temperatures well above 80°F, I feel no discomfort. My fingers and toes retain their full dexterity and sensation, and the involuntary gasp that accompanies a sudden plunge into cold water doesn't materialize. With two staff watching for the approach of bears, I work quickly, but cleaning the camera lens this time is a surprisingly refreshing and comfortable task.

The typical weather patterns over Katmai and Bristol Bay have provided salmon with ideal migrating and spawning conditions for thousands of years, and the fish have evolved to thrive in cold, highly oxygenated water. The heat wave, however, was producing water temperatures that were outright dangerous (Figure 1).

On July 1, an automated temperature logger located at the outlet of Lake Brooks where the river begins recorded an average daily water temperature of 61°F, while the high was 66°. On July 4, the average temperature climbed above 66°F, and from July 6 to July 12 it averaged more than 70°. During this latter stretch, which represented the height of the heat wave, daytime high water temperatures exceeded 76°F for six consecutive days and low temperatures remained above 70° during four days. At 6 p.m. on July 7, the data logger recorded a daily high of 78.5°F. The next day at 6 p.m., the water temperature reached a tropical 79.6°F.

For salmon, water temperatures at this level are more than simply uncomfortable. Depending on a salmon's prior acclimation, thermal stress

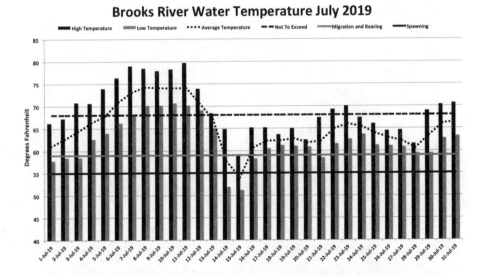

Figure 1: Average water temperatures (dotted line) at the head of Brooks River exceeded the State of Alaska's water temperature threshold for freshwater fish migration (solid gray horizontal line) on all but two days in July 2019. The average daily water temperature exceeded the state's "not to exceed at any time" threshold (dashed horizontal line) from July 6 to 12. Vertical bars represent daily high and low water temperatures.

can set in at temperatures as low as 63°F, and a salmon's migration can cease when temperatures reach the upper 60s and low 70s. Besides delaying migration and spawning, elevated water temperatures deplete a salmon's energy stores by increasing the fish's metabolism and need for oxygen. It can cause their eggs to deform and can decrease the viability of their sperm, while infection and disease can gain a foothold more easily and spread more quickly. Warmer water also holds less dissolved oxygen, making it harder for salmon to breathe. Finally, if the water temperature rises high enough, it can kill otherwise healthy fish.

Upstream migration and spawning is the most energetically demanding time in a salmon's life, and the river's temperatures tested their resiliency like never before. The sockeye responded by pausing the run. They sought refuge in Naknek Lake below the thermocline where conditions were closer to optimal for their respiratory and metabolic needs. Salmon resumed their migration only after the heat wave broke. Most salmon likely made their final destinations, but the warm conditions continued for much of the rest of the summer and delayed spawning in many streams.

Although lakes in the region provided salmon with a refuge during the worst of the heat wave, these water bodies are also warming. Over 60 years, springtime air temperatures have increased in the Iliamna Lake area, resulting in a trend toward a longer ice-free season and a longer growing season for plankton. The warming trend, so far, has likely improved fresh-water habitat conditions for juvenile sockeye. They are growing faster, and a higher proportion of smolts are leaving fresh water for the sea after one year rather than two years. Yet, adults are not returning at younger ages. Ocean conditions could be the biggest wildcard affecting change in Kat-mai's ecosystems.

The oceans have absorbed 25 to 30 percent of all anthropogenic carbon emissions since the industrial revolution. This has slowed the rate of atmospheric warming. More carbon dioxide (CO_2) in the oceans means less available CO_2 to warm the atmosphere, but it also comes at a high price. Carbon dioxide entering the ocean is increasing the acidity of the water.

When atmospheric CO_2 enters the oceans, it combines with water to form carbonic acid (H_2CO_3). Most of the carbonic acid then breaks down into bicarbonate (HCO_3^-) and releases a free hydrogen atom. The latter serves to lower ocean pH levels as it seeks a home and combines with carbonate ions (CO_3^{2-}) to form more bicarbonate.

Surface ocean waters have increased in acidity by about 0.11 pH units since the beginning of the industrial revolution. Because the pH scale is logarithmic, not linear, a change of one pH unit, from 8 (slightly alkaline) to 7 (neutral) for example, corresponds to an order of magnitude change in acidity. Therefore, a 0.11 pH decrease is a solution 30 percent more acidic than before. Under high CO_2 emission scenarios, the acidity of the ocean is projected to increase nearly 150 percent by the end of the 21st century relative to preindustrial levels, a level of acidity that the oceans haven't experienced in 20 million years.

The issue with ocean acidification isn't that we will notice. A person taking a swim at the beach won't feel a difference. For small sea creatures that rely on calcium carbonate to build their shells, however, the souring of the seas will create a significant hardship, one with ramifications that domino up the food chain.

Pteropods are planktonic, free-swimming snails. Along with other zooplankton, they play a large role in the health of ocean food webs. In the North Pacific, pteropods compose more than 60 percent of the diet of juvenile pink salmon in some years. They are also eaten by some krill species, which are one of the most important foods for sockeye.

Since ocean water is normally supersaturated with calcium carbonate, pteropods sequester ample amounts of it to support their shells, keeping their populations healthy and abundant. With ocean acidification, however, high latitude regions are projected to become undersaturated in calcium carbonate minerals such as aragonite as early as 2050. Some pteropods are already showing signs of severe shell dissolution in the ocean off the US West Coast. If pteropods do not adapt to living in those conditions, their ranges will contract to lower latitudes and possibly away from areas used by sea-faring salmon. The oceans will become less suitable to the survival of salmon even as there are no visible changes to the water that we can see.

At the same time, sea surface temperatures may further restrict where salmon can survive. Given what we know about the thermal tolerances of salmon and their preferred marine habitats during the 1980s and comparing that to different carbon emission scenarios for the mid- and late 21st century, Omar Abdul-Aziz and colleagues from the University of Washington concluded that by 2080 increased sea surface temperatures in the North Pacific will reduce sockeye habitat by as much as 50 percent in July and 41 percent in December. While conditions in parts of the Arctic Ocean could become more amenable to sockeye and other salmon, the gains in the Arctic would not make up for the habitat losses farther south. The highest CO_2 emission scenarios would result in ocean warming that would completely eliminate the Gulf of Alaska as a rearing area for seagoing sockeye salmon. During that dystopian future, if sockeye and Chinook salmon still found suitable spawning habitat in British Columbia and the US West Coast, they would be forced to migrate across large areas of the Pacific unfavorable to their survival.

Humans have already burned enough fossil fuels to push average global surface temperatures about 1°C above preindustrial levels. The effects of climate change are already pronounced across Alaska, including in King Salmon where the average annual air temperatures from 1947 to 2018 show an increase of 4.8°F over that time period. Chinook, chum, coho, and sockeye salmon in Alaska are now smaller than they were historically, with the rate of decline having accelerated since the year 2000 due to climate and competition at sea. The growing intensity of heat waves, droughts, wildfires, and floods—all fueled by warmer atmospheric and ocean conditions— serve as a prelude for the future. No matter our efforts to mitigate climate change (and we must do so), we've already set an unalterable course toward a warmer world, one in which national parks will become different places than we have come to know. Instead of trying to preserve parks as a form of ecological museum, the NPS has increasingly begun to manage park landscapes for continuous change.

On Lake Superior, warmer winters and a lack of ice bridges have increasingly isolated Isle Royale National Park's wolves from the mainland. Without the periodic immigration of mainland wolves into the park, Isle Royale's wolves became inbred and the population began to die. To stave off the local extinction and restore the population, the NPS captured and transported wolves from nearby mainland areas to Isle Royale.

But why intervene on the behalf of wolves at all? Wolves, as a species, don't need Isle Royale to survive. As the NPS reasons, it's less for them and more for the park. Without wolf predation to suppress the moose population, plant communities would shift dramatically. Heavy browsing pressure from moose would cause a cascade of effects and perhaps cause the island's vegetation to become less resilient in the face of climate change.

Scenarios like that of Isle Royale will only become more common in our parks as we continue to fragment habitat, accidentally introduce and promote the spread of non-native species, and change the climate. Not that we want it to be this way. Ideally park ecosystems would remain healthy enough and function normally enough so native species and biodiversity are protected without our heavy-handed interventions, but unless we shift our priorities dramatically then we'll find ourselves stepping in at ever-increasing rates. National parks were never truly "vignettes of primitive America." They are vignettes of what humans have chosen to save.

The heat wave breaks on July 12 as a storm front pushes across the region. An easterly wind stirs the lakes and drizzle dampens the land. Salmon that schooled near the river mouth in Naknek Lake begin to surge upstream. I watch the run gain momentum that evening. One dozen, then two dozen fish jump each minute. Just after 9 p.m., with the air temperature dipping to near 60°F, I make my last count for the day. One hundred and twenty fish attempted the leap; eight of those found success.

We can never know precisely how climate change will alter Katmai until it happens, but the heat wave provided a glimpse of the conditions bears and salmon will experience more frequently in the near future. Summer 2019 was anomalously hot from a 20th-century perspective, but by the end of this century, it will be average or even cooler than average. Summer heat that threatens to undo the salmon migration will be a recurring event. Even so, Katmai is poised to remain resilient in a rapidly changing world. Outside of a few isolated pockets, non-native species have yet to gain much of a foothold, offering us a chance to prevent future arrivals and control the spread of existing introductions. The region's clean, deep lakes provide sockeye salmon refuge during extreme conditions. Its bears are adaptable enough to exploit new opportunities if fewer traditional foods are available.

Katmai's size and well-preserved landscapes will buffer against effects that smaller protected areas cannot weather as well. Its wildness will remain even as its landscape shifts to something different. How much change we are willing to impose on this place and the planet is a decision entirely within our control.

CHAPTER 18

CHALLENGE

A 1,200 foot-long, immaculate new bridge spans Brooks River. Beginning at the lodge, the 8- to 10-foot-high bridge extends southward over a soupy marsh and across the main river channel. Constructed in the winter and spring of 2019, it offers tremendous views of the lower river, Dumpling Mountain, and Naknek Lake. Spacious platforms extend off its middle and south sections, providing ample room to watch bears in comfort. Compared to its predecessor, the new bridge adds a layer of convenience never seen here before.

The National Park Service and the Alaska congressional delegation speak proudly of what the bridge offers. During an early July 2019 ribbon-cutting ceremony, Lucy Murfitt, a staffer for US Senator Lisa Murkowski, said that with the new bridge "bear jams are going to be a thing of the past." Bert Frost, director of the NPS Alaska Region, took the podium to explain the NPS has "two missions" and called the bridge "the essence of what the National Park Service is about."

The bridge, however, is less of a balance between wildlife protection and visitor enjoyment, and more of a forced compromise imposed on wildlife. After decades of debate about what we will allow Brooks River to be, the NPS has established that at the most famous bear-viewing site in the world, human convenience continues to come first.

A few days after the polite applause and giant ceremonial scissors welcomed people to enjoy the new bridge, I linger on the platform attached to its south end. A mother bear and two yearlings swim through the main upstream channel, while a mom and a single yearling rest on the far side of the river mouth. A pile of people forms at the ramp behind me, bear jammed by two subadults resting on the road.

While waiting for the bear jam to clear and looking for a better view of the mom and yearling, seven people descend the stairs from the bridge and walk to the river mouth. At the lakeshore, they turn left onto a spit of gravel and proceed to the water's edge.

Their position on the spit is compromised when the subadult sisters, 909 and 910, arrive on the beach behind them. A low rise of gravel separates the people from the bears, and although I can see all of them, they clearly can't see each other. The group keeps its attention focused across the river until the twins walk into view. With the bears about 25 to 30 yards away, a reluctant do-si-do follows, with five of the seven visitors departing slowly. Two decide there's no rush and eagerly snap photos of the bears along the shoreline.

Rangers see all of this, but their hands are full trying to manage the people closer to the bridge and they seem reluctant to encourage people to stay on the elevated deck. I didn't want to spend my time watching people unnecessarily close to bears, so I wander, a bit frustrated, into camp only to stumble into a more chaotic scene.

One-seven-one has treed her two spring cubs in a balsam poplar about 15 feet from an entrance to the lodge dining hall. As I approach the lodge, two rangers try to corral people, but they're losing the battle. Utility vehicles, staff, and tourists wander to the beach, not 40 yards from the bears. At the same time a mother and her two yearlings walk along the lake's edge. They swing behind the tail of a floatplane just as the pilot starts the engine. Startled, the family turns into the trees and runs within 30 yards of where I stand.

The bedlam cools after the second family departs. However, 171 and her cubs remain on the other side of the lodge, so I join a ranger escort along the beach to reach a destination farther away from the mayhem. Returning to the visitor center a half-hour later, I encounter a temporary wooden barricade plastered with a laminated sign. "Stop. Area behind this sign closed due to bear activity."

The morning was foggy, delaying flights from King Salmon, so now, around 1 p.m., the camp area is especially busy. About 35 people fill the orientation room inside the visitor center, a scant 50 yards from 171. They'll soon graduate from bear school to find their easiest and most obvious route to the lodge and falls blocked. Another 20 people mingle outside the visitor center, waiting their turn to attend the orientation. Several anglers and day-trippers eat lunch in the picnic area across the trail. On the far side of the lodge, maybe 30 yards from 171, guests and staff shuffle about with the business of the hour. Inside the lodge, lunch-goers feast with a mother bear a few feet outside the window.

By now, I'm looking to return to the bridge area, so I decide to try an alternative route. Following a path heading perpendicular to the lakeshore, I bear left at the park's auditorium to a series of guest cabins overlooking the river, only to find this route would also bring me too close to the family. I stall at the porch of a cabin where the current tenants politely allow me to stand and view the bears.

One-seven-one huffs frequently as she stands guard below her two cubs. They cling to a crook in the tree trunk about 30 feet above the ground. After a quiet moment, one cub gains the courage to descend. Proceeding butt first, it uses its sharp claws to bite into the tree bark. It's nearly to the ground when a plane engine chokes to life. The propeller wash sweeps through the trees and over the family. The cub scurries back up the trunk.

The attention that swarms Brooks Camp today is a far cry from the dearth of federal resources devoted to the area after the monument's creation. For the first 30 years of Katmai National Monument's existence—a time frame described by historian Frank Norris as Katmai's "Era of Neglect"—very few tourists made their way to Katmai, and the NPS could hardly get itself to pay attention to what was then the nation's largest national monument. The NPS had tried, from time to time, to secure funding for a ranger to patrol the monument, but Congress repeatedly rebuffed the request. When Victor

Cahalane and Mount McKinley National Park Superintendent Frank Been explored Katmai in the fall of 1940, they were the first NPS personnel to visit the monument on foot. Another 10 years would pass before any rangers would find a home here, and only after an entrepreneur approached the NPS with a novel idea.

Ray Petersen started flying in southwest Alaska in 1935. An ardent fisherman, he soon became familiar with the exceptional quality of Katmai's angling opportunities and began flying salmon cannery superintendents to Brooks River so they could also enjoy the experience of casting their lines in pristine waters. Looking to expand his small regional flight service, Northern Consolidated Airlines, into the tourism business, Petersen approached the NPS in the winter of 1949–50 with a proposal to develop two fishing camps in Katmai—Coville Camp on the west end of Lake Grosvenor and Brooks Camp at the outlet of Brooks River.

Petersen's offer was timely for the NPS. Officers and enlisted men stationed at the Naknek Air Base had increasingly sought Brooks River's fishing opportunities since the station opened in 1941, but reports from US Fish and Wildlife Service researchers suggested the level of catch-and-keep fishing pressure was unsustainable. Without funding to hire rangers for the monument, the NPS was in no position to enforce fishing regulations or encourage a conservation-based fishing ethic.

Meanwhile, many local residents and state officials questioned the monument's existence. In 1947, the Alaska Territory's governor Ernest Gruening and congressional delegate Edward Bartlett suggested the monument be eliminated. Their calls echoed the sentiments of a former territorial governor, Thomas Riggs, who in 1920 claimed, "Katmai National Monument serves no purpose and should be abolished." If tourist lodges were established within Katmai's boundaries, then the NPS hoped the clientele would embrace conservation principles, visitors from across the nation would see the monument's value, and Katmai's existence as a protected area would finally be legitimized.

Brooks Camp opened for business in the summer of 1950 and the NPS assigned William Nancarrow to become Katmai's first ranger that summer. The scenery, fishing opportunities, and remoteness of Brooks Camp combined to make it a mecca for anglers, and its reputation grew quickly. By 1959, over 1,000 people visited the camp, and most everyone came to fish.

The visitor boom was not isolated to Katmai. Between 1940 and 1954, visitation to US national park areas had more than tripled, but after years of funding and staff shortages the parks were poorly prepared to handle the surge. NPS Director Conrad Wirth saw that the parks needed an upgrade to accommodate a larger and more mobile citizenry, leading him to conceive Mission 66, a 10-year program to modernize and expand the capacity of parks by the 50th anniversary of the establishment of the National Park Service.

Although Katmai's tourist industry was still in its infancy, park staff aimed to capitalize on the Mission 66 program. With the area's recreational potential far below its capacity, an expansion of visitor services in Katmai was an opportunity for Ray Petersen, if he played his cards right. The NPS, however, wished to disperse visitor use outside of the Brooks and Coville camps. When the park's Mission 66 plan was unveiled in 1956, it proposed a series of dispersed developments such as small campgrounds, trails, and a road from the mouth of Ukak River on Iliuk Arm to the foot of the Valley of Ten Thousand Smokes. Other than a small campground, the plan didn't include improvements at Brooks River.

Ray Petersen had advocated for a road to the Valley as early as September 1950, and continued to argue that Brooks Camp was the best place for it to begin. By using his political connections and agreeing to upgrade facilities at Brooks Camp, Petersen persuaded the NPS to abandon its original Mission 66 plans and construct the Valley road from Brooks Camp.

It was a shrewd business move. A road to the Valley from anywhere else would have subtracted from Petersen's bottom dollar and dispersed visitation away from Brooks Camp. Instead, the completed road centralized most of the park's visitor services at Brooks Lodge. It would not be the last time the concessioner held sway over park plans.

Brooks Camp's infrastructure slowly expanded through the 1960s and 1970s. The concessioner constructed the modern lodge in 1960 and a motel-like "Skytel" building in 1965. The NPS added large diesel-powered generators and built employee housing, trails, boat docks, food caches, campground shelters, and a septic system. It facilitated the excavation and partial reconstruction of a traditional semisubterranean Alaska Native house exhibit and repurposed structures used by other agencies and contractors into housing, storage, and work space.

The discovery of extensive archeological resources complicated development matters. Don Dumond from the University of Oregon found the lodge and its structures sat upon a village site dating to about AD 1200. Additional archeological sites were soon discovered behind the lodge, along the modern lake shorelines, and buried in the old beach and river terraces lining the river. There was hardly a spot of dry ground near the river that hadn't been previously occupied.

Protection of these sensitive and irreplaceable resources ran headlong into the expansion of lodge and NPS facilities. In 1974 and 1975, the NPS, via a contractor, installed underground fuel tanks, water lines, and sewer lines. The contractor worked at such a rapid rate that the NPS's on-site archeologist couldn't keep pace with the development. Near the Skytel and the cabins overlooking the river, the utility installation desecrated Alaska Native graves by laying waterlines directly on top of fully articulated skeletons.

Over the same time frame, human food and garbage concentrations brought increasing numbers of bears to the river, and the NPS began to evaluate the presence of Brooks Camp in regard to bear and human conflict. With growing concern over the frequency of bear encounters, habituation issues, and the difficulty protecting archeological resources, a somewhat radical idea began to circulate within the NPS: move Brooks Lodge.

By the early 1970s, NPS planning officials were openly suggesting that Brooks Camp be eventually phased out due to concerns about the growing rate of bear and human conflict, and the idea persisted over the next decade. In 1980, Will Troyer noted the NPS facilities and lodge "could not have been placed in a worse location to interfere with regular movement patterns of bear when they fish the river.

"The camp is like a barricade to the bear's [sic] normal movement and almost forces bear to wander in and around buildings. . . . Serious consideration should be given to relocating this camp or portions of it. Moving it closer to the campground would be a vast improvement; even removing the immediate facilities next to the river would assist greatly as this would provide a small corridor for bears to pass through." Troyer also recommended the NPS consider closing portions of the river to fishing when bear activity was high.

By October 1980, the NPS officially suggested that the lodge might be relocated to an unspecified "interior woods site," a "Naknek Lake site," or a "Brooks River view site." Wien Airlines, the concessioner at the time, had little interest in spending money to relocate facilities and the idea was tabled.

In 1982, when Wien sold the concession to Katmailand, owned by Ray Petersen, bear watching had become a major attraction at the river, and increasing visitation challenged the NPS's ability to manage the situation. Three commercial licensees brought about 60 day-trippers to Brooks in 1981. Eight years later, with bear watching now the main attraction, some 16 licensees flew more than 1,850 visitors to the camp. By the early 1990s, total annual visitation climbed to over 10,000. More people than ever before were coming into close contact with bears, and bears "stealing" fish from anglers became a regular occurrence.

In 1988, the park initiated a long-term development plan in an attempt to figure out a way to stem the tide of bear-human conflict and overcrowding. After several years of public meetings, drafts, and revisions, the NPS released its Final Brooks Camp Development Concept Plan (DCP) in 1996. The DCP outlined the conceptual steps the NPS would take to reduce visitor interactions with brown bears, establish use limits that would protect a high-quality experience, and preserve archeological resources. It was a guide rather than an instruction manual, hence a plan in concept only, and it offered no time line to meet its goals.

The DCP outlined five alternatives plus the requisite "no action" as required by the National Environmental Policy Act. Alternative One called for the bare minimum of improvements. The lodge and main visitor facilities would remain in place, the campground would be updated, an elevated bridge would be built over the river, and an expanded platform complex would be built at the falls. Alternatives Two, Three, and Five called for removing all facilities north of the river except the Dumpling Mountain Trail. The lodge, campground, and employee housing would be rebuilt south of the river in an area traversed by fewer bears. The differences between these alternatives revolved around where the lodge would be rebuilt and the role the town of King Salmon would serve as a gateway community. Alternative Four proposed the biggest departure from the status quo. It called for the removal of all overnight facilities and would make Brooks Camp day-use only. Each alternative called for day-use limits, construction of new wildlife-viewing platforms, seasonal sport fishing closures during times of high bear activity, a catch-and-release policy for the river when fishing is permitted, and people-free zones along the river. Day use would be capped to July 1992 numbers with 60 lodge guests, 60 campers, and 80 day-trippers.

The NPS chose alternative Five, which called for the relocation of Brooks Lodge to a terrace almost a mile south of its current location. Few of the people who commented publicly on the final DCP agreed this was the best choice. Commenting on behalf of the Bristol Bay Native Corporation, Tom Hawkins thought the DCP should emphasize more attention to gateway communities. Many environmental groups and biologists supported the day-use-only option. The sport fishing community was united in its opposition to any restrictions on their preferred pastime. The Alaska Office of the Governor was leery of visitation restrictions and emphasized that the state had authority over fishing seasons and regulations at the river. Raymond F. (Sonny) Petersen, president of Katmailand and son of Brooks Lodge founder Raymond I. Petersen, questioned the NPS's decision-making process and recommended the park build a raised bridge across the river. Petersen wrote, "I for the life of me cannot understand why the NPS keeps convincing themselves that there is such a huge problem. Doesn't the fact that there are lots of bears and satisfied visitors mean something besides a crisis[?]"

Over the next several years, the NPS tried to implement its preferred alternative only to meet significant pushback from the Alaska congressional delegation. US Senator Ted Stevens, in particular, was adamant in his opposition, calling the DCP "a bunch of nonsense." Stevens used his influential position on the Senate appropriations committee to stonewall the NPS's effort to move the lodge. A Senate committee report on the 1998 Department of Interior appropriations bill bluntly stated, "The Committee does not agree with the Park Service's proposal to move Brooks River

Lodge in Katmai National Park and has prohibited the use of any funds to do so. The Committee expects the Park Service to find alternative means to manage increased day use through the improvement or expansion of existing facilities, boardwalks, and boat landings, without instituting or utilizing a quota system on visitors." Stevens also included a rider in a 1999 spending bill that granted Sonny Petersen permanent rights to the NPS concession contract at Brooks River.

Stevens lost his reelection bid in 2008 and Petersen sold Katmailand to Bristol Bay Native Corporation in 2016, but their persistent opposition to the park's DCP forced the NPS to try other ways to accomplish its goal of moving the lodge.

As political battles proliferated over development and visitation along the river, the NPS was able to implement some of the DCP's goals in the late 1990s and early 2000s. The State of Alaska adopted catch-and-release fishing regulations along the river. The NPS constructed an expanded wildlife-viewing platform at the falls, eliminated public fish cleaning facilities, closed the falls platform at night, and closed the area near the falls to foot traffic in early summer. Yet, the consistent political opposition curtailed any substantive efforts to move the lodge or place limits on visitation. With existing facilities like park housing continuing to deteriorate (why invest in buildings that are supposed to be removed?), the NPS tried a different tactic. The agency requested funding to replace parts of Brooks Camp, starting with the less controversial (that is, nonpublic, nonconcession) facilities in an attempt to relocate it a little at a time. In 2009, the park constructed a new maintenance facility south of the river off the Valley of Ten Thousand Smokes Road. That same year, construction began on new NPS housing near the maintenance yard to replace dilapidated tent frames.

When the park finalized construction of the elevated bridge, one of the most unique aspects of Brooks River also disappeared.

On an overcast early September day, I gaze at schools of sockeye holding steady in the lower river. Two bears snorkel in the water adjacent to the floating bridge, while another rests on an abandoned pathway directly across the river. Downstream of the resting bear, a dozen people stand with a ranger on the Corner, an elbow in the gravel footpath leading to the bridge from the lodge. Joining me on the platform are about 20 people who spent much of the morning either here or at the falls. Lunchtime nears for this bear-watching crowd, but they'll have to wait at least a few more minutes because the bears have other ideas. We are bear jammed.

The bears were unlikely to gain the motivation to climb over or break through wooden railings and 2-inch-wide slats of the floating bridge. The people waiting on either side of the bridge could probably cross safely. The Corner ranger and I, however, hold our groups with us.

While we wait, a family of four—retired parents, their son, and daughter-in-law—arrive on the ground in front of me. They seem ready to cross the bridge and may not have experienced anything like this before, so I explain the park's bridge management rationale.

"If you are looking to cross, the bridge is closed right now because of the bears next to it. We need to give them space so they have the opportunity to fish and rest. Once the bears move far enough away, I'll let you know when you can continue. In the meantime, please join us on the platform. If we consolidate in one place, then the bears have more room and we are less likely to impede their progress."

When they climb the stairs to my level I provide more info. "The bears in the water next to the bridge are both adult females. The bear upstream is 410. She's probably the oldest bear at the river."

The tiny bit of basic info piques the visitors' curiosity, which was my intended outcome. I'm bombarded with questions as we watch the bears swim and fish. How old is she? Can she still have cubs? How do you know it's her? How many fish do they eat in a day? We chat for several minutes until I must pause the conversation to update my cross-river partner over the radio.

"Corner, Platform."

"Corner."

"The bears fishing in the water have moved more than 50 yards from the bridge, so we are just waiting for the bear on the closed trail."

"Copy."

Unlike my position on the lower river platform, the Corner ranger stands on the ground. She has no elevated refuge to retreat to and her sightlines are limited by vegetation. Close encounters with bears are frequent at the Corner and she is relying on my eyes to keep tabs on bears that she cannot see.

After finishing the update, I expand on my decision-making process for the people standing near me.

"I know many of you are waiting to cross the bridge. I'll let you know as soon as it is clear to do so. Right now, the bear on the other side of the river is still within 50 yards of the bridge. She's a subadult bear, probably 4.5 years old, who first experienced the river as a cub with her mother."

Upstream, three additional bears appear. I point out a mother and two yearlings who have walked into view. Most everyone's attention focuses in that direction. I sense they appreciate the update. There was a time when I would not have known that was a bear family either.

The running commentary and updates are a bit self-serving. State the obvious, I reason, because the circumstances at the bridge are unique; they aren't obvious to those who don't experience it frequently. Provided with the information, my audience doesn't peer at me with confusion or frustration. Even if some would rather not give the remaining bear 50 yards of space, they at least know why I'm doing it. I can't let people approach bears within 50 yards, as per regulation, but the bridge closure was less for human safety and more to ensure bears had free access to the river and food they need to survive. I corralled people on the platform and the Corner ranger kept her people in place to provide a wildlife-viewing opportunity that minimized disturbance to the bears.

The bear on the trail stands and looks at the water, then turns to walk downstream along the bank. The Corner ranger's view is obscured, so I call to inform her.

"Corner, the bear on your side is walking toward you on the closed trail. It's about 60 yards from your location."

She doesn't immediately respond, which is fine because I can determine from her group's reaction that she's received the message. The visitors on the Corner, who had been settled into photographing a bear downstream, rouse their attention upstream as the ranger begins to direct them to walk on the trail toward the lodge.

"The bear is at the bridge gates, camp side, and moving downstream."

The Corner ranger blurts out a quick "Copy" while gesturing further instructions to her group. She shuffles them out of the bear's line of travel, a move designed to preempt a close encounter. I watch them disappear in the forest along the trail to the lodge. Once the bear reaches the recently vacated Corner, it continues along the riverbank through a small grove of spruce and birch to the beach. From there, it enters the water and swims to the other side of the river.

While juggling radio communications with the Corner and keeping track of the bears' movements, I've also readied my audience for the opportunity to cross.

"With that bear moving to the river mouth, the trail and bridge look clear. I just need to wait for the ranger on the other side to return and if nothing changes, then the bridge will be open."

I turn my attention to the ranger on the other side. "Corner. Platform."

"Corner."

"The Corner is clear to reapproach. When you get there, the bridge will be open unless you see something I don't."

The ranger emerges from the trees with her visitors. "Your side looks clear to me."

"Bridge open."

I repeat the call to open the bridge to my visitors on the platform and thank them for their patience as they leave. Bear jam cleared.

Bear jams at the bridge were a unique phenomenon and managing them well was a uniquely challenging duty. It required knowing the bears individually; recognizing, for example, Holly and 410's tendencies to tolerate the close proximity of people, giving us an opportunity to linger closer to the 50-yard boundary than we might with other bears. I had to identify signs of hesitation in bears—the pauses and other body language that suggested they wanted to proceed but couldn't—so that we could react appropriately. I needed to know which bears were prone to take fish from people, so anglers could consider not fishing when those bears approached. I used my best judgment to anticipate how bears would react to each other. A meeting between two subadults could result in a friendly touching of muzzles or a vigorous chase where my group would have mere seconds to react. I needed to understand the tangential risk caused by a large adult male wandering through the lower river, scattering every bear in sight. And each situation required me to explain my decision-making process to the people with me. It was not only good service, but it helped the audience better understand the behavior of the bears and the reasons why we needed to give them space.

I made mistakes, plenty of them in fact. During long delays I was apt, like most other rangers, to push the boundaries of the bears' personal space to allow visitors and staff to cross the bridge. On many occasions, I mis-interpreted or wrongly predicted the direction bears would travel, caus-ing too-close encounters or forcing a halt to traffic, which is problematic because people eager to use the bathroom or eat lunch react less like a flock of flying shorebirds and more like a slow-moving locomotive.

The pressure to open the bridge under questionable circumstances usu-ally didn't come from visitors. It was encouraged, although not explicitly, through park policies and work culture. Rangers who managed the bridge often experienced disdain for their work by other NPS staff, concession employees, and private fishing and bear-viewing guides who believed their own convenience and work schedules should take priority. Interpreters and bear techs were placed in an impossible position when tasked to give bears space when a small, yet vocal contingent questioned their authority and methods. The conflict between priorities and calls for greater convenience led the NPS to reimagine the bridge and the future of Brooks Camp.

In May 2009, as park staff finalized their weeks of preparation for Brooks Camp's June 1 opening, we gathered in the auditorium for an all-employee meeting. It was a chance for the park's leadership to meet field staff, con-duct mandatory training sessions, and provide updates on the upcoming season and future efforts. The annual event typically contained a fair share of attaboy encouragement and we're-here-for-you speeches from higher-level supervisors, but there were occasional gems of presentations, such as when seasonal staff were threatened with "short seasons" if they attempted to "subvert management" or when one of the park's former administrative officers sexually harassed the park employees during the anti-sexual harass-ment training.

This meeting took a twist of a different sort when Katmai Superintendent Ralph Moore presented a surprising plan. He announced that the park would replace the floating bridge with an elevated bridge. Ralph explained that a new bridge was necessary to replace failing infrastructure, to provide dependable access, and to facilitate the move of Brooks Camp. The project's estimated cost was several million dollars and by the early 2020s, the lodge would be moved to the south side of the river.

One of the seasonal bear technicians immediately questioned the rationale, asking how a permanent, multimillion-dollar bridge would convince anyone of the necessity of moving the lodge. Ralph rejected the question's premise and reiterated his talking points.

The idea of an elevated bridge was not new. It was considered then rejected in the DCP process of the 1990s, because the "development footprint and zone of human influence would be greatly expanded in the Brooks River area." As the NPS reasoned, "This would have a negative effect on overall bear use at Brooks River" and continue the presence of intensive development on nationally significant archeological resources. However, the bridge idea was not without its supporters. In his comments on the final draft of the DCP, Katmailand's Sonny Petersen recommended the park build an elevated boardwalk and bridge, and in a 1999 review of the bear and people management strategy at Brooks River, biologist Terry DeBruyn concluded the same.

The idea gained more supporters when issues caused by aging and inadequate infrastructure came to the forefront. As Petersen explained in 2013, "I remember this whole bridge thing started at a planning meeting that Brooks Lodge Manager Jim Albert and I attended a few years ago. That meeting was about the leach field failing and the sub-standard NPS employee housing. The plan was to get some money to move some NPS employees to the south side and they asked us if we would be willing to move some also. . . . We agreed to move a few employees, but we also brought up the access issue."

In February 2008, Senator Stevens's office received a funding request for $4.9 million to build a replacement bridge over Brooks River. The request stated, "The degraded bridge at Brooks threatens public health and safety and could adversely impact park resources. Without the bridge replacement, visitation to the Lodge could be reduced or terminated for health and safety reasons."

The park reiterated these claims and others in detail within an internal NPS project tracking system. The bridge was needed to "provide dependable access across the river." Bear jams caused "several park visitors and park staff to miss scheduled flights or boat transport due to the long delays." The bridge was also detrimental to wildlife and hard to maintain. It impeded the movement of bears and delayed the salmon migration. When the bridge's floats were damaged, its foam interior broke apart, floated downstream, and was eaten by birds and fish. "The current bridge and trail are damaged every year from storms, from the installation and removal process . . . and most of all by bears."

Safety concerns were one of the park's biggest justifications. The trail to the bridge was hazardous, for example. "If a visitor fell into the river at [the Corner], the swift current would quickly sweep him/her into Naknek Lake, where rescue might be extremely difficult." Close contact with bears was an extreme danger. "The lack of an elevated walk way and bridge will continue to place park visitors utilizing Brooks Camp in a precarious position where they will come close to wild Alaska brown bears on the ground level. . . . A life-endangering bear encounter is the greatest danger that all Brooks Camp visitors and employees face every day. . . . Park management is very concerned that someday a visitor or employee will be mauled or killed by a bear in the river corridor. An elevated boardwalk and bridge will be a major step in preventing this event."

What would happen if the bridge were not built? "Closing Brooks Camp, the most visited area in the park, even for one season, would generate considerable outcry from the public, the concessionaire, commercial operators, the tourist industry and the congressional delegation. . . . No practical, viable, non-construction alternatives exist to resolve all of these issues."

This litany seems dire. It's also mostly false.

Maintaining the floating bridge had proved to be time consuming. Its installation required the attention of most of the Brooks Camp maintenance staff for a day in the spring and again to remove it in October. When water levels in the lake were high, wind-driven waves could damage bridge supports and erode the adjacent banks. Bears would occasionally chew on its wooden railings out of curiosity or playfulness, and they would claw its floats. But foam pieces from the bridge were not a consistent or even common source of litter in the river.

While the floating bridge was an obstacle that bears either swam under or walked around, it was not an absolute physical or mental barrier for them. With the exception of food availability, the presence of people was, and remains, the most important influence on bear movements in the lower river.

Bear jams certainly caused many frustrations, and it's easy to grow impatient when standing in a cold drizzle while a bear slurps down its umpteenth salmon or rests unseen in the trees near the Corner. Rangers sometimes hazed bears away from the trail to allow human foot traffic to move through. The presence of multiple bears in close proximity, cubs, and the recognition that bears needed access to the river to fish precluded hazing under most circumstances though.

Perhaps the most stressful bear jams for visitors were those that threatened to delay outgoing flights, which could potentially set off a chain reaction that caused people to miss a connection in King Salmon or beyond. The most disappointing bear jams, however, were those that truly disrupted a person's once-in-a-lifetime trip. A many-hours-long closure in July 2017 resulted in some day visitors not reaching the falls. One visitor cried as she took a photo of webcam footage of Brooks Falls that was broadcasting in the visitor center, her dream of watching bears standing on the lip dashed, ironically, by bears.

These disappointments and discomforts could have been partly alleviated with proper expectations. After giving hundreds of bear orientations and speaking with thousands of people on the Corner and lower platform, it was clear to me that many day-trippers weren't well informed by their air taxis or guides about the nature of the experience. Moreover, guides frequently advertised "day-trip" bear viewing tours that gave clients less than four hours at the river. The NPS justified its need for a new bridge largely on unfortunate situations like these, using them to illustrate a dire situation when access was already dependable, just not always timely or convenient.

The duration of bear jams and, concurrently, the need for an elevated bridge was frequently based on assertions rather than hard data. When the bridge plan was announced in 2009, the NPS lacked any information on the frequency or length of bear jams. About the only things known was that they happened and some people found them inconvenient. Needing evidence, the park began to track bridge closures in 2011. Staff and volunteers monitored the bridge for more than 500 hours during July and September 2011 to 2014. The bridge was closed 44 percent of the time, including 39 percent of survey time in July and 55 percent of the time in September. However, most documented closures during July lasted less than 15 minutes, while September bear jams averaged 15 minutes. The combined average length of a bridge closure across both months was 10.7 minutes. A change to park policy in which rangers escorted small groups of visitors within 50 yards of bears under controlled circumstances further reduced the amount of time people spent waiting. On average, ranger escorts guided 890 people per year during situations when the bridge was otherwise closed. Over the three years of monitoring, only nine closures lasted longer than one hour. The longest bridge closure during the survey period was 171 minutes on July 8, 2012.

Although visitors would express frustration when the bridge was closed, most rolled with it and even enjoyed bear jams. In 2007, 48 percent of visitors reported that bear-caused delays "added to" their experience, 32 percent said it had no effect, and only 7 percent reported that it detracted from their experience. A 2014 survey reported almost the exact same statistics. The NPS's final environmental impact statement for the elevated bridge admitted this too, stating, "Bear jams add to visitor experience by providing an intimate yet safe bear encounter. The presence of uniformed rangers provides reassurance of safety, while the proximity to wild bears gives visitors a sense of adventure."

The concentration of people and bears in the Corner area had its moments of unease, but everywhere else at Brooks River poses the same risks, perhaps more so because staff do not regularly monitor or manage those situations. Anglers and photographers routinely have close encounters with bears in the river, as do people who walk the roads and trails. The only time I was seriously charged by a bear was on the falls trail during a surprise encounter. Around the lodge, buildings and vegetation limit sightlines, and closely mowed grass attracts habituated bears that want some salad in their diet. It is not uncommon to walk around the corner of a building and suddenly stand face to face with a bear or find yourself needing to avoid running bears. In 2018, a bear running through the lodge area "pawed" a Brooks Lodge employee, while in a separate incident a different bear pawed a visitor's pant leg after approaching the visitor in a curious manner. On an evening when rangers were absent from the Brooks Falls platform, in perhaps one of the greatest "hold-my-beer" moments in history, a man left the platform and walked into the river to take selfie photos with bears in the background. The claim that bear encounters near the floating bridge were more dangerous than any place on the river is demonstrably false.

National Park Service leadership, in fairness, did seem to believe a permanent elevated bridge would eventually lead to the relocation of Brooks Lodge, although this logic was hard for me to accept, not with the concessioner and the Alaska congressional delegation's history of opposition to the idea. As part of Brooks Camp's phased relocation, the NPS planned to create a separate environmental impact statement to evaluate moving the lodge and campground. However, only a year after the final bridge environmental impact statement was issued, the Department of the Interior and the NPS reversed their position.

In a 2014 Senate hearing, Senator Lisa Murkowski expressed her opposition to moving the lodge. "I'm troubled by the fact that this bridge is part of what I view as an outdated Development Concept Plan completed in 1996 that also calls for moving the entire existing Brooks Lodge to the other side of the river. I completely disagree with that not only because it would be totally cost prohibitive, but also because of the historic significance of this facility. . . . I don't want to see the construction of this bridge if it is part of an effort by the Park Service to move Brooks Lodge."

Murkowski then put Department of Interior Secretary Sally Jewell on the spot asking, "Is it still the DOI's position that the Brooks Lodge facility must be moved to the other side of the Brooks River?"

Jewell replied, "The National Park Service (NPS) does not plan to move the historic Brooks Lodge facility. Once the bridge is finished, the NPS will complete the supporting infrastructure. . . and move the majority of NPS housing to the south side. This combined effort will significantly reduce development on the north side, mitigating impact to cultural resources and bear use areas. It will greatly improve the visitor experience. The lodge, campground, cultural exhibits, and limited concessioner housing will remain on the north side." Just to be sure, Senator Murkowski included language in the next appropriations bill directing the NPS to not move the lodge.

Writing before the final 1996 DCP was issued, historian Frank Norris presaged the plan's reception. "Regardless of what decisions are made when the development concept plan is completed, it is unlikely that existing conflicts will diminish any time soon. If the DCP recommends the removal of Brooks Camp, the political process that will likely ensue may escalate into a major confrontation, either within the agency or between the agency and outside pressure groups. If it recommends the status quo, however, the existing resource conflicts will only worsen in the future. When viewed in retrospect, the present DCP may likely be seen as an opening volley in a long-term engagement."

Norris could not have been more right. Brooks Camp has become a centerpiece in our evolving relationship with the lands we call national parks and the wildlife within them. Every time we step outside our cabins, cross the bridge, stand on the platforms, and wade into the river, we become part of the story.

When I'm able to speak to a bear tech and ask what precipitated 171's most recent excursion into the lodge area, he informs me that the family had been resting in the forest near camp until they were spooked by the approach of another bear. To avoid it, 171 and her cubs ran into camp where they encountered people and the cubs sought safety in the tree.

One-seven-one apparently felt they were safe, because she eventually left them in the tree to go fishing in the river. Now the risk had shifted slightly. A person could unknowingly walk between the cubs and 171 when she returned. I have no need to add to the dilemma, so I remain at the guest cabin waiting for the scenario to resolve. Although I have never quite become used to witnessing these situations, they have become a normal part of the Brooks Camp experience.

The bridge, like the platforms at the falls, will soon become normalized as well. An expanded human footprint has become our new baseline for the Brooks River experience, along with record-high visitation. Summer 2019 became the busiest in Brooks Camp's history. More than 14,000 people attended the mandatory bear orientation, almost double the number from 2009. On July 16 alone, about 500 people were present at Brooks River, a level of humanity the NPS had once considered unacceptable. With the bridge, Brooks Camp now accommodates more people. Travel across the river is more convenient than ever. Yet without additional protections for bears, the NPS prioritized enjoyment over conserving "the scenery and the natural and historic objects and wildlife therein."

In front of the lodge, I see rangers wave people onto the porch when 171 returns along the beach. A lodge employee, perhaps unaware of the cubs or the mom only 30 feet away, emerges from a kitchen door and heads to the adjacent bathhouse. A floatplane taxis to shore, roaring its 100-decibel turbine engine.

The plane cuts its engine and for a moment the landscape is quiet. One-seven-one stands under the tree and huffs at her cubs. They stir and begin to climb down. Reunited, the family walks in our direction.

We need to get out of their way quickly, so I cram inside the small guest cabin with its tenants. Bear techs move on the bears' position. They clap and scuff their feet to try and get the family to leave. It almost works until 171 begins jaw-popping. This alarms her cubs and they ascend a tree only 10 feet from the cabin. Rangers stop their efforts. We remain quiet inside.

To my relief, the cubs aren't eager to make home in this tree. They climb to the ground and follow their mother to the edge of camp. Rangers resume the light hazing. "Keep going," they tell her along with a slow loud clap. I watch the family pass the cabin's open front door and disappear into the riverside marsh. The challenge of managing this family has momentarily ended. The challenge of meeting the wants of people while protecting the needs of wildlife may never be resolved. Although a highly convenient bridge spans the river, the status quo of bear-human conflict at Brooks River remains very much the same.

FUTURE

"The importance of Brooks River transcends Katmai National Park. It is perhaps the most iconic wildlife-viewing site found within any US national park. As such its care sets a standard for both the National Park System and the National Park Service."

—Ray Bane, Katmai National Park
Superintendent 1987–1990

Brooks River occupies a unique position. Its salmon, bears, and human history combine to make it one of the most storied and dynamic places in all of America's national parks. In an increasingly human-dominated world we must ask ourselves, how much of its evolution are we willing to shape?

Nearly everyone who has spent a few hours at Brooks River has an opinion on how the place should be used and managed. Any proposed changes, though, must be reconciled with the hand that has been dealt; namely, people and our infrastructure will continue to occupy the river and influence its wild inhabitants. With a permanent bridge now spanning the river, Brooks

Camp isn't going anywhere. Bears and people will indefinitely occupy the same spaces.

But conflict is not an inherent outcome when people interact with wildlife. Conflict occurs most often when we don't value the needs of wildlife and aren't willing to change our behavior to accommodate them. The National Park Service has accomplished a lot to protect bears at Brooks River. Yet, unlimited visitation and increased development have substantially altered the face of the river and affect the bears that use it. Just as adding an extra lane to a freeway doesn't alleviate traffic jams, we can no longer expect to build our way out of crowding and wildlife conflict issues in national parks. Careful planning and a collective willingness to practice greater levels of self-restraint are now necessary to ensure bears have the space they need while we continue to enjoy the experience of watching them.

It begins by devoting more of the river exclusively to bears. Currently, the only area on the river closed to people is the immediate area surrounding Brooks Falls between June 15 and August 15. Fishing opportunities for nonhabituated bears have slowly evaporated as more people visit the river, enter the river for fishing and photography, and the tourist season expands into early October. Although it is a rare occurrence, bears obtaining fish from anglers and consequently becoming food-conditioned remain ongoing concerns. Well-constructed regulatory closures would further reduce the risk of food conditioning and the frequency of close encounters. Importantly, it would grant more opportunities for habituated and nonhabituated bears alike to use the river, which would help the park to better meet its legislative mandate to provide habitat for high concentrations of brown bears.

During the early summer and September through October peaks in bear activity, a closure should extend from a point 100 yards upstream of Brooks Falls downstream to the river mouth and include the area within 50 yards of the adjacent riverbanks. Within this zone, human entry into the river and along the immediate riverbanks would be prohibited. Bear-viewing opportunities would take place from the bridge, platforms, and sites adjacent to the lodge. Hard closures would extend from June 15 to August 1 and September 1 to October 15, dates that correspond with predictable peaks in bear activity. Outside of those periods the NPS could allow for limited river access, determined on a week-by-week basis, if bear activity is below a certain threshold. The rule would not apply to the Katmai descendants partici-pating in the traditional redfish harvest at the river mouth.

At the end of the summer season, the lodge should continue to close on September 18. Given a strong trend of increased campground use in late September, the NPS should consider closing the campground on the same date as the lodge unless bear monitoring studies determine that increased visitation during the bears' hyperphagic period does not negatively influ-ence bear use of the river.

Among all the hair-pulling debates over day-use limits, the river's human-carrying capacity has never been scientifically evaluated. The NPS should investigate Brooks River's real and perceived visitor-carrying capac-ity. Armed with that knowledge, daily visitation could be capped at thresh-olds that preserve a high-quality experience and do not require expanding infrastructure to accommodate more people. In some ways, this is admit-tedly spinning the wheels of the 1996 Brooks Camp Development Concept Plan, but so much at the river has changed since the early 1990s when day-use limits were proposed. Fresh studies are necessary to evaluate what sort of experience and crowding the visiting public is willing to accept.

It pains me to suggest that national park areas place restrictions on visi-tation. I treasure my time in parks and I want to share that experience with others. Unfortunately, there is no longer room for increased visitation in many popular park areas without substantially expanding infrastructure or allowing overwhelming traffic (auto, foot, plane, or otherwise) to degrade the parks. At Brooks River, no new wildlife-viewing platforms or elevated walkways should be constructed. We should live within our means and establish a threshold for visitation that we are not willing to exceed.

Surprise encounters between people and bears are a frequent occur-rence along the road and trail to Brooks Falls, and rangers maintain only a cursory presence in these areas. During periods of high bear activity, access between the bridge and falls should be by guided escort only. Rangers and guides would make context-specific determinations on whether or not to approach bears within 50 yards. Day-use limits and a modest increase in staffing would allow this system to become feasible.

Visiting the river in person is an amazing experience, but it is inacces-sible to most of the public because of time constraints, financial limitations, cultural differences, health and accessibility issues, and other barriers. Everyone, however, deserves the chance to appreciate and understand nature and the importance of national parks and wild places. Therefore, the NPS should forever maintain its webcams along the river. It should devote at least three rangers (one full-time year-round ranger and two seasonal rangers) to the most watched webcams in the National Park System so that anyone with an internet connection can have a meaningful bear-viewing opportunity and national park experience.

Lastly, I hope you are able to visit Brooks River in person. It remains an incredible experience. Preserving one of the most special places in North America will require an increased level of dedication and cooperation. Through the Brooks River Pledge, a personal pledge made between you and the brown bears that use Brooks River as their home, you can help protect brown bears and the experience of watching them.

When I visit Brooks River, I pledge to protect its bears by following proper wildlife-viewing ethics, setting a good example for others, and sharing my experience responsibly.

Put the pledge into action while you visit:

- I will learn to recognize signs of alarm and stress in bears, including subtle cues that indicate my presence has altered a bear's behavior.
- I will avoid activities that may disturb bears or alter the behavior of bears.
- I will ensure that my presence does not impede bears by giving them the right-of-way in places where they frequently travel, like the beach and trails.
- I will give bears space, not approaching bears within 50 yards or remaining within 50 yards of bears, except when directed by a ranger, inside a building, or while watching from a designated wildlife-viewing platform.
- I will cooperate with the instructions given by park rangers.
- On the bridge and elevated walkways, I will walk quietly until I reach a viewing platform, where a consolidated human presence is less likely to interfere with bear movement.

- I will remain on designated trails as much as possible. I will avoid entering the river, standing along the riverbank, or otherwise lingering in areas where bears travel frequently so that bears have the most opportunity to gain access to the resources they need to survive.
- I will place the bears' welfare equal to my own, understanding that I may need to yield space to bears.
- I will be patient with the bears, fully acknowledging that Brooks River is their home. It is a place that operates on "bear time" where their daily activities like resting and feeding can cause inconveniences for people.
- I will share my experience with others so they can better understand and appreciate how special Brooks River is.

The COVID-19 pandemic affected Brooks Camp in significant ways. All newly arriving staff were required to quarantine in King Salmon for 2 weeks before traveling to Brooks Camp. The National Park Service reduced staffing levels and delayed opening Brooks Camp to the public until early July 2020, and then only for day visitors. The lodge didn't open until August 10 and the campground never opened. A reduced capacity on the wildlife-viewing platform at Brooks Falls allowed for more space between people. Despite the measures to protect rangers and public health, two park staff contracted SARS-CoV-2—the coronavirus behind the disease COVID-19. Both rangers were asymptomatic and, thankfully, the outbreak at Brooks Camp was detected early through routine, repeated testing before it could spread to other staff.

The bears and salmon, having no conception of humankind's issues, went about their business as normal and Bristol Bay experienced another large and healthy sockeye run. Even though the commercial salmon fishery in Bristol Bay ran at near capacity and caught tens of millions of fish, the sockeye run in Naknek River set an all-time record high for escapement when more than 4 million salmon entered the river. From July 4 to July 15, the average daily escapement in Naknek River approached 300,000 salmon. At Brooks River, salmon stacked thickly against the falls for weeks. The exceptional run, combined with the presence of far fewer people than a typical summer, provided bears with greater opportunities to make a living throughout the river. No bear appeared to have trouble getting its fill of salmon or finding space to fish.

Along with millions of other people, I watched the events play out through the webcams at the river and took comfort in viewing the scene of wild health. I find solace and inspiration in watching bears and salmon at Brooks River, and I want future generations to enjoy the experience gifted to me. Katmai National Park remains one of the wildest and healthiest landscapes in North America. It's a place where we needn't consult history books or imagine the abundance of an ecosystem operating at its fully realized potential. We witness it.

Brooks River's bears and salmon have become iconic symbols of wildness and ecosystem health. They inspire through their stories of hardship and perseverance, their triumphs and adaptive feats, their instincts and character. And they survive within an increasingly human-dominated world. Brooks River's fate, along with that of its bears and salmon, is intertwined with humanity's struggle to resolve our role on the landscape.

ACKNOWLEDGMENTS

No book is a completely solo endeavor, not even for an extreme introvert such as me. I'm indebted to many people who provided information, support, and guidance. Any mistakes are mine alone.

To all the other authors in the world, you have my undying respect. Although I had my suspicions, I never truly understood how difficult writing a book would be until I tried myself.

Thanks to Ally Machate at The Writer's Ally for her initial suggestions on improving my original proposal and connecting me with Carl Lennertz for editorial advice. Carl was instrumental in helping me develop and focus my vision for this book. Thanks also to Michael Tizzano, associate editor at The Countryman Press, for his advice and direction.

I spoke with many scientists and other experts during the last 12 years who helped me better understand the nature of bears and salmon. I'd like to thank Sherri Anderson, Krista Bartz, Barbara Bodenstein, Linda Chisolm, Bruce Finney, Troy Hamon, Grant Hilderbrand, Susan Knowles, Katja Mocnik, Katie Myers, Tamara Olson, Richard Russell, Michael Saxton, Leslie Skora, Carissa Turner, and Imes Vaughn. They all showed a great deal of tolerance for my inane questions.

Roy Wood, my supervisor at Katmai and friend, believed enough in me to allow me to hone my interpretive skills and make good mistakes. I'm the interpreter I am today because of that opportunity. Katmai National Park's staff has continued to welcome me to Brooks Camp even after I left the ranks of the NPS. Readers, know these people work very hard and don't get paid enough. Tell your congresspersons.

I'm especially grateful for the support expressed by the small but highly dedicated team at explore.org led by Courtney Huq, Joe Pifer, Candice Rusch, and Charlie Weingarten. During my time as a ranger and afterward, they helped me reach audiences around the world, and their platform has provided millions of people with meaningful opportunities to fall in love with Katmai. The fanatical bearcam audience is the most passionate and curious lot of national park stewards I've ever had the pleasure of working with. I sleep a little easier knowing they care about Katmai and its bears as much as I do.

My parents, Jan and Mick, always encouraged me to explore my dreams. I've never taken the opportunity to publicly thank them. Thank you, Mom and Dad.

Finally, I must extend my deepest gratitude for Jeanne Roy. She took the chance that allowed us to discover Katmai and Brooks River for ourselves. Through this project, through the days and nights when I was cranky, restless, and full of self-doubt, she offered unwavering support and encouragement when I needed it most.

REFERENCES

Chapter 1

Adleman, Jennifer. "The Great Eruption of 1912." *Alaska Park Science* 1, no. 1 (2002). irma.nps.gov/DataStore/DownloadFile/522766.

Clemens, Janet, and Frank Norris. *Building in an Ashen Land: Historic Resource Study of Katmai National Park and Preserve*. Alaska: National Park Service, Alaska Support Office, 1999. www.nps.gov/parkhistory/online_books/katm/hrs/hrs.htm.

Griggs, Robert. *The Valley of Ten Thousand Smokes*. Washington, DC: National Geographic Society, 1922.

———. "The Valley of Ten Thousand Smokes: National Geographic Society Explorations in the Katmai District of Alaska." *National Geographic Magazine*, January 1917.

Hildreth, Wes, and Judy Fierstein. *The Novarupta-Katmai Eruption of 1912—Largest Eruption of the Twentieth Century: Centennial Perspectives*. US Geological Survey Professional Paper 1791, 2012. pubs.usgs.gov/pp/1791/.

Hussey, John. *Embattled Katmai: A History of Katmai National Monument*. Historic Resource Study, US Office of History and Historic Architecture, Western Service Center, National Park Service, 1971. www.nps.gov/parkhistory/online_books/katm/embattled_katmai.pdf.

Martin, George. "The Recent Eruption of Katmai Volcano in Alaska: An Account of One of the Most Tremendous Volcanic Explosions Known in History." *National Geographic Magazine*, February 1913.

Schaaf, Jeanne. *Witness: Firsthand Accounts of the Largest Volcanic Eruption in the Twentieth Century*. National Park Service, 2004. www.nps.gov/articles/aps-v11-i1-c9.htm.

Sigurdsson, Haraldur, ed. *Encyclopedia of Volcanoes*, 1st ed. San Diego: Academic Press, 1999.

Spurr, Josiah. "A Reconnaissance in Southwestern Alaska in 1898." USGS Annual Report. US Geological Survey, 1898.

Chapter 2

Alaska National Interest Lands Conservation Act (ANILCA), Pub. L. No. 96–487 (1980).

Griggs, Robert. "The Valley of Ten Thousand Smokes: An Account of the Discovery and Exploration of the Most Wonderful Volcanic Region in the World." *National Geographic Magazine*, February 1918.

———. *The Valley of Ten Thousand Smokes*. Washington, DC: National Geographic Society, 1922.

Hoover, Herbert. Presidential Proclamation 1950, April 24, 1931.

Norris, Frank. *Isolated Paradise: An Administrative History of the Katmai and Aniakchak NPS Units, Alaska*. National Park Service, 1996. www.nps.gov/parkhistory/online_books/katm/adhi/.

Wilson, Woodrow. Proclamation, No. 1487, September 24, 1918.

Chapter 3

Brubaker, Linda B., Patricia M. Anderson, and Feng Sheng Hu. "Vegetation Ecotone Dynamics in Southwest Alaska during the Late Quaternary." *Quaternary Science Reviews*, Beringian Paleoenvironments—Festschrift in Honour of D. M. Hopkins, 20, no. 1 (January 1, 2001): 175–88. doi.org/10.1016/S0277-3791(00)00124-4.

Bundy, Barbara, Dale Vinson, and Don Dumond. "Brooks River Cutbank: An Archeological Data Recovery Project in Katmai National Park." University of Oregon Anthropological Papers No. 64. University of Oregon, 2005.

Detterman, Robert. "Glaciation of the Alaska Peninsula." In *Glaciation in Alaska: The Geologic Record*. Anchorage: Alaska Geological Society, 1986.

Dumond, Don. *A Naknek Chronicle: Ten Thousand Years in a Land of Lakes and Rivers and Mountains of Fire*. National Park Service, 2005. www.nps.gov/parkhistory/online_books/katm/naknek_chronicle.pdf.

———. "Archeology on the Alaska Peninsula: The Naknek Region, 1960–1975." University of Oregon Anthropological Papers No. 21. University of Oregon, 1981.

———. "Prehistoric Human Occupation in Southwestern Alaska: A Study of Resource Distribution and Site Location." University of Oregon Anthropological Papers No. 36. University of Oregon, 1987.

Eastman, John. *The Book of Swamp and Bog: Trees, Shrubs, and Wildflowers of Eastern Freshwater Wetlands*. Mechanicsburg, PA: Stackpole Books, 1995.

Finney, Bruce. "Paleolimnology of Selected Lakes in the Southwest Alaska Network: Understanding Past Trends of Salmon Abundance and Lake Productivity." National Park Service, 2006.

Hambrey, Michael. *Glacial Environments.* Vancouver, BC: UBC Press, 1994.

Hults, Chad. "Katmai National Park and Preserve and Alagnak Wild River Geologic Resources Inventory Report." Natural Resource Report NPS/NRSS/GRD/NRR 2016/1314. National Park Service, 2016. irma.nps.gov/DataStore/Reference/Profile/2235401.

Kaufman, Darrell, and Karen Stilwell. "Preliminary Evaluation of Post Glacial Shore-lines." In *Geologic Studies in Alaska,* edited by Julie Dumoulin and John Gray. US Geological Survey Professional Paper 1574. US Geological Survey, 1997.

Mann, Daniel H., and Dorothy M. Peteet. "Extent and Timing of the Last Glacial Maximum in Southwestern Alaska." *Quaternary Research* 42, no. 2 (September 1, 1994): 136–48. doi.org/10.1006/qres.1994.1063.

National Park Service. "Top Six Reasons Brooks Camp Is an Archeological Gem—Katmai National Park & Preserve (US National Park Service)." Accessed February 13, 2017. www.nps.gov/katm/learn/historyculture/top-six-reasons.htm.

Chapter 4

Barboza, Perry S., Sean D. Farley, and Charles T. Robbins. "Whole-Body Urea Cycling and Protein Turnover during Hyperphagia and Dormancy in Growing Bears (*Ursus americanus* and *U. arctos*)." *Canadian Journal of Zoology* 75, no. 12 (December 1, 1997): 2129–36. doi.org/10.1139/z97-848.

Craighead, Frank C., and John J. Craighead. "Data on Grizzly Bear Denning Activities and Behavior Obtained by Using Wildlife Telemetry." *Bears: Their Biology and Management* 2 (1972): 84. doi.org/10.2307/3872573.

———. "Grizzly Bear Prehibernation and Denning Activities as Determined by Radiotracking." *Wildlife Monographs,* no. 32 (1972): 3–35. www.jstor.org/stable/3830494.

Dittmer, D. K., and R. Teasell. "Complications of Immobilization and Bed Rest. Part 1: Musculoskeletal and Cardiovascular Complications." *Canadian Family Physician* 39 (June 1993): 1428–37. www.ncbi.nlm.nih.gov/pmc/articles/PMC2379624/.

Doherty, Alison H., Gregory L. Florant, and Seth W. Donahue. "Endocrine Regulation of Bone and Energy Metabolism in Hibernating Mammals." *Integrative and Comparative Biology* 54, no. 3 (September 1, 2014): 463–83. doi.org/10.1093/icb/icu001.

Donahue, Seth W., Meghan E. McGee, Kristin B. Harvey, Michael R. Vaughan, and Charles T. Robbins. "Hibernating Bears as a Model for Preventing Disuse Osteoporosis." *Journal of Biomechanics* 39, no. 8 (January 1, 2006): 1480–88. doi.org/10.1016/j.jbiomech.2005.03.030.

Donahue, Seth W., Michael R. Vaughan, Laurence M. Demers, and Henry J. Donahue. "Bone Formation Is Not Impaired by Hibernation (Disuse) in Black Bears *Ursus americanus.*" *Journal of Experimental Biology* 206, no. 23 (December 1, 2003): 4233–39. doi.org/10.1242/jeb.00671.

Evans, A. L., N. J. Singh, A. Friebe, J. M. Arnemo, T. G. Laske, O. Fröbert, J. E. Swenson, and S. Blanc. "Drivers of Hibernation in the Brown Bear." *Frontiers in Zoology* 13, no. 1 (February 11, 2016): 7. doi.org/10.1186/s12983-016-0140-6.

Glenn, Leland P., and Leo H. Miller. "Seasonal Movements of an Alaska Peninsula Brown Bear Population." *Bears: Their Biology and Management* 4 (1980): 307. doi.org/10.2307/3872885.

Harlow, H. J., T. Lohuis, R. C. Anderson-Sprecher, and T. D. I. Beck. "Body Surface Temperature of Hibernating Black Bears May Be Related to Periodic Muscle Activity." *Journal of Mammalogy* 85, no. 3 (June 1, 2004): 414–19. doi.org/10.1644/1383936.

Heinrich, Bernd. *Winter World: The Ingenuity of Animal Survival.* New York: Harper-Collins, 2004.

Hissa, Raimo, Esa Hohtola, Terhi Tuomala-Saramäki, Tommi Laine, and Heikki Kallio. "Seasonal Changes in Fatty Acids and Leptin Contents in the Plasma of the European Brown Bear (*Ursus arctos arctos*)." *Annales Zoologici Fennici* 35, no. 4 (1998): 215–24. www.jstor.org/stable/23735612.

Iaizzo, Paul A., Timothy G. Laske, Henry J. Harlow, Carolyn B. McClay, and David L. Garshelis. "Wound Healing during Hibernation by Black Bears (*Ursus americanus*) in the Wild: Elicitation of Reduced Scar Formation." *Integrative Zoology* 7, no. 1 (2012): 48–60. doi.org/10.1111/j.1749-4877.2011.00280.x.

Jørgensen, Peter Godsk, Jon Arnemo, Jon E. Swenson, Jan S. Jensen, Søren Galatius, and Ole Frøbert. "Low Cardiac Output as Physiological Phenomenon in Hibernating, Free-Ranging Scandinavian Brown Bears (*Ursus* arctos)—An Observational Study." *Cardiovascular Ultrasound* 12, no. 1 (September 16, 2014): 36. doi.org/10.1186/1476-7120-12-36.

Klok, M. D., S. Jakobsdottir, and M. L. Drent. "The Role of Leptin and Ghrelin in the Regulation of Food Intake and Body Weight in Humans: A Review." *Obesity Reviews: An Official Journal of the International Association for the Study of Obesity* 8, no. 1 (January 2007): 21–34. doi.org/10.1111/j.1467-789X.2006.00270.x.

Laske, Timothy G., David L. Garshelis, and Paul A. Iaizzo. "Monitoring the Wild Black Bear's Reaction to Human and Environmental Stressors." *BMC Physiology* 11, no. 1 (August 17, 2011): 13. doi.org/10.1186/1472-6793-11-13.

Lennox, Alanda R., and Allen E. Goodship. "Polar Bears (*Ursus maritimus*), the Most Evolutionary Advanced Hibernators, Avoid Significant Bone Loss during Hibernation." *Comparative Biochemistry and Physiology Part A: Molecular & Integrative Physiology* 149, no. 2 (February 1, 2008): 203–8. doi.org/10.1016/j.cbpa.2007.11.012.

Lohuis, T. D., H. J. Harlow, T. D. I. Beck, and P. A. Iaizzo. "Hibernating Bears Conserve Muscle Strength and Maintain Fatigue Resistance." *Physiological and Biochemical Zoology* 80, no. 3 (May 1, 2007): 257–69. doi.org/10.1086/513190.

Mayo Clinic. "When You Lose Weight, Where Does the Lost Body Fat Go?" Accessed June 25, 2020. www.mayoclinic.org/healthy-lifestyle/weight-loss/expert-answers/body-fat/faq-20058251.

McGee-Lawrence, Meghan E., Samantha J. Wojda, Lindsay N. Barlow, Thomas D.

Drummer, Alesha B. Castillo, Oran Kennedy, Keith W. Condon, et al. "Grizzly Bears (*Ursus arctos horribilis*) and Black Bears (*Ursus americanus*) Prevent Trabecular Bone Loss during Disuse (Hibernation)." *Bone* 45, no. 6 (December 2009): 1186–91. doi.org/10.1016/j.bone.2009.08.011.

Ratigan, Emmett D., and Dianne B. McKay. "Exploring Principles of Hibernation for Organ Preservation." *Transplantation Reviews* 30, no. 1 (January 1, 2016): 13–19 . doi.org/10.1016/j.trre.2015.08.002.

Rigano, Kimberly Scott. "Reversible Insulin Sensitivity in Grizzly Bears (*Ursus arctos horribilis*): The Roles of Cell Autonomous and Exogenous Factors in Seasonal Glucose Metabolism." Master's of Science thesis, Washington State University, 2015. www.dissertations.wsu.edu/Thesis/Fall2015/K_Rigano_112715.pdf.

Robbins, Charles T., Claudia Lopez-Alfaro, Karyn D. Rode, Øivind Tøien, and O. Lynne Nelson. "Hibernation and Seasonal Fasting in Bears: The Energetic Costs and Consequences for Polar Bears." *Journal of Mammalogy* 93, no. 6 (December 17, 2012): 1493–1503. doi.org/10.1644/11-MAMM-A-406.1.

Sahdo, Berolla, Alina L. Evans, Jon M. Arnemo, Ole Fröbert, Eva Särndahl, and Stéphane Blanc. "Body Temperature during Hibernation Is Highly Correlated with a Decrease in Circulating Innate Immune Cells in the Brown Bear (*Ursus arctos*): A Common Feature among Hibernators?" *International Journal of Medical Sciences* 10, no. 5 (March 11, 2013): 508–14. doi.org/10.7150/ijms.4476.

Schoen, John W., Lavern R. Beier, Jack W. Lentfer, and Loyal J. Johnson. "Denning Ecology of Brown Bears on Admiralty and Chichagof Islands." *Bears: Their Biology and Management* 7 (1987): 293. doi.org/10.2307/3872636.

Schwartz, Charles, Sterling Miller, and Albert Franzmann. "Denning Ecology of Three Black Bear Populations in Alaska." *Bears: Their Biology and Management* 7 (January 1, 1987). doi.org/10.2307/3872635.

Sommer, Felix, Marcus Ståhlman, Olga Ilkayeva, Jon M. Arnemo, Jonas Kindberg, Johan Josefsson, Christopher B. Newgard, Ole Fröbert, and Fredrik Bäckhed. "The Gut Microbiota Modulates Energy Metabolism in the Hibernating Brown Bear *Ursus arctos*." *Cell Reports* 14, no. 7 (February 2016): 1655–61. doi.org/10.1016/j .celrep.2016.01.026.

Stenvinkel, Peter, Ole Fröbert, Björn Anderstam, Fredrik Palm, Monica Eriksson, Ann-Christin Bragfors-Helin, Abdul Rashid Qureshi, et al. "Metabolic Changes in Summer Active and Anuric Hibernating Free-Ranging Brown Bears (*Ursus arctos*)." *PLOS ONE* 8, no. 9 (September 9, 2013): e72934. doi.org/10.1371/journal .pone.0072934.

Stenvinkel, Peter, Alkesh H. Jani, and Richard J. Johnson. "Hibernating Bears (Ursidae): Metabolic Magicians of Definite Interest for the Nephrologist." *Kidney International* 83, no. 2 (February 1, 2013): 207–12. doi.org/10.1038/ki.2012.396.

Storey, Kenneth. "Out Cold: Biochemical Regulation of Mammalian Hibernation—A Mini-Review." *Gerontology* 56 (August 1, 2009): 220–30. doi .org/10.1159/000228829.

Teasell, R., and D. K. Dittmer. "Complications of Immobilization and Bed Rest. Part 2: Other Complications." *Canadian Family Physician* 39 (June 1993): 1440–46.

Troyer, Will. "Distribution and Density of Brown Bear Denning, Katmai Area, Alaska." Unpublished Report. National Park Service, 1974.

―――. "Movements and Dispersal of Brown Bear at Brooks River, Alaska." Unpublished Report. National Park Service, 1980.

Troyer, Will, and James Faro. "Brown Bear Studies—Katmai." Unpublished Report. National Park Service, 1976.

Van Daele, Lawrence J., Victor G. Barnes, and Roger B. Smith. "Denning Characteristics of Brown Bears on Kodiak Island, Alaska." *Bears: Their Biology and Management* 8 (1990): 257. doi.org/10.2307/3872927.

Why Fat Grizzly Bears Don't Get Diabetes. SciTech Now, 2015. www.youtube.com/watch?v=zapPpPYOoUQ&feature=youtu.be.

Chapter 5

Auchly, Bruce. "Inside the Bear Nursery." *Montana Outdoors*, June 2020. fwp.mt.gov/mtoutdoors/HTML/articles/backporch/2012/MA12bearhibernation.htm.

Ben-David, Merav, Kimberly Titus, and LaVern R. Beier. "Consumption of Salmon by Alaskan Brown Bears: A Trade-off between Nutritional Requirements and the Risk of Infanticide?" *Oecologia* 138, no. 3 (February 1, 2004): 465–74. doi.org/10.1007/s00442-003-1442-x.

Egbert, Allan. "The Social Behavior of Brown Bears at McNeil River, Alaska." PhD dissertation, Utah State University, 1978. digitalcommons.usu.edu/etd/2101.

Farley, Sean D., and Charles T. Robbins. "Lactation, Hibernation, and Mass Dynamics of American Black Bears and Grizzly Bears." *Canadian Journal of Zoology* 73, no. 12 (December 1, 1995): 2216–22. doi.org/10.1139/z95-262.

Friebe, Andrea, Alina L. Evans, Jon M. Arnemo, Stéphane Blanc, Sven Brunberg, Günther Fleissner, Jon E. Swenson, and Andreas Zedrosser. "Factors Affecting Date of Implantation, Parturition, and Den Entry Estimated from Activity and Body Temperature in Free-Ranging Brown Bears." PLOS ONE 9, no. 7 (July 2, 2014): e101410. doi.org/10.1371/journal.pone.0101410.

Glenn, Leland P., and Leo H. Miller. "Seasonal Movements of an Alaska Peninsula Brown Bear Population." *Bears: Their Biology and Management* 4 (1980): 307. doi.org/10.2307/3872885.

Herrero, Stephen. *Bear Attacks: Their Causes and Avoidance.* Guilford, CT: The Lyons Press, 2002.

Jenness, Robert, Albert W. Erickson, and John J. Craighead. "Some Comparative Aspects of Milk from Four Species of Bears." *Journal of Mammalogy* 53, no. 1 (1972): 34–47. doi.org/10.2307/1378825.

Kilham, Ben. "The Social Black Bear: What Bears Have Taught Me About Being Human." Talk given at the College of the Atlantic, 2010. www.youtube.com/watch?v=6LWBH3zLCaU.

Morehouse, Andrea T., Tabitha A. Graves, Nate Mikle, and Mark S. Boyce. "Nature vs. Nurture: Evidence for Social Learning of Conflict Behaviour in Grizzly Bears." PLOS ONE 11, no. 11 (November 16, 2016). doi.org/10.1371/journal .pone.0165425.

North American Bear Center. "Care of Newborn Cubs," January 10, 2008. bear.org/ care-of-newborn-cubs.

Oftedal, Olav T., Gary L. Alt, Elsie M. Widdowson, and Michael R. Jakubasz. "Nutrition and Growth of Suckling Black Bears (*Ursus americanus*) during Their Mothers' Winter Fast." *British Journal of Nutrition* 70, no. 1 (July 1993): 59–79. doi .org/10.1079/BJN19930105.

Pajetnov, Valentin S., and Sergey V. Pajetnov. "Food Competition and Grouping Behavior of Orphaned Brown Bear Cubs in Russia." *Ursus* 10 (1998): 571–74.

Ramsay, Malcolm A., and Robert L. Dunbrack. "Physiological Constraints on Life History Phenomena: The Example of Small Bear Cubs at Birth." *The American Naturalist* 127, no. 6 (June 1, 1986): 735–43. doi.org/10.1086/284522.

Robbins, Charles T., Merav Ben-David, Jennifer K. Fortin, and O. Lynne Nelson. "Maternal Condition Determines Birth Date and Growth of Newborn Bear Cubs." *Journal of Mammalogy* 93, no. 2 (April 30, 2012): 540–46. doi .org/10.1644/11-MAMM-A-155.1.

Robbins, Charles T., Claudia Lopez-Alfaro, Karyn D. Rode, Øivind Tøien, and O. Lynne Nelson. "Hibernation and Seasonal Fasting in Bears: The Energetic Costs and Consequences for Polar Bears." *Journal of Mammalogy* 93, no. 6 (December 17, 2012): 1493–1503. doi.org/10.1644/11-MAMM-A-406.1.

Schwartz, Charles, Sterling Miller, and Mark Haroldson. "Grizzly Bear." In *Wild Mammals of North America: Biology, Management, and Conservation,* 2nd ed. Edited by George Feldhamer, Bruce Thompson, and Joseph Chapman. Baltimore: Johns Hopkins University Press, 2003.

Woodford, Riley. "Bear Milk." Alaska Fish and Wildlife News, June 2007. www.adfg .alaska.gov/index.cfm?adfg=wildlifenews.view_article&articles_id=296.

Wright, Patricia A., Martyn E. Obbard, Brendan J. Battersby, Andrew K. Felskie, Paul J. LeBlanc, and James S. Ballantyne. "Lactation during Hibernation in Wild Black Bears: Effects on Plasma Amino Acids and Nitrogen Metabolites." *Physiological and Biochemical Zoology* 72, no. 5 (September 1, 1999): 597–604. doi .org/10.1086/316691.

Chapter 6

Bear, Mark F., Barry W. Connors, and Michael A. Paradiso. *Neuroscience : Exploring the Brain.* Philadelphia : Lippincott Williams & Wilkins, 2007. archive.org/details/ neuroscienceexpl00mark.

Bellemain, Eva, Jon E. Swenson, and Pierre Taberlet. "Mating Strategies in Relation to Sexually Selected Infanticide in a Non-Social Carnivore: The Brown Bear." *Ethology* 112, no. 3 (2006): 238–46. doi.org/10.1111/j.1439-0310.2006.01152.x.

Craighead, L., D. Paetkau, H. V. Reynolds, E. R. Vyse, and C. Strobeck. "Microsatellite Analysis of Paternity and Reproduction in Arctic Grizzly Bears." *The Journal of Heredity* 86, no. 4 (August 1995): 255–61. doi.org/10.1093/oxfordjournals .jhered.a111578.

Dahle, Bjørn, and Jon E. Swenson. "Seasonal Range Size in Relation to Reproductive Strategies in Brown Bears *Ursus arctos*." *Journal of Animal Ecology* 72, no. 4 (2003): 660–67. doi.org/10.1046/j.1365-2656.2003.00737.x.

Hessing, Pauline, and Larry Aumiller. "Observations of Conspecific Predation by Brown Bears, *Ursus arctos*, in Alaska." *Canadian Field-Naturalist* 108, no. 3 (1994): 332–36.

Himelright, Brendan M., Jenna M. Moore, Ramona L. Gonzales, Alejandra V. Mendoza, Penny S. Dye, Randall J. Schuett, Barbara S. Durrant, Betsy A. Read, and Thomas J. Spady. "Sequential Ovulation and Fertility of Polyoestrus in American Black Bears (*Ursus americanus*)." *Conservation Physiology* 2, no. 1 (November 25, 2014). doi.org/10.1093/conphys/cou051.

Jamison, Michael. "Neurosurgeon: Griz Are Sniffing Champs of the Wild." Missoulian.com (July 29, 2007). missoulian.com/news/state-and-regional/neurosurgeon -griz-are-sniffing-champs-of-the-wild/article_e90b9662-7629-5442-8568- 3c0c50826899.html.

Larivière, Serge, and Steven H. Ferguson. "Evolution of Induced Ovulation in North American Carnivores." *Journal of Mammalogy* 84, no. 3 (August 29, 2003): 937–47. doi.org/10.1644/BME-003.

Lukas, Dieter, and Elise Huchard. "The Evolution of Infanticide by Males in Mammalian Societies." *Science* 346, no. 6211 (November 14, 2014): 841–44. doi .org/10.1126/science.1257226.

McDonough, Thomas J., and Aaron M. Christ. "Geographic Variation in Size, Growth, and Sexual Dimorphism of Alaska Brown Bears, *Ursus arctos*." *Journal of Mammalogy* 93, no. 3 (June 28, 2012): 686–97. doi.org/10.1644/11-MAMM-A-010.1.

McLellan, Bruce N. "Sexually Selected Infanticide in Grizzly Bears: The Effects of Hunting on Cub Survival." *Ursus* 16, no. 2 (November 2005): 141–56. doi.org/10.2192/ 1537-6176(2005)016[0141:SSIIGB]2.0.CO;2.

Nielsen, Jennifer, and Sara Graziano. "Individual Genotypes, Relatedness, and the Circadian Rhythm Gene Clock in Brown Bears (*Ursus arctos*) at Brooks River, Katmai National Park and Preserve, Alaska." NRPP PMIS-5561: Unpublished Progress Report June 2008. US Geological Survey, June 20, 2008.

Okano, Tsukasa, Sachiko Nakamura, Rumiko Nakashita, Takeshi Komatsu, Tetsuma Murase, Makoto Asano, and Toshio Tsubota. "Incidence of Ovulation without Coital Stimuli in Captive Japanese Black Bears (*Ursus Thibetanus japonicus*) Based on Serum Progesterone Profiles." *Journal of Veterinary Medical Science* 68, no. 10 (2006): 1133–37. doi.org/10.1292/jvms.68.1133.

Olson, Tamara. "Using DNA Fingerprinting to Assess Parentage in Brooks River Brown Bears." PowerPoint presentation, Brooks Camp, July 21, 2009.

Sienkiewicz, T., A. Sergiel, D. Huber, R. Maślak, M. Wrzosek, P. Podgórski, S. Reljić, and Ł. Paśko. "The Brain Anatomy of the Brown Bear (Carnivora, *Ursus arctos* L., 1758) Compared to That of Other Carnivorans: A Cross-Sectional Study Using MRI." *Frontiers in Neuroanatomy* 13 (August 29, 2019): 1–28. doi.org/10.3389/fnana.2019.00079.

Steyaert, S. M. J. G., C. Reusch, S. Brunberg, J. E. Swenson, K. Hackländer, and A. Zedrosser. "Infanticide as a Male Reproductive Strategy Has a Nutritive Risk Effect in Brown Bears." *Biology Letters* 9, no. 5 (October 23, 2013). doi.org/10.1098/rsbl.2013.0624.

Swenson, Jon, Sven Brunberg, and Peter Segerstrom. "Factors Associated with Loss of Brown Bear Cubs in Sweden." *Ursus* 12 (January 1, 2001).

Zedrosser, Andreas, Eva Bellemain, Pierre Taberlet, and Jon E. Swenson. "Genetic Estimates of Annual Reproductive Success in Male Brown Bears: The Effects of Body Size, Age, Internal Relatedness and Population Density." *Journal of Animal Ecology* 76, no. 2 (2007): 368–75. doi.org/10.1111/j.1365-2656.2006.01203.x.

Chapter 7

Bidon, Tobias, Axel Janke, Steven R. Fain, Hans Geir Eiken, Snorre B. Hagen, Urmas Saarma, Björn M. Hallström, Nicolas Lecomte, and Frank Hailer. "Brown and Polar Bear Y Chromosomes Reveal Extensive Male-Biased Gene Flow within Brother Lineages." *Molecular Biology and Evolution* 31, no. 6 (June 1, 2014): 1353–63. doi.org/10.1093/molbev/msu109.

Cahill, James A., Richard E. Green, Tara L. Fulton, Mathias Stiller, Flora Jay, Nikita Ovsyanikov, Rauf Salamzade, et al. "Genomic Evidence for Island Population Conversion Resolves Conflicting Theories of Polar Bear Evolution." *PLOS Genetics* 9, no. 3 (March 14, 2013). doi.org/10.1371/journal.pgen.1003345.

Dahle, Bjørn, and Jon E. Swenson. "Family Breakup in Brown Bears: Are Young Forced to Leave?" *Journal of Mammalogy* 84, no. 2 (May 30, 2003): 536–40. doi.org/10.1644/1545-1542(2003)084<0536:FBIBBA>2.0.CO;2.

Davison, John, Simon Y. W. Ho, Sarah C. Bray, Marju Korsten, Egle Tammeleht, Maris Hindrikson, Kjartan Østbye, et al. "Late-Quaternary Biogeographic Scenarios for the Brown Bear (*Ursus arctos*), a Wild Mammal Model Species." *Quaternary Science Reviews* 30, no. 3 (February 1, 2011): 418–30. doi.org/10.1016/j.quascirev.2010.11.023.

Glenn, Leland P., and Leo H. Miller. "Seasonal Movements of an Alaska Peninsula Brown Bear Population." *Bears: Their Biology and Management* 4 (1980): 307. doi.org/10.2307/3872885.

Hall, E. Raymond. *Geographic Variation among Brown and Grizzly Bears (Ursus arctos) in North America*. Special publicaton of the Museum of National History. No.13 (1984). University of Kansas, 1984. www.biodiversitylibrary.org/item/22659.

McLellan, Bruce N., and Frederick W. Hovey. "Natal Dispersal of Grizzly Bears." *Canadian Journal of Zoology* 79, no. 5 (May 1, 2001): 838–44. doi.org/10.1139/z01-051.

Merriam, C. Hart. "Review of the Grizzly and Big Brown Bears of North America

(Genus Ursus) with Description of a New Genus, Vetularctos." North American Fauna. US Department of Agriculture Bureau of Biological Survey, February 9, 1918. www.biodiversitylibrary.org/item/164187#page/9/mode/1up.

Miller, Webb, Stephan C. Schuster, Andreanna J. Welch, Aakrosh Ratan, Oscar C. Bedoya-Reina, Fangqing Zhao, Hie Lim Kim, et al. "Polar and Brown Bear Genomes Reveal Ancient Admixture and Demographic Footprints of Past Climate Change." *Proceedings of the National Academy of Sciences of the United States of America* 109, no. 36 (September 4, 2012): E2382–90. doi.org/10.1073/pnas.1210506109.

Rausch, Robert L. "Geographic Variation in Size in North American Brown Bears, *Ursus arctos* L., as Indicated by Condylobasal Length." *Canadian Journal of Zoology* 41, no. 1 (January 1, 1963): 33–45. doi.org/10.1139/z63-005.

Schwartz, Charles, Sterling Miller, and Mark Haroldson. "Grizzly Bear." In *Wild Mammals of North America: Biology, Management, and Conservation,* 2nd ed., Edited by George Feldhamer, Bruce Thompson, and Joseph Chapman. Baltimore: Johns Hopkins University Press, 2003.

Sellers, Richard, and Larry Aumiller. "Brown Bear Population Characteristics at McNeil River, Alaska." *Bears: Their Biology and Management* 9, no. 1 (1994).

Sellers, Richard, Sterling Miller, and Tom Smith. "Population Dynamics of a Naturally Regulated Brown Bear Population on the Coast of Katmai National Park and Preserve." Resource Report NPS/AR/NRTR—99/36. National Park Service and Alaska Department of Fish and Game, 1999. www.adfg.alaska.gov/static/home/library/pdfs/wildlife/research_pdfs/population_dynamics_brown_bear_katmai_national_park.pdf.

Talbot, Sandra L., Judy R. Gust, George K. Sage, Anthony Fischbach, Kristin Amstrup, William Leacock, and Larry Van Daele. "Genetic Characterization of Brown Bears of the Kodiak Archipelago." Final Report to Kodiak National Wildlife Refuge, February 2, 2006. www.arlis.org/docs/vol1/69123188.pdf.

Waits, Lisette, David Paetkau, and Curtis Strobeck. "Genetics of the Bears of the World." In *Bears: Status Survey and Conservation Action Plan,* edited by Christopher Servheen, Stephen Herrero, and Bernard Peyton. International Union for Conservation of Nature, 1999. portals.iucn.org/library/node/7503.

Waits, Lisette, David Paetkau, Curtis Strobeck, and Richard Ward. "A Comparison of Genetic Diversity in North American Brown Bears." *Ursus* 10 (1998): 307–14. www.bearbiology.org/publications/ursus-archive/a-comparison-of-genetic-diversity-in-north-american-brown-bears/.

Waits, Lisette P., Sandra L. Talbot, R. H. Ward, and G. F. Shields. "Mitochondrial DNA Phylogeography of the North American Brown Bear and Implications for Conservation." *Conservation Biology* 12, no. 2 (1998): 408–17. doi.org/10.1111/j.1523-1739.1998.96351.x.

White, P. J., Kerry A. Gunther, Frank T. Van Manen, and Daniel D. Bjornlie, eds. *Yellowstone Grizzly Bears: Ecology and Conservation of an Icon of Wildness.* Yellowstone Forever, Yellowstone National Park; US Geological Survey, Northern Rocky Mountain Science Center, 2017. www.nps.gov/yell/learn/nature/upload/Yellowstone_Grizzlies_Web.pdf.

Chapter 8

Clapham, Melanie, Owen T. Nevin, Andrew D. Ramsey, and Frank Rosell. "A Hypothetico-Deductive Approach to Assessing the Social Function of Chemical Signalling in a Non-Territorial Solitary Carnivore." *PLOS ONE* 7, no. 4 (April 18, 2012). doi.org/10.1371/journal.pone.0035404.

De Waal, Frans. *Are We Smart Enough to Know How Smart Animals Are?* New York: W. W. Norton and Company, 2016.

Drews, Carlos. "The Concept and Definition of Dominance in Animal Behaviour." *Behaviour* 125, no. 3/4 (1993): 283–313. www.jstor.org/stable/4535117.

Green, Gerald I., and David J. Mattson. "Tree Rubbing by Yellowstone Grizzly Bears *Ursus arctos*." *Wildlife Biology* 9, no. 4 (March 2003): 1–9. doi.org/10.2981/wlb.2003.002.

Lamb, Clayton T., Garth Mowat, Sophie L. Gilbert, Bruce N. McLellan, Scott E. Nielsen, and Stan Boutin. "Density-Dependent Signaling: An Alternative Hypothesis on the Function of Chemical Signaling in a Non-Territorial Solitary Carnivore." *PLOS ONE* 12, no. 10 (October 5, 2017): e0184176. doi.org/10.1371/journal.pone.0184176.

Rosell, F., S. M. Jojola, K. Ingdal, B. A. Lassen, J. E. Swenson, J. M. Arnemo, and A. Zedrosser. "Brown Bears Possess Anal Sacs and Secretions May Code for Sex." *Journal of Zoology* 283, no. 2 (2011): 143–52. doi.org/10.1111/j.1469-7998.2010.00754.x.

Sergiel, Agnieszka, Javier Naves, Piotr Kujawski, Robert Maślak, Ewa Serwa, Damián Ramos, Alberto Fernández-Gil, et al. "Histological, Chemical and Behavioural Evidence of Pedal Communication in Brown Bears." *Scientific Reports* 7, no. 1 (April 21, 2017): 1052. doi.org/10.1038/s41598-017-01136-1.

Stonorov, Derek, and Allen W. Stokes. "Social Behavior of the Alaska Brown Bear." *Bears: Their Biology and Management* 2 (1972): 232–42. doi.org/10.2307/3872587.

Tomiyasu, Jumpei, Daisuke Kondoh, Yojiro Yanagawa, Yoshikazu Sato, Hideyuki Sakamoto, Naoya Matsumoto, Kazuyoshi Sasaki, Shingo Haneda, and Motozumi Matsui. "Testicular Regulation of Seasonal Change in Apocrine Glands in the Back Skin of the Brown Bear (*Ursus arctos*)." *The Journal of Veterinary Medical Science* 80, no. 6 (June 2018): 1034–40. doi.org/10.1292/jvms.17-0689.

Chapter 9

Bunnel, Fred, and Tony Hamilton. "Forage Digestibility and Fitness in Grizzly Bears." In *Bears: Their Biology and Management* 5 (1983): 179–85. www.bearbiology.org/publications/ursus-archive/forage-digestibility-and-fitness-in-grizzly-bears/.

Coogan, Sean C. P., David Raubenheimer, Gordon B. Stenhouse, Nicholas C. Coops, and Scott E. Nielsen. "Functional Macronutritional Generalism in a Large Omnivore, the Brown Bear." *Ecology and Evolution* 8, no. 4 (2018): 2365–76. doi.org/10.1002/ece3.3867.

Erlenbach, Joy A., Karyn D. Rode, David Raubenheimer, and Charles T. Robbins. "Macronutrient Optimization and Energy Maximization Determine Diets of Brown Bears." *Journal of Mammalogy* 95, no. 1 (February 2014): 160–68. doi .org/10.1644/13-MAMM-A-161.

Hendry, Andrew, and Ole Berg. "Secondary Sexual Characters, Energy Use, Senescence, and the Cost of Reproduction in Sockeye Salmon." *Canadian Journal of Zoology* 77, no. 11 (December 1, 1999): 1663–75. doi.org/10.1139/z99-158.

Heymsfield, Steven B., Nicole M. Avena, Leslie Baier, Phillip Brantley, George A. Bray, Lisa C. Burnett, Merlin G. Butler, et al. "Hyperphagia: Current Concepts and Future Directions Proceedings of the 2nd International Conference on Hyperphagia." *Obesity (Silver Spring, MD)* 22, no. 01 (February 2014): S1–17. doi .org/10.1002/oby.20646.

Hilderbrand, Grant. "Brown Bears, Sea Otters, and Seals, Oh My!" PowerPoint presentation, USGS Alaska Science Center, March 2017. www.youtube.com/watch?v= -jqCAzIKsDA.

Hilderbrand, Grant, Charles Schwartz, C. T. Robbins, M. E. Jacoby, T. A. Hanley, Stephen Arthur, and Chris Servheen. "The Importance of Meat, Particularly Salmon, to Body Size, Population Productivity, and Conservation of North American Brown Bears." *Canadian Journal of Zoology* 77 (July 1, 1999): 132–38. doi .org/10.1139/cjz-77-1-132.

Kunce, Kaitlyn. "Changing Tides—More Questions Than Answers." Katmai National Park & Preserve, Alaska. US National Park Service. *Katmai Terrane* (blog), June 8, 2016. www.nps.gov/katm/blogs/changing-tides-more-questions -than-answers.htm.

———."In the Eye of the Camera." Katmai National Park & Preserve, Alaska. US National Park Service. *Katmai Terrane* (blog), September 1, 2016. www.nps.gov/ katm/blogs/in-the-eye-of-the-camera.htm.

López-Alfaro, Claudia, Sean C. P. Coogan, Charles T. Robbins, Jennifer K. Fortin, and Scott E. Nielsen. "Assessing Nutritional Parameters of Brown Bear Diets among Ecosystems Gives Insight into Differences among Populations." *PLOS ONE* 10, no. 6 (June 17, 2015): e0128088. doi.org/10.1371/journal.pone.0128088.

Olson, Tamara. "Resource Partitioning among Brown Bears at Brooks River in Katmai National Park and Preserve, Alaska." Master's of Science thesis, Utah State University, 1993. digitalcommons.usu.edu/etd/6967.

Quinn, Thomas. *The Behavior and Ecology of Pacific Salmon and Trout,* 2nd ed. Seattle: University of Washington Press, 2018.

Rode, Karyn D., Charles T. Robbins, and Lisa A. Shipley. "Constraints on Herbivory by Grizzly Bears." *Oecologia* 128, no. 1 (June 1, 2001): 62–71. doi.org/10.1007/ s004420100637.

Schwab, Clarissa, Bogdan Cristescu, Joseph M. Northrup, Gordon B. Stenhouse, and Michael Gänzle. "Diet and Environment Shape Fecal Bacterial Microbiota Composition and Enteric Pathogen Load of Grizzly Bears." *PLOS ONE* 6, no. 12 (December 15, 2011). doi.org/10.1371/journal.pone.0027905.

Sellers, Richard A., Sterling Miller, and Tom Smith. "Population Dynamics of a Naturally Regulated Brown Bear Population on the Coast of Katmai National Park and Preserve." Resource Report NPS/AR/NRTR—99/36. National Park Service and Alaska Department of Fish and Game, 1999. www.adfg.alaska.gov/static/home/library/pdfs/wildlife/research_pdfs/population_dynamics_brown_bear_katmai_national_park.pdf.

Smith, Tom S., and Steven T. Partridge. "Dynamics of Intertidal Foraging by Coastal Brown Bears in Southwestern Alaska." *The Journal of Wildlife Management* 68, no. 2 (2004): 233–40. doi.org/10.2193/0022-541X(2004)068[0233:DOIFBC]2.0.CO;2.

Welch, Christy A., Jeffrey Keay, Katherine C. Kendall, and Charles T. Robbins. "Constraints on Frugivory by Bears." *Ecology* 78, no. 4 (1997): 1105–19. doi.org/10.1890/0012-9658(1997)078[1105:COFBB]2.0.CO;2.

Chapter 10

Gadsby, David C. "Ion Channels versus Ion Pumps: The Principal Difference, in Principle." *Nature Reviews. Molecular Cell Biology* 10, no. 5 (May 2009): 344–52. doi.org/10.1038/nrm2668.

Groot, Cornelius, and Leo Margolis. *Pacific Salmon Life Histories*. Vancouver, BC: UBC Press, 1991.

Lohmann, Kenneth J., Nathan F. Putman, and Catherine M. F. Lohmann. "Geomagnetic Imprinting: A Unifying Hypothesis of Long-Distance Natal Homing in Salmon and Sea Turtles." *Proceedings of the National Academy of Sciences of the United States of America* 105, no. 49 (December 9, 2008): 19096–101. doi.org/10.1073/pnas.0801859105.

The Lohmann Lab—University of North Carolina at Chapel Hill. "Magnetoreception." Accessed December 21, 2019. lohmannlab.web.unc.edu/magnetoreception.

Mann, Stephen, N. Sparks, M. Walker, and J. Kirschvink. "Ultrastructure, Morphology and Organization of Biogenic Magnetite from Sockeye Salmon, *Oncorhynchus nerka*: Implications for Magnetoreception." *The Journal of Experimental Biology* 140 (December 1, 1988): 35–49.

Markowitz, Tim, and Michael Link. "Estimating the Effects of Smolt Predation by Beluga Whales on Kvichak River Sockeye Salmon." Unpublished report prepared by LGL Alaska Research Associates, Inc., Anchorage, AK, for the North Pacific Research Board, Anchorage, Alaska, and the Bristol Bay Science and Research Associates, Dillingham, Alaska, 2006.

Pollack, Lisa. "That Nest of Wires We Call the Imagination: A History of Some Key Scientists Behind the Bird Compass Sense." Historical Series: Magnetic Sense of Birds, May 2012. www.ks.uiuc.edu/History/magnetoreception.

Putman, Nathan F. "Inherited Magnetic Maps in Salmon and the Role of Geomagnetic Change." *Integrative and Comparative Biology* 55, no. 3 (September 1, 2015): 396–405. doi.org/10.1093/icb/icv020.

Quinn, Thomas. *The Behavior and Ecology of Pacific Salmon and Trout*, 2nd ed. Seattle: University of Washington Press, 2018.

Scanlan, Michelle M., Nathan F. Putman, Amanda M. Pollock, and David L. G. Noakes. "Magnetic Map in Nonanadromous Atlantic Salmon." *Proceedings of the National Academy of Sciences* 115, no. 43 (October 23, 2018): 10995–99. doi.org/10.1073/pnas.1807705115.

Strange, Richard. "WFS 550 Fish Physiology—Osmoregulation/Gill Function." Online Fish Physiology: Osmoregulation, 2007. web.utk.edu/~rstrange/wfs550/html-con-pages/t-osmo-gill.html.

Theoretical and Computational Biophysics Group. "Cryptochrome and Magnetic Sensing." NIH Center for Macromolecular Modeling & Bioinformatics, University of Illinois at Urbana-Champaign. Accessed December 21, 2019. www.ks.uiuc.edu/Research/cryptochrome.

USGS Water Science School. "Dictionary of Water Terms." Accessed December 17, 2019. www.usgs.gov/special-topic/water-science-school/science/dictionary-water-terms?qt-science_center_objects=0#F.

Chapter 11

Dittman, Andrew, and Thomas Quinn. "Homing in Pacific Salmon: Mechanisms and Ecological Basis." *The Journal of Experimental Biology* 199 (1996): 83–91.

Groot, Cornelius, and Leo Margolis. *Pacific Salmon Life Histories*. Vancouver, BC: UBC Press, 1991.

Hendry, Andrew, and Ole Berg. "Secondary Sexual Characters, Energy Use, Senescence, and the Cost of Reproduction in Sockeye Salmon." *Canadian Journal of Zoology* 77, no. 11 (December 1, 1999): 1663–75. doi.org/10.1139/z99-158.

Ioannou, Christos. "Predator Swamping." In *Encyclopedia of Evolutionary Psychological Science*, edited by Todd K. Shackelford and Viviana A. Weekes-Shackelford, 1–3. Cham, Switzerland: Springer International Publishing, 2017. doi.org/10.1007/978-3-319-16999-6_2702-1.

Knapp, Gunnar, Mouhcine Guetttabi, and Scott Goldsmith. "The Economic Importance of the Bristol Bay Salmon Industry Prepared for the Bristol Bay Regional Seafood Development Association." Institute of Social and Economic Research, University of Alaska Anchorage, April 2013. www.fishermenforbristolbay.org/wp-content/uploads/2013/02/CFBB-ISER-full-report-FINAL-4-19-2013.pdf.

Lehnert, Sarah. "Why Are Salmon Red? Proximate and Ultimate Causes of Flesh Pigmentation in Chinook Salmon." University of Windsor, 2016. scholar.uwindsor.ca/etd/5909.

Lohmann, Kenneth J., Nathan F. Putman, and Catherine M. F. Lohmann. "Geomagnetic Imprinting: A Unifying Hypothesis of Long-Distance Natal Homing in Salmon and Sea Turtles." *Proceedings of the National Academy of Sciences of the United States of America* 105, no. 49 (December 9, 2008): 19096–101. doi.org/10.1073/pnas.0801859105.

Nevitt, G. A., A. H. Dittman, T. P. Quinn, and W. J. Moody. "Evidence for a Peripheral Olfactory Memory in Imprinted Salmon." *Proceedings of the National Academy of Sciences of the United States of America* 91, no. 10 (May 10, 1994): 4288–92.

Quinn, Thomas. *The Behavior and Ecology of Pacific Salmon and Trout*, 2nd ed. Seattle: University of Washington Press, 2018.

Quinn, Thomas P., Curry J. Cunningham, and Aaron J. Wirsing. "Diverse Foraging Opportunities Drive the Functional Response of Local and Landscape-Scale Bear Predation on Pacific Salmon." *Oecologia* 183, no. 2 (February 1, 2017): 415–29. doi .org/10.1007/s00442-016-3782-3.

Walton, Izaak, and Charles Cotton. *The Compleat Angler*. John Lane, 1897. archive .org/details/compleatangler00gallgoog.

Williams, Kathy S., Kimberly G. Smith, and Frederick M. Stephen. "Emergence of 13-Yr Periodical Cicadas (Cicadidae: Magicicada): Phenology, Mortality, and Predators Satiation." *Ecology* 74, no. 4 (1993): 1143–52. doi. org/10.2307/1940484.

Chapter 12

"2018 Bristol Bay Salmon Season Summary." Alaska Department of Fish and Game, September 18, 2018. www.adfg.alaska.gov/static/applications/dcfnewsrelease/ 989536277.pdf.

"2019 Bristol Bay Salmon Season Summary." Alaska Department of Fish and Game, September 17, 2019. www.adfg.alaska.gov/static/applications/dcfnewsrelease/ 1114049452.pdf.

Bilby, Robert E., Brian R. Fransen, and Peter A. Bisson. "Incorporation of Nitrogen and Carbon from Spawning Coho Salmon into the Trophic System of Small Streams: Evidence from Stable Isotopes." *Canadian Journal of Fisheries and Aquatic Sciences* 53, no. 1 (January 1, 1996): 164–73. doi.org/10.1139/f95-159.

Bilby, Robert E., Brian R. Fransen, Peter A. Bisson, and Jason K. Walter. "Response of Juvenile Coho Salmon (*Oncorhynchus kisutch*) and Steelhead (*Oncorhynchus mykiss*) to the Addition of Salmon Carcasses to Two Streams in Southwestern Washington, USA." *Canadian Journal of Fisheries and Aquatic Sciences* 55, no. 8 (August 1, 1998): 1909–18. doi.org/10.1139/f98-094.

Bond, Morgan H., Jessica A. Miller, and Thomas P. Quinn. "Beyond Dichotomous Life Histories in Partially Migrating Populations: Cessation of Anadromy in a Long-Lived Fish." *Ecology* 96, no. 7 (2015): 1899–1910. doi.org/10.1890/14-1551.1.

Brennan, Sean R., Daniel E. Schindler, Timothy J. Cline, Timothy E. Walsworth, Greg Buck, and Diego P. Fernandez. "Shifting Habitat Mosaics and Fish Production across River Basins." *Science* 364, no. 6442 (May 24, 2019): 783–86. doi .org/10.1126/science.aav4313.

"David S. Hobbie (Alaska District, US Army Corps of Engineers) to James Fueg (Pebble Limited Partnership)." August 20, 2020. www.documentcloud.org/ documents/7043034-Notification-Letter-002.html.

"David S. Hobbie (Alaska District, US Army Corps of Engineers) to James Fueg (Pebble Limited Partnership)." November 25, 2020. documentcloud.org/documents/20417239-poa-2017-00271_denial_letterappeal_form-3.

Genetic Status of Atlantic Salmon in Maine: Interim Report from the Committee on Atlantic Salmon in Maine. Board on Environmental Studies and Toxicology, Ocean Studies Board, National Research Council. Interim Report from the Committee on Atlantic Salmon in Maine. Washington, DC: National Academies Press, 2002. www.nap.edu/catalog/10273.html.

Gresh, Ted, Jim Lichatowich, and Peter Schoonmaker. "An Estimation of Historic and Current Levels of Salmon Production in the Northeast Pacific Ecosystem: Evidence of a Nutrient Deficit in the Freshwater Systems of the Pacific Northwest." *Fisheries* 25, no. 1 (January 1, 2000): 15–21. doi.org/10.1577/1548-8446(2000)025<0015:AEOHAC>2.0.CO;2.

Hilborn, Ray, Thomas P. Quinn, Daniel E. Schindler, and Donald E. Rogers. "Biocomplexity and Fisheries Sustainability." *Proceedings of the National Academy of Sciences* 100, no. 11 (May 27, 2003): 6564–68. doi.org/10.1073/pnas.1037274100.

Hilderbrand, Grant, Sean Farley, Charles Schwartz, and Charles Robbins. "Importance of Salmon to Wildlife: Implications for Integrated Management." *Ursus* 15, no. 1 (2004): 1–9.

Hilderbrand, G. V., S. D. Farley, C. T. Robbins, T. A. Hanley, K. Titus, and C. Servheen. "Use of Stable Isotopes to Determine Diets of Living and Extinct Bears." *Canadian Journal of Zoology* 74, no. 11 (November 1, 1996): 2080–88. doi.org/10.1139/z96-236.

Jaecks, Troy, and Thomas P. Quinn. "Ontogenetic Shift to Dependence on Salmon-Derived Nutrients in Dolly Varden Char from the Iliamna River, Alaska." *Environmental Biology of Fishes* 97, no. 12 (December 1, 2014): 1323–33. doi.org/10.1007/s10641-014-0221-3.

McDonough, Thomas J., and Aaron M. Christ. "Geographic Variation in Size, Growth, and Sexual Dimorphism of Alaska Brown Bears, *Ursus arctos.*" *Journal of Mammalogy* 93, no. 3 (June 28, 2012): 686–97. doi.org/10.1644/11-MAMM-A-010.1.

Meyers, Donald. "Remembering Celilo Falls 62 Years after It Was Silenced by The Dalles Dam." *Yakima Herald,* May 12, 2019. www.yakimaherald.com/news/local/remembering-celilo-falls-62-years-after-it-was-silenced-by-the-dallesdam/article_be6c698a-93a9-11e8-b4d1-538eaf5535d0.html.

National Oceanic and Atmospheric Administration. "Atlantic Salmon (Protected)." Accessed April 2, 2020. www.fisheries.noaa.gov/species/atlantic-salmon-protected.

National Oceanic and Atmospheric Administration. "Threatened and Endangered Species Directory Page | NOAA Fisheries," Accessed April 2, 2020. www.fisheries.noaa.gov/species-directory/threatened-endangered.

Pebble Partnership, The. "Fact Sheet: Protecting Water," No Date. pebblepartnership.com/protecting-water.

Quinn, Thomas P., James M. Helfield, Catherine S. Austin, Rachel A. Hovel, and Andrew G. Bunn. "A Multidecade Experiment Shows That Fertilization by Salmon

Carcasses Enhanced Tree Growth in the Riparian Zone." *Ecology* 99, no. 11 (2018): 2433–41. doi.org/10.1002/ecy.2453.

Schindler, Daniel E., Jonathan B. Armstrong, Kale T. Bentley, KathiJo Jankowski, Peter J. Lisi, and Laura X. Payne. "Riding the Crimson Tide: Mobile Terrestrial Consumers Track Phenological Variation in Spawning of an Anadromous Fish." *Biology Letters* 9, no. 3 (June 23, 2013). doi.org/10.1098/rsbl.2013.0048.

Stanek, Ashley E., Nathan Wolf, Grant V. Hilderbrand, Buck Mangipane, Douglas Causey, and Jeffrey M. Welker. "Seasonal Foraging Strategies of Alaskan Gray Wolves (*Canis lupus*) in an Ecosystem Subsidized by Pacific Salmon (*Oncorhynchus* spp.)." *Canadian Journal of Zoology* 95, no. 8 (May 9, 2017): 555–63. doi.org/10.1139/cjz-2016-0203.

US Army Corps of Engineers. Pebble Project EIS. "Chapter 4: Environmental Consequences." In *Pebble Mine Draft Environmental Impact Statement,* 2019.

———. "Executive Summary." In *Pebble Mine Draft Environmental Impact Statement,* 2019.

———. *Record of Decision for Application Submitted by Pebble Limited Partnership to: The United States Army Corps of Engineers* (Department of the Army Permit # POA-2017-00271), 2020. www.pebbleprojecteis.com/documents/finaleis.

Washington State Recreation and Conservation Office. "Salmon Recovery: Problem." Accessed April 2, 2020. rco.wa.gov/salmon-recovery/problem.

Watts, Dominique E., and Seth D. Newsome. "Exploitation of Marine Resources by Wolves in Southwestern Alaska." *Journal of Mammalogy* 98, no. 1 (February 8, 2017): 66–76. doi.org/10.1093/jmammal/gyw153.

Willson, Mary F., Scott M. Gende, and Brian H. Marston. "Fishes and the Forest: Expanding Perspectives on Fish-Wildlife Interactions." *BioScience* 48, no. 6 (June 1, 1998): 455–62. doi.org/10.2307/1313243.

Wipfli, Mark S., John Hudson, and John Caouette. "Influence of Salmon Carcasses on Stream Productivity: Response of Biofilm and Benthic Macroinvertebrates in Southeastern Alaska, USA." *Canadian Journal of Fisheries and Aquatic Sciences* 55, no. 6 (June 1, 1998): 1503–11. doi.org/10.1139/f98-031.

Chapter 13

Chomel, B. B., R. W. Kasten, G. Chappuis, M. Soulier, and Y. Kikuchi. "Serological Survey of Selected Canine Viral Pathogens and Zoonoses in Grizzly Bears (*Ursus arctos horribilis*) and Black Bears (*Ursus americanus*) from Alaska." *Revue Scientifique et Technique (International Office of Epizootics)* 17, no. 3 (December 1998): 756–66. doi.org/10.20506/rst.17.3.1134.

Creevy, Kate. "Overview of Infectious Canine Hepatitis—Generalized Conditions." Merck Veterinary Manual, June 2013. www.merckvetmanual.com/generalized-conditions/infectious-canine-hepatitis/overview-of-infectious-canine-hepatitis?query=canine%20adenovirus%201.

Knowles, Susan, Barbara L. Bodenstein, Troy Hamon, Michael W. Saxton, and Jeffrey S. Hall. "Infectious Canine Hepatitis in a Brown Bear (*Ursus arctos horribilis*) from Alaska, USA." *Journal of Wildlife Diseases* 54, no. 3 (2018): 642–45. doi .org/10.7589/2017-10-245.

Masson, Jeffery, and Susan McCarthy. *When Elephants Weep: The Emotional Lives of Animals*. New York: Delta, 1996.

Pinto, A. C., and F. Etxebarría. "Description of Pathological Conditions in the Skeleton of an Adult Male Brown Bear *Ursus arctos* from the Cantabrian Range of Mountains (Reserva Nacional de Caza de Riaño, León)" 26 (2001): 564–477.

Ramey, Andrew M., Christopher A. Cleveland, Grant V. Hilderbrand, Kyle Joly, David D. Gustine, Buck Mangipane, William B. Leacock, et al. "Exposure of Alaska Brown Bears (*Ursus arctos*) to Bacterial, Viral, and Parasitic Agents Varies Spatiotemporally and May Be Influenced by Age." *Journal of Wildlife Diseases* 55, no. 3 (December 17, 2018): 576–88. doi.org/10.7589/2018-07-173.

Sellers, Richard A., Sterling Miller, and Tom Smith. "Population Dynamics of a Naturally Regulated Brown Bear Population on the Coast of Katmai National Park and Preserve." Resource Report NPS/AR/NRTR—99/36. National Park Service and Alaska Department of Fish and Game, 1999, 54. www.adfg.alaska.gov/static/ home/library/pdfs/wildlife/research_pdfs/population_dynamics_brown_ bear_katmai_national_park.pdf.

Zarnke, Randall L., and Mary Beth Evans. "Serologic Survey for Infectious Canine Hepatitis Virus in Grizzly Bears (*Ursus arctos*) from Alaska, 1973 to 1987." *Journal of Wildlife Diseases* 25, no. 4 (October 1, 1989): 568–73. doi.org/10.7589/ 0090-3558-25.4.568.

Chapter 14

Brown, Gary. *The Great Bear Almanac*, 1st ed. New York: The Lyons Press, 1993.

Cronon, William. "The Trouble with Wilderness; or Getting Back to the Wrong Nature." In *Uncommon Ground: Rethinking the Human Place in Nature*. Edited by William Cronon. New York: W. W. Norton and Company, 1996.

Drugs.com. "Telazol [for veterinary use]." Accessed February 21, 2019. www.drugs .com/vet/telazol.html.

Dumond, Don. *A Naknek Chronicle: Ten Thousand Years in a Land of Lakes and Rivers and Mountains of Fire*. Research / Resources Management Report AR/CRR-2005- 54. National Park Service, 2005.

Hussey, John. *Embattled Katmai: A History of Katmai National Monument*. Historic Resource Study, US Office of History and Historic Architecture, Western Service Center, National Park Service, 1971.

Johnson, Lyndon. Proclamation, No. 3890, January 20, 1969.

Mangipane, Lindsey S., Jerrold L. Belant, Tim L. Hiller, Michael E. Colvin, David D. Gustine, Buck A. Mangipane, and Grant V. Hilderbrand. "Influences of Landscape Heterogeneity on Home-Range Sizes of Brown Bears." *Mammalian Biology* 88 (January 1, 2018): 1–7. doi.org/10.1016/j.mambio.2017.09.002.

Nielsen, Mary Jane. "The Pelagia Story." Master's of Arts thesis, University of Alaska Fairbanks, 2005.

Norris, Frank. *Isolated Paradise: An Administrative History of the Katmai and Aniakchak NPS Units, Alaska.* National Park Service, 1996. www.nps.gov/parkhistory/online_books/katm/adhi/index.htm.

"Omnibus Parks and Public Lands Management Act of 1996." Public Law No. 104–333, § 1035 (1996).

Ringsmuth, Katherine. *At the Heart of Katmai: An Administrative History of the Brooks River Area, with Special Emphasis on Bear Management in Katmai National Park and Preserve 1912–2006.* Research / Resource Management Report NPS/AR/CRR/2013-77. US Department of the Interior, National Park Service, 2013. nps history.com/publications/katm/at-the-heart-of-katmai.pdf.

Roosevelt, Franklin D. Proclamation, No. 2564, August 4, 1942.

Troyer, Will. "Movements and Dispersal of Brown Bear at Brooks River, Alaska." Unpublished Report. National Park Service, 1980.

White, P. J., Kerry A. Gunther, Frank T. Van Manen, and Daniel D. Bjornlie, eds. *Yellowstone Grizzly Bears: Ecology and Conservation of an Icon of Wildness.* Yellowstone Forever, Yellowstone National Park; US Geological Survey, Northern Rocky Mountain Science Center, 2017. www.nps.gov/yell/learn/nature/upload/Yellowstone_Grizzlies_Web.pdf.

Wilson, Woodrow. Proclamation, No. 1847, September 24, 1918.

Chapter 15

Act of March 27, 1978, Public Law No. 95–250 (1978).

"An Act to establish a National Park Service, and for other purposes," Public Law No. 64–235 (1916).

Aumiller, Larry, and Colleen Matt. "Management of McNeil River State Game Sanctuary for Viewing of Brown Bears." *International Association for Bear Research and Management* 9, no. 1 (1994): 51–61.

Bennett, Bo. *Rods and Wings: A History of the Fishing Lodge Business in Bristol Bay.* Publication Consultants, 2000.

Cahalane, Victor. "A Biological Survey of Katmai National Monument." Smithsonian Institution, 4376, 1959.

Crupi, Anthony P. "Foraging Behavior and Habitat Use Patterns of Brown Bears (*Ursus arctos*) in Relation to Human Activity and Salmon Abundance on a Coastal Alaskan Salmon Stream." Master's of Science thesis, Utah State University, 2003. digitalcommons.usu.edu/etd/4777.

Fair, Jeff. *In Wild Trust: Larry Aumiller's 30 Years Among the McNeil River Brown Bears.* Fairbanks: University of Alaska Press, 2017.

Gunther, Kerry. "Visitor Impact on Grizzly Bear Activity in Pelican Valley, Yellowstone National Park." *Bears: Their Biology and Management* 8 (1990): 73–78.

Herrero, Stephen, Tom Smith, Terry D. DeBruyn, Kerry Gunther, and Colleen A.

Matt. "From the Field: Brown Bear Habituation to People—Safety, Risks, and Benefits." *Wildlife Society Bulletin* 33, no. 1 (2005): 362–73. doi.org/10.2193/0091-7648 (2005)33[362:FTFBBH]2.0.CO;2.

Jope, Katherine L. "Implications of Grizzly Bear Habituation to Hikers." *Wildlife Society Bulletin (1973–2006)* 13, no. 1 (1985): 32–37. www.jstor.org/stable/3781944.

Leong, Kristen, Bill Stiver, Lindsey Donaldson, and Scott Bates. "A Behavior-Based Framework for Managing Human-Wildlife Interactions in Parks." National Park Service, August 2016. irma.nps.gov/dsscholar/abstracts/2233045.html.

National Park System General Authorities Act, Public Law No. 91–383 (1970).

Nevin, Owen, and Barrie Gilbert. "Perceived Risk, Displacement and Refuging in Brown Bears: Positive Impacts of Ecotourism?" *Biological Conservation* 121 (February 1, 2005): 611–22. doi.org/10.1016/j.biocon.2004.06.011.

———. "Measuring the Cost of Risk Avoidance in Brown Bears: Further Evidence of Positive Impacts of Ecotourism." *Biological Conservation* 123 (June 1, 2005): 453–60. doi.org/10.1016/j.biocon.2005.01.007.

Olson, Tamara. "Resource Partitioning Among Brown Bears at Brooks River in Katmai National Park and Preserve, Alaska." Master's of Science thesis, Utah State University, 1993. digitalcommons.usu.edu/etd/6967.

Olson, Tamara L., Barrie K. Gilbert, and Ronald C. Squibb. "The Effects of Increasing Human Activity on Brown Bear Use of an Alaskan River." *Biological Conservation* 82, no. 1 (October 1, 1997): 95–99. doi.org/10.1016/S0006-3207(96)00151-6.

Olson, Tamara, Ronald C. Squibb, and Barrie Gilbert. "Brown Bear Diurnal Activity and Human Use: A Comparison of Two Salmon Streams." *Bears: Their Biology and Management* 10 (1998): 547–55.

Ringsmuth, Katherine. *At the Heart of Katmai: An Administrative History of the Brooks River Area, with Special Emphasis on Bear Management in Katmai National Park and Preserve 1912–2006.* Research/Resource Management Report NPS/AR/CRR/2013-77. US Department of the Interior, National Park Service, 2013. nps history.com/publications/katm/at-the-heart-of-katmai.pdf.

Rode, Karyn, Sean Farley, and Charles Robbins. "Behavioral Responses of Brown Bears Mediate Nutritional Effects of Experimentally Introduced Tourism." *Biological Conservation* 133 (2006): 70–80. doi.org/10.1016/j.biocon.2006.05.021.

Smith, Tom. "Effects of Human Activity on Brown Bear Use of the Kulik River, Alaska." *Ursus* 13 (2002): 257–67. www.bearbiology.org/wp-content/uploads/2017/10/Smith_13.pdf.

Squibb, Ronald, and Tamara Olson. *Brown Bears of Brooks River.* Salt Lake City: Lorraine Press, 1993.

Stringham, Stephen F. "Fear of Humans by Bears and Other Animals (Anthropophobia): How Much Is Natural?" *Journal of Behavior.* Accessed July 2, 2020. www.jscimedcentral.com/Behavior/behavior-2-1009.php.

"Traffic Jams at Brooks River: Humans and Bruins Mingle at the Popular Site, but the National Park Service and US Senator Ted Stevens Differ over the Agency's

Plan to Move the Camp and Limit Visitor Encounters." *Anchorage Daily News,* July 26, 1998.

Turner, Carissa. "Determining the Effectiveness of Park Management Strategies at a Coastal Brown Bear Viewing Site in Katmai National Park, Alaska." Master's of Science thesis, University of Victoria, 2001.

"Visitor Use." US National Park Service, Southwest Alaska Network. April 10, 2020. www.nps.gov/articles/visitor-use.htm.

Warner, Susan. "Visitor Impact on Brown Bears, Admiralty Island, Alaska." *International Association for Bear Research and Management* 7 (1987): 377–82. www .bearbiology.org/publications/ursus-archive/visitor-impact-on-brown-bears -admiralty-island-alaska/.

Winks, Robin. "The National Park Service Act of 1916: 'A Contradictory Mandate'?" *74 Denver University Law Review 575,* 1997. npshistory.com/publications/winks.htm.

Chapter 16

"36 CFR §13.920 Wildlife Distance Conditions," July 1, 2020. www.ecfr.gov.

"36 CFR §13.1206 Wildlife Distance Conditions," July 1, 2020. www.ecfr.gov.

"Bear Human Conflict Management Plan: Katmai National Park and Preserve, Aniakchak National Monument and Preserve, Alagnak Wild River." National Park Service, March 2006. www.nps.gov/katm/learn/management/upload/KATM BMP06.pdf.

"Bear Safety—Glacier National Park (US National Park Service)," November 17, 2017. www.nps.gov/glac/planyourvisit/bears.htm.

Cahalane, Victor. "A Biological Survey of Katmai National Monument." 4376. Smithsonian Institution, 1959.

Ditmer, Mark A., John B. Vincent, Leland K. Werden, Jessie C. Tanner, Timothy G. Laske, Paul A. Iaizzo, David L. Garshelis, and John R. Fieberg. "Bears Show a Physiological but Limited Behavioral Response to Unmanned Aerial Vehicles." *Current Biology* 25, no. 17 (August 31, 2015): 2278–83. doi.org/10.1016/j.cub.2015.07.024.

Ditmer, Mark A., Leland K. Werden, Jessie C. Tanner, John B. Vincent, Peggy Callahan, Paul A. Iaizzo, Timothy G. Laske, and David L. Garshelis. "Bears Habituate to the Repeated Exposure of a Novel Stimulus, Unmanned Aircraft Systems." *Conservation Physiology* 7, no. 1 (January 1, 2020). doi.org/10.1093/conphys/coy067.

Egbert, Allan. "'The Social Behavior of Brown Bears at McNeil River, Alaska' by Allan L. Egbert." PhD dissertation, Utah State University, 1978. digitalcommons .usu.edu/etd/2101.

Fitz, Michael. "The Last Bear Killed at Brooks Camp" Katmai National Park & Preserve, Alaska. US National Park Service. *Katmai Terrane* (blog). January 29, 2014. www.nps.gov/katm/blogs/the-last-bear-killed-at-brooks-camp.htm.

Herrero, Stephen, Tom Smith, Terry DeBruyn, Kerry Gunther, and Colleen Matt. "Brown Bear Habituation to People: Safety, Risks, and Benefits." *Wildlife Society Bulletin* 33 (January 1, 2005): 362–73. doi.org/10.2193/0091-7648(2005)33[362:FTF BBH]2.0.CO;2.

Leopold, A. Starker, S. A. Cain, C. M. Cottam, I. N. Gabrielson, and T. L. Kimball. "Wildlife Management in the National Parks: The Leopold Report," March 4, 1963. www.nps.gov/parkhistory/online_books/leopold/leopold.htm.

Norris, Frank. *Isolated Paradise: An Administrative History of the Katmai and Aniakchak NPS Units, Alaska*. National Park Service, 1996.

Olson, Tamara, Eric Groth, Katja Mocnik, and Carlton Vaughn. "Bear Management at Brooks River, Katmai National Park, 2003–2006." Alaska Region Natural Resources Technical Report NPS/AR/NRTR-2009-73. National Park Service, 2009. www.nps.gov/parkhistory/online_books/katm/adhi/index.htm.

Ringsmuth, Katherine. *At the Heart of Katmai: An Administrative History of the Brooks River Area, with Special Emphasis on Bear Management in Katmai National Park and Preserve 1912–2006*. Research/Resource Management Report NPS/AR/CRR/2013-77. National Park Service, 2013. npshistory.com/publications/katm/at-the-heart-of-katmai.pdf.

Schullery, Paul. "What Is Natural? Philosophical Analysis and Yellowstone Practice." *Western North American Naturalist* 61, no. 3 (2001). scholarsarchive.byu.edu/wnan/vol61/iss3/1.

Smith, Tom, Stephen Herrero, and Terry DeBruyn. "Alaskan Brown Bears, Humans, and Habituation." *Ursus* 16, no. 1 (2005): 1–10.

"Superintendent's Compendium," Yellowstone National Park (US National Park Service). September 17, 2019. www.nps.gov/yell/learn/management/compendium.htm.

Treadwell, Timothy, and Jewel Palovak. *Among Grizzlies: Living with Wild Bears in Alaska*. New York: Random House Publishing, 1999.

Troyer, Will. "Movements and Dispersal of Brown Bear at Brooks River, Alaska." Unpublished Report. National Park Service, 1980.

Chapter 17

"2019 Was 2nd Hottest Year on Record for Earth Say NOAA, NASA." National Oceanic and Atmospheric Administration. January 15, 2020. www.noaa.gov/news/2019-was-2nd-hottest-year-on-record-for-earth-say-noaa-nasa.

"Climate in Katmai." National Park Service Southwest Alaska Network, March 2020. irma.nps.gov/DataStore/DownloadFile/637857.

Abdul-Aziz, Omar I., Nathan J. Mantua, and Katherine W. Myers. "Potential Climate Change Impacts on Thermal Habitats of Pacific Salmon (*Oncorhynchus* spp.) in the North Pacific Ocean and Adjacent Seas." *Canadian Journal of Fisheries and Aquatic Sciences* 68, no. 9 (September 1, 2011): 1660–80. doi.org/10.1139/f2011-079.

"A Primer on pH." PMEL Carbon Program, National Oceanic and Atmospheric

Administration. Accessed April 4, 2020. www.pmel.noaa.gov/co2/story/A+primer
+on+pH.

Barber, Valerie A., Glenn Patrick Juday, and Bruce P. Finney. "Reduced Growth of Alaskan White Spruce in the Twentieth Century from Temperature-Induced Drought
Stress." *Nature* 405, no. 6787 (June 2000): 668–73. doi.org/10.1038/35015049.

Carlson, Stephanie M. "Synchronous Timing of Food Resources Triggers Bears to
Switch from Salmon to Berries." *Proceedings of the National Academy of Sciences* 114,
no. 39 (September 26, 2017): 10309–11. doi.org/10.1073/pnas.1713968114.

Cline, Timothy J., Jan Ohlberger, and Daniel E. Schindler. "Effects of Warming Climate
and Competition in the Ocean for Life-Histories of Pacific Salmon." *Nature Ecology & Evolution* 3, no. 6 (June 2019): 935–42. doi.org/10.1038/s41559-019-0901-7.

Deacy, William W., Jonathan B. Armstrong, William B. Leacock, Charles T. Robbins,
David D. Gustine, Eric J. Ward, Joy A. Erlenbach, and Jack A. Stanford. "Phenological Synchronization Disrupts Trophic Interactions between Kodiak Brown Bears
and Salmon." *Proceedings of the National Academy of Sciences* 114, no. 39 (September
26, 2017): 10432–37. doi.org/10.1073/pnas.1705248114.

Doney, Scott C., Victoria J. Fabry, Richard A. Feely, and Joan A. Kleypas. "Ocean
Acidification: The Other CO_2 Problem." *Annual Review of Marine Science* 1, no. 1
(2009): 169–92. doi.org/10.1146/annurev.marine.010908.163834.

"Final Development Concept Plan Environmental Impact Statement, Brooks River
Area, Katmai National Park and Preserve, Alaska." National Park Service, 1996.
www.nps.gov/katm/learn/management/upload/BrooksDCP.pdf.

"Isle Royale National Park Environmental Impact Statement to Address the Presence
of Wolves." National Park Service, March 2018. parkplanning.nps.gov/showFile
.cfm?projectID=59316&filename=ISRO_Wolf_FEIS_March_2018_508_final
.pdf&sfid=317805

Jiang, Li-Qing, Brendan R. Carter, Richard A. Feely, Siv K. Lauvset, and Are
Olsen. "Surface Ocean pH and Buffer Capacity: Past, Present and Future."
Scientific Reports 9, no. 1 (December 2019): 18624. doi.org/10.1038/
s41598-019-55039-4.

Jorgenson, M. Torre, Gerald Frost, and Will Lentz. "Photographic Monitoring of
Landscape Change in the Southwest Alaska Network of National Parklands,
2006." NPS/AKRSWAN/NRTR-2006/03. Southwest Alaska Network Inventory
and Monitoring Program, National Park Service, November 2006.

"July 2019 Was Hottest Month on Record for the Planet." National Oceanic and Atmospheric Administration. August 15, 2019. www.noaa.gov/news/july-2019-was
-hottest-month-on-record-for-planet.

Livingston, Ian. "Alaska's Exceptional Heat Wave Delivers State's Hottest Days on
Record." *The Washington Post*, July 9, 2019, sec. Capital Weather Gang. www
.washingtonpost.com/weather/2019/07/09/alaskas-exceptional-heat-wave
-delivers-states-hottest-days-record.

Oke, K. B., C. J. Cunningham, P. a. H. Westley, M. L. Baskett, S. M. Carlson, J.
Clark, A. P. Hendry, et al. "Recent Declines in Salmon Body Size Impact Ecosys-

tems and Fisheries." *Nature Communications* 11, no. 1 (August 19, 2020): 4155. doi .org/10.1038/s41467-020-17726-z.

Olson, Tamara. "Resource Partitioning Among Brown Bears at Brooks River in Katmai National Park and Preserve, Alaska." Master's of Science thesis, Utah State University, 1993. digitalcommons.usu.edu/etd/6967.

Potter, Christopher, and Olivia Alexander. "Changes in Vegetation Phenology and Productivity in Alaska Over the Past Two Decades." *Remote Sensing* 12, no. 10 (January 2020): 1546. doi.org/10.3390/rs12101546.

Quinn, Thomas. *The Behavior and Ecology of Pacific Salmon and Trout,* 2nd ed. Seattle: University of Washington Press, 2018.

Sousa, Emily. "Geomorphic and Climatic Influences on White Spruce Growth Near the Forest-Tundra Ecotone in Southwestern Alaska." Master's of Science thesis, University of Alaska Fairbanks, 2015.

Van Dien, Kevin, and Debbi Stone. "The Effects of Ocean Acidification on the Marine Food Chain." Climate Interpreter. Accessed April 4, 2020. climateinterpreter.org/ content/effects-ocean-acidification-marine-food-chain.

Zeebe, Richard E. "History of Seawater Carbonate Chemistry, Atmospheric CO_2, and Ocean Acidification." *Annual Review of Earth and Planetary Sciences* 40, no. 1 (2012): 141–65. doi.org/10.1146/annurev-earth-042711-105521.

Chapter 18

Anderson, Sherri, and Troy Hamon. "Katmai National Park Bridge Traffic Monitoring 2011–2014." National Park Service, Draft Unpublished Report 2015.

"Brooks River Visitor Access Final Environmental Impact Statement." National Park Service, 2013. parkplanning.nps.gov/document.cfm?parkID=13&projectID=242 54&documentID=51483.

Congressional Record."Proceedings and Debates of the 113th Congress, Second Session." 113th Cong, 2nd sess. Vol. 160, No. 151, December 11, 2014.

"Final Development Concept Plan Environmental Impact Statement, Brooks River Area, Katmai National Park and Preserve, Alaska." National Park Service, 1996.

"Fiscal Year 2009 Project Request Form: Replacement Bridge Over Brooks River." Fax submitted to the office of Ted Stevens, United States Senator for Alaska, February 15, 2008.

Hussey, John. *Embattled Katmai: A History of Katmai National Monument.* Historic Resource Study, US Office of History and Historic Architecture, Western Service Center, National Park Service, 1971.

Katmai National Park and Preserve. "Charges Pending For Visitors Who Approached Bears in Closed Area." News Release, August 10, 2018. www.nps.gov/katm/learn/ news/charges-pending-for-visitors-who-approached-bears-in-closed-area.htm.

Katmai National Park and Preserve. "No Injuries in Two Minor Bear Incidents." News Release, July 26, 2018. www.nps.gov/katm/learn/news/no-injuries-in-two-minor -bear-incidents.htm.

Littlejohn, Margaret, and Steven Hollenhorst. "Katmai National Park and Preserve Visitor Study Summer 2006." Visitor Services Project Report 182. Park Studies Unit, University of Idaho, 2006. sesrc.wsu.edu/doc/182_KATM_rept.pdf.

"Lodge's Future Assured: Bill Rider Let's Owner Retain Katmai Facility." *Anchorage Daily News,* October 21, 1998, sec. B1.

Murkowski, Lisa, US Senator of Alaska. "Murkowski Interior Subcommittee Leadership Brings Results for Alaska Tribal Health, Lands and Parks in Spending Bill." News Release, December 12, 2014. www.murkowski.senate.gov/press/release/murkowski-interior-subcommittee-leadership-brings-results-for-alaska-tribal-health-lands-and-parks-in-spending-bill.

Norris, Frank. *Isolated Paradise: An Administrative History of the Katmai and Aniakchak NPS Units, Alaska.* National Park Service, 1996. www.nps.gov/parkhistory/online_books/katm/adhi/index.htm.

"Replace Floating Bridge and Access Trail with Elevated Bridge and Boardwalk PMIS139730." National Park Service, February 2008.

Ringsmuth, Katherine. *At the Heart of Katmai: An Administrative History of the Brooks River Area, with Special Emphasis on Bear Management in Katmai National Park and Preserve 1912–2006.* Research / Resource Management Report NPS/AR/CRR/2013-77. National Park Service, 2013. npshistory.com/publications/katm/at-the-heart-of-katmai.pdf.

Stawn, Matthew, and Yen Le. "Katmai National Park and Preserve Visitor Study Summer 2014." SESRC Technical Report 15-023. Social and Economic Sciences Research Center, Washington State University, 2015. www.nps.gov/katm/learn/management/upload/KATM14-report-final.pdf.

"Stevens Fights Katmai Quotas." *Anchorage Daily News,* September 27, 1997, sec. A1.

Troyer, Will. "Movements and Dispersal of Brown Bear at Brooks River, Alaska." Unpublished Report. National Park Service, 1980.

US Congress, House of Representatives, Conference Report. "Making Appropriations for the Department of the Interior and Related Agencies, for the Fiscal Year Ending September 30, 1998, and for Other Purposes." 105th Cong, 1st sess., H. Report 105–337, October 22, 1997.

US Congress, Senate. "Department of the Interior and Related Agencies Appropriations Bill, 1998." 105th Cong, 1st Sess, Report 105-56, July 22, 1997.

US Congress, Senate. Subcommittee of the Committee on Appropriations. "Department of the Interior, Environment, and Related Agencies Appropriations for Fiscal Year 2015." 113th Cong, 2nd sess., March 26, 2014.

Epilogue

Repanshek, Kurt. "Bridge And Boardwalk To Span Brooks River At Katmai National Park Gets Park Service Approval," November 16, 2016. www.nationalparktraveler.org/2016/11/bridge-and-boardwalk-span-brooks-river-katmai-national-park-gets-park-service-approval.

INDEX